MW00565193

"*The Silent Shore* is a must-read account of the 1931 lynching of a young Black man on a December evening in downtown Salisbury, Maryland. The event was a seminal one—an act of racial terrorism that, along with other lynchings on the Eastern Shore of Maryland, shaped the dynamics of race and power across the state for decades to come. Chavis digs deep, finding documents never before seen publicly, to present a rich and revealing story of how lynchings were planned and executed, and the conspiracy of silence among white people in the region that shrouded the perpetrators of lynching from accountability. The story resonates with power and caution for our contemporary efforts to address racial violence and discrimination."

—**Sherrilyn Ifill**, author of *On the Courthouse Lawn: Confronting the Legacy of Lynching in the Twenty-First Century*

"*The Silent Shore* is a poignant and revelatory reflection on lynching, violence, and racism. Seemingly southern in its heritage of slavery and white supremacy, the 'Free State' of Maryland also had a robust tradition of Black activism. In this prodigiously researched and gracefully told story, Charles Chavis reveals the clash of these two traditions while tracing a surprising story of political courage and community resolve in the wake of the gruesome execution of Matthew Williams."

—**W. Fitzhugh Brundage**, author of *Civilizing Torture: An American Tradition*

"Excellent and essential reading. By recovering the tragic story of Matthew Williams, Chavis enriches the history of lynching in America. Deeply researched and brimming with important insights, this book locates the 'Free State' of Maryland as a critical site of contestation over race, democracy, and citizenship in ways that continue to reverberate in the age of Black Lives Matter."

—**Penial E. Joseph**, author of *The Sword and the Shield*

"Chavis's book brings the painful truth of antiblack violence to light and breaks the silence that, up until now, surrounded the murder of Matthew Williams. For nearly 90 years, this lynching has haunted the Eastern Shore; now, Chavis's investigative work helps heal old wounds and opens new ones by revealing Williams's killers and those who assisted them. The detailed retelling of these fateful events—reconstructed from sources never before used by scholars—is powerful, timely, and devastating."

—**Aston Gonzalez**, author of *Visualizing Equality: African American Rights and Visual Culture in the Nineteenth Century*

"Chavis, who has discovered period sources that shed new light on the lynching of Matthew Williams, a Black man who was killed by a mob in Salisbury, Maryland, in 1931, brings the sensibilities of both a scholar and a history detective to bear in scrutinizing the ins and outs of an often complicated story and narrative arc. This book is further enhanced by a number of excellent photographs and other illustrations."

—**Claude A. Clegg III**, author of *The Black President: Hope and Fury in the Age of Obama*

The Silent Shore

The
Silent Shore

The Lynching
of Matthew Williams
and the Politics
of Racism
in the Free State

Charles L. Chavis Jr.

Johns Hopkins University Press

Baltimore

© 2021 Johns Hopkins University Press
All rights reserved. Published 2021
Printed in the United States of America on acid-free paper
2 4 6 8 9 7 5 3 1

Johns Hopkins University Press
2715 North Charles Street
Baltimore, Maryland 21218-4363
www.press.jhu.edu

Library of Congress Cataloging-in-Publication Data

Names: Chavis, Charles L. author.
Title: The silent shore : the lynching of Matthew Williams and the politics of
    racism in the free state / Charles L. Chavis Jr.
Description: Baltimore, Maryland : Johns Hopkins University Press, 2021. |
    Includes bibliographical references and index.
Identifiers: LCCN 2021011260 | ISBN 9781421442921 (hardcover) |
    ISBN 9781421442938 (ebook)
Subjects: LCSH: Williams, Matthew, 1908–1931. | Lynching—Maryland—
    Salisbury—History—20th century.
Classification: LCC HV6462.M3 C43 2021 | DDC 364.1/34—dc23
LC record available at https://lccn.loc.gov/2021011260

A catalog record for this book is available from the British Library.

Frontispiece: The lynching of Matthew Williams, in Salisbury, Maryland.
Lithographic print, c. 1931. Courtesy of Smithsonian National Museum of African
American History and Culture.

Special discounts are available for bulk purchases of this book. For more information,
please contact Special Sales at specialsales@jh.edu.

To the victims of anti-Black violence in Maryland,
known and unknown, and to Black truth-tellers,
who risk their lives for the sake of Justice

Whisper Their Names in Sacred Prayer

Matthew Williams

Unknown

Howard Purnell

Anton Black

Freddie Carlos Gray Jr.

Dr. Arthur D. Brown

Maslin Frysinger Pinkett Sr.

These aren't good times for a Negro man to be too proud, step too high.
There are a lot of white men hard up. There are a lot of white men
out of work. They won't be wanting to see a big proud black man getting
along. They'll be lynchings now.

Sherwood Anderson, "Lookout, Brown Man," *The Nation* (1930)

Fear and anger are a threat to justice. They can infect a community, a
state, or a nation, and make us blind, irrational, and dangerous.

Bryan Stevenson, *Just Mercy* (2014)

[Contents]

[Preface]
Hidden in Full View
Confronting the Specter of White Supremacy
in Black Life and Historical Research

History, despite its wrenching pain, cannot be unlived, but if faced with courage, need not be lived again.

Maya Angelou, "On the Pulse of Morning," January 20, 1993

On January 6, 2021, while finalizing revisions of the manuscript for this book, I took a break just after midnight to check on the returns coming in from the Georgia Senate runoff election. By then it was clear that Reverend Dr. Raphael Gamaliel Warnock, the son of sharecroppers, had defeated Republican incumbent Kelly Loeffler, becoming the first Black Democratic US senator elected in the South and only the eleventh Black senator elected in US history. Especially given the heightened racial divisions in the country over the previous four years, Warnock's victory was a triumph for African Americans and our democracy.

The next morning, I went back to writing and called my six-year-old son, Noah, down the stairs and held him in my arms, thinking about what Rev. Warnock's victory meant for my son's future. Indeed, as in the Reconstruction era, my celebration and hopefulness following November 3, 2020, were short-lived, for also on January 6 I learned that a mob of pro-Trump insurrectionist-rioters had descended on the United States Capitol following the start of a joint session of Congress to tally the electoral college votes for president-elect Joe Biden and vice-president-elect Kamala Harris.

As I watched footage of the white mob, with nooses and Confederate battle flags, wearing tactical gear and plain clothes, I saw on live television the mob spirit that I had been studying for more than five years. However, like the records that I would salvage—historical records detailing those involved, those who were complicit, and those who witnessed the lynching of Matthew Williams—this mob spirit, much like white supremacy, has been hidden in full view.[1]

Indeed, incidents of overt racial violence can often pull our attention away from systemic racism. While the two are not the same, they produce the same outcomes in that they function as a mechanism of control and oppression. Failing to understand the elusive nature of white supremacy makes room for well-intentioned whites to dismiss the overt acts of racial violence, personified in the manifestation of lynch mobs, neo-Nazis, and the alt-right, as being anecdotal one-offs and the actions of a deranged marginal faction. Their solution is to ignore or to root out and prosecute such backward, uncivilized, and "un-American" actors. This prosecution must be carried out. But how do we deal with the anti-Blackness and white supremacy that manifest themselves within our institutions, practices, and behaviors and every system of our society? To deal with these systemic manifestations of white power and anti-Blackness, we must realize that white supremacy thrives on the suppression of narratives, narratives of the oppressed, marginalized, and outcast.

Salvaging the Narratives of the Oppressed

As a historian and civil rights activist, I confront white supremacy by salvaging the narratives of the oppressed—in this case, the ninety-year-old narrative of a young man and the impact of his death on the Black community of Salisbury, on Maryland's Eastern Shore. In retrieving these narratives, I was again made aware that archival institutions were not designed to preserve oppressed people's narratives and memory.[2] For this reason, historians must be salvaging experts, understanding that we must first review the existing story, literature, and research, and then determine what is missing.

I have followed this advice here by looking at the groundbreaking work of Sherrilyn Ifill and the sources she consulted, including the Baltimore *Afro-American* and the research files located at the Edward H. Nabb Center for Delmarva Studies at Salisbury University. After consulting the known causes and the scholarship surrounding Williams's lynching, I was able to determine what was missing. I decided to follow the trail outlined in both primary and secondary sources, which pointed to two individuals who had played central roles in investigating the lynching: Attorney General Preston Lane and Governor Albert Ritchie.

Because both Lane and Ritchie were government officials, I headed to the Maryland State Archives to see what I could find. Upon arriving at the archives, I noticed the difference in practices followed by various archival repositories. Unlike the Nabb Center, the Maryland State Archives had processed its records not to facilitate research but to appeal to patrons seeking access to such government documents as copies of deeds and marriage and divorce records. Despite this difficulty, I pressed on and began looking at the records of Albert Ritchie, Maryland's forty-ninth governor, during whose tenure the Maryland Interracial Commission (MIC) was created in 1927.[3] Knowing that he had tasked members with investigating the lynching, I requested the MIC records for the years leading up to and following the lynching. Once the boxes arrived, I was shocked to discover that some were empty, while others were full of newspapers having nothing to do with the commission. I informed the reference archivist on duty, who called upstairs to Chris Haley, director of the Legacy of Slavery Program at the Maryland State Archives and manager of "Judge Lynch's Court," an online case study project documenting lynching in the state of Maryland. (Chris Haley is also a nephew of author Alex Haley.)

Mr. Haley was dismayed and confused upon learning of the situation. Knowing what I knew about the secrecy associated with the investigations of lynching throughout the country, I was nevertheless inspired to continue. I looked at the records of the attorney general, who had been in charge of leading the investigation, for the years following the lynching. I could find no correspondence, however, concerning the lynching or the related investigation. Not taking no for an answer, I spent a week going through the online catalog and pulling files that I thought might contain records related to the lynching.

After four days of searching the massive database, I stumbled upon a pdf document more than eight hundred pages long, labeled "restricted." Among the investigations led by the Maryland Attorney General's Office that were listed in the document were those of Matthew Williams and George Armwood. I immediately requested these items, only to find out that they were stored offsite and their retrieval would take a few days. After two days, the boxes arrived, and what their contents revealed was unbelievable. Each box contained the original contemporaneous witness statements taken following Matthew Williams's lynching in 1931 and George Armwood's in 1933.

The boxes also contained the reports of officers who had been at the scene of the lynchings and the records of the secret investigation authorized by Governor Ritchie. I doubled back to Ifill's work and saw no reference to these statements. I quickly realized that this was evidence that had not yet been referenced in any publications. I reflected upon my discovery and the problems I'd had locating evidence related to the case in the Maryland State Archives. When I spoke with Mr. Haley, he expressed confusion about why the files were listed as restricted, as the statute of limitations had passed. Thus, I began to question why this evidence had been buried for all these years.

In speaking with David Taft Terry, the former director of the Legacy of Slavery Program (2001–4), I was able to gain insight into how records are processed in the archives. Professor Terry informed me that he had known staff working with the same collection in the early 2000s. He attributed the difficulties that I was experiencing in locating accurate and complete cataloging of the collection's contents to their being part of a transfer series—a collection yet to be fully processed by the archive but made available anyway. The state archives—and most other repositories—have some version of this protocol.

If this evidence had been released, it would have stained the modern legacy of the Free State and the legacy of one of its leading political figures. Indeed, this is not new evidence; it is newly considered evidence that was hidden in full view for almost ninety years.

The Silent Shore

Introduction

Our country's national crime is lynching. It is not the creature of an hour,
the sudden outburst of uncontrolled fury, or the unspeakable brutality of
an insane mob. It represents the cool, calculating deliberation of intelligent
people who openly avow that there is an "unwritten law" that justifies
them in putting human beings to death without complaint under oath,
without trial by jury, without opportunity to make defense,
and without right of appeal.

Ida B. Wells-Barnett, "Lynch Law in America" (1900)

On December 16, 2016, just weeks before leaving office, President Barack Obama made history by signing the Emmett Till Civil Rights Crimes Reauthorization Act. The act extended the responsibilities of the Department of Justice and the Federal Bureau of Investigation (FBI) to the prosecution of civil rights violations that occurred before 1980. According to a White House summary, the bill would require "full accounting of all victims whose deaths or disappearances were the result of racially motivated crimes."[1]

Till's lynching is one of the darker episodes in American history. However, it represents only one of many thousands of lynchings of Black men and women that date back to the founding of the United States. Consider the evolution of this phenomenon into modern-day lynchings, the "strange fruit in the age of Obama." In 2015 alone, 102 unarmed African Americans were the victims of what many describe as modern-day lynchings by police officers, 35 more African Americans than the number lynched in 1910, when

Jack Johnson defeated Jim Jeffries in Reno, Nevada, and became the first African American heavyweight champion.[2]

In suggesting that such modern-day forms of lynching exist, I open myself to the long-standing debate over the definition of lynching. Recently, scholars such as Ersula Ore have highlighted the "continued debate over the definition of lynching and the ways such debate reflects an ongoing tradition to rhetorically save face through denial of lynching's adaptive and transformative nature."[3]

African American artist Scott Tyler (Dread Scott), the artist behind the flag entitled *A Man Was Lynched by Police Yesterday* in 2015, echoes this perspective in arguing, "Many people think of lynching as a horror from the past, and rightly so—by and large black people are not found strung up from trees in 2020—but the inheritors of lynch mob terror are the police."[4] Scott provides a provocative framing of white supremacy's role in shaping how things are defined. Indeed, racial terror lynching must be understood as one of the many offspring that birthed out of white supremacy. Like a virus that evolves to preserve itself, white supremacy grows along with whatever offspring it produces. The minute that a "definition of lynching" or a "vaccine" is established, the virus of white supremacy and its offspring mutate for the sake of their survival, and by excluding one element of its original signature, the practice and legacy of lynching and what it represents continues to live on under a different name. This is why the victims and targets of racial terror lynching must have a say in how it is defined. For this reason, I employ a broader definition of lynching that sees it as "adaptive and transformative" and may include the destructive act of violence as carried out by public officials or by private individuals or mobs.

In 1894, Frederick Douglass, Maryland's native son, a formerly enslaved Black man, responded to the lynching crisis of his day, weeks before his death, by describing the nature and structure of the mob spirit:

> In its thirst for blood and its rage for vengeance, the mob has blindly, boldly and defiantly supplanted sheriffs, constables and police. It has assumed all the functions of civil authority. It laughs at legal processes, courts and juries, and its red-handed murderers range abroad unchecked and unchallenged by law or by public opinion. If

the mob is in pursuit of Negroes who happen to be accused of crime, innocent or guilty, prison walls and iron bars afford no protection. Jail doors are battered down in the presence of unresisting jailors, and the accused, awaiting trial in the courts of law, are dragged out and hanged, shot, stabbed or burned to death, as the blind and irresponsible mob may elect.[5]

Douglass sheds light on the nature of the lynch mob and foresees the trajectory of the culture of race lynching in the United States through the twentieth century. The longevity of this culture and mob structure coincides with the system of silence that sought to protect white society and customs, not only in Maryland but also in counties and states across the United States.

On December 4, 1931, Matthew Williams was found lying unconscious in the office of his employer, Daniel "D. J." Elliot, a local box factory and lumberyard owner, in a pool of blood. According to witnesses, two shots had been heard; when authorities arrived, Daniel "D. J." Elliott was dead, and Williams, severely wounded, lay incapacitated. Shortly thereafter, Williams was taken to the "Negro" wing of Peninsula General Hospital in downtown Salisbury, Maryland. After citizens heard that Williams was alive, a lynch mob began to form, and a crowd of more than a thousand gathered outside the hospital, demanding Williams be released to them. Eventually, the mob reached Williams, who had been straitjacketed, and threw him out of the window, delivering him to the angry crowd below. Williams was stabbed and dragged three blocks to the courthouse lawn, where his unconscious body was hanged twenty-five feet above the earth. Shortly thereafter, onlookers witnessed the traditional conclusion to the vast majority of racial terror lynchings as Williams's lifeless body was doused with gasoline and set ablaze.[6]

Following this horrific incident, the state's leading political figure, Governor Albert C. Ritchie, became one of the first political leaders to respond by condemning both Williams's alleged actions and the actions of the nameless mob.[7] On December 6, two days following the lynching, Ritchie told the *Baltimore Sun*, "The crime of the Negro Williams was a shocking thing but he could have paid the penalty for it through the established legal machinery. The action of the mob in lynching him must bring the blush of shame to every law-abiding Marylander, whether on or off the eastern shore."[8]

Rabbi Edward L. Israel, an emerging progressive and interracialist from the historic Har Sinai congregation in Baltimore, wrote from his sickbed to Governor Ritchie, calling for "the demonstration of a strong, courageous character on the part of Annapolis."[9] Furthermore, he raised the questions:

> What is going to be the answer of the constituted authorities? Are we going to witness in Maryland the usual conclusion to these barbaric scenes?
>
> Is a travesty of a coroner's inquest going to gather with fake solemnity and declare that the negro came to his death at "the hands of persons unknown" while all the while the identity of the mob leaders is a matter of public knowledge?[10]

Israel then critiqued Ritchie and the state for attempting to politicize the lynching of Williams, asking him whether leaders were going "to find their real courage or [persist in] petty politics which prates of State's rights yet will do nothing to uphold the dignity of those rights in the face of possible loss of political prestige?"[11]

Inspired by Rabbi Israel's response, this book focuses on the politics of anti-Blackness. It presents a narrative dominated by white politicians (Albert Ritchie and white Eastern Shoremen), white-centered political scenarios, and white protagonists. I seek to uncover the secret investigation into one of the most overlooked lynchings in US history, the 1931 lynching of Matthew Williams. I also examine Governor Albert Ritchie's abortive attempt to make lynching a political avenue toward securing an incipient Black urban vote.

Once slavery ended in the United States, Jim Crow segregation emerged and thrived, and race lynching became the symbol of its longevity and success. By the turn of the twentieth century, anti-lynching crusader Ida B. Wells-Barnett had identified a formula common to lynchings in the American South: what she called the "old threadbare lie," the alleged social and sexual violation of white female purity that was used to justify these horrendous acts.[12] Lost within this pretext for such acts is the victims' human story and the communities that witnessed these crimes against humanity. Following the "old threadbare lie," silence rang out when it was time to identify the members of the lynch mobs.

Many historical conceptualizations of race lynching in America present an image almost solely rooted in the Deep South; in fact, this historical perspective overemphasize the areas that registered the highest number of lynchings. Like the numbers game in historical scholarship on the transatlantic slave trade, where the quantification and abstractions of Black bodies overshadow the humanity of the millions of enslaved Africans, another numbers game has threatened to merely quantify the scores of Black lives that were taken as a result of race lynching in America.[13]

The strong focus on the Deep South areas that registered the highest numbers of lynching incidents has left a significant gap in the scholarship.[14] Lost in the abstractions are the human stories of at least forty-one souls (between 1854 and 1933) in Maryland whose lives were cut short at the hands of bloodthirsty mobs. One of these souls was Matthew Williams. Overlooked alongside these people is the role of the "Free State" as, to use historian Barbara Jeanne Fields's term, a "Middle Ground." Maryland's unique position as a border state and its comparatively low number of lynchings have largely shielded it from historical analysis.[15]

Notwithstanding the focus on more national studies of lynching, several scholars have taken case study approaches to understanding these instances of human injustice. This book stands among a growing number of historical narratives on lynchings, including James McGovern's *Anatomy of Lynching: The Killing of Claude Neal* (1982) and Howard Smead's *Blood Justice: The Lynching of Mack Charles Parker* (1985).[16] More recent studies in this developing field explore the hidden histories of lynching in local communities in and outside the Deep South, including border states such as Maryland.[17] Among the most relevant scholarship is the work of Claude A. Clegg III, *Troubled Ground: A Tale of Murder, Lynching, and Reckoning in the New South* (2010), a deeply personal turn-of-the-century examination of a triple lynching in Salisbury, North Carolina, and lynching prosecutions in the United States.[18] Beyond these brief regional histories, the most significant contribution to the historiography of lynching in Maryland appeared in Sherrilyn Ifill's groundbreaking 2007 study, *On the Courthouse Lawn: Confronting the Legacy of Lynching in the Twenty-First Century*.[19] Ifill's contributions center on the intersections of memory and racial violence involved in the lynching of Williams (1931) and George Armwood (1933) on Maryland's Eastern Shore.[20]

A System of Silence

The practice of lynching persisted, in part, due to the silence that emerged to control the collective memory of southern white communities. This silence would lead to the traditional verdict that concluded almost all lynching investigations: the lynching had taken place "at the hands of persons unknown."[21] Sherrilyn Ifill describes this as a "conspiracy of silence"; however, a conspiracy requires organization and collective effort to carry out an unlawful and harmful scheme.[22] Accessing newly discovered evidence, this book allows for more sophisticated analysis. While the phrase "conspiracy of silence" can be applied to the white perpetrators behind the lynching, to use it in reference to vulnerable Black citizens is problematic at the very least. The term must be understood in relationship to power, a power denied to African Americans in the United States. Without doubt, "criminal conspiracies" played a part in allowing lynchings to go unchecked; however, it was instead a *system of silence* that saturated communities such as Salisbury well before the lynching of Matthew Williams.

The words of Czech writer and politician Václav Havel illuminate this system of silence. The central figure in Havel's groundbreaking essay "The Power of the Powerless," is the greengrocer who displays a sign in his store window indicating allegiance to communist ideals: "Workers of the World Unite!"[23] The greengrocer's willingness to display this sign is not motivated by a desire to communicate his enthusiasm for unity among workers of the world. Nor did his supervisor wish to create such unity. Rather, the sign is a symbol used to avoid trouble and signal conformity. Havel translates the sign's slogan as "I am afraid and therefore, unquestioningly obedient."[24] He explains how people operate in this system of silence:

> Individuals need not believe all these mystifications, but they must behave as though they did, or they must at least tolerate them in silence, or get along well with those who work with them. For this reason, however, they must live within a lie. They need not accept the

lie. It is enough for them to have accepted their life with it and in it. For by this very fact, individuals confirm the system, fulfill the system, make the system, are the system.[25]

In writing those words more than forty-six years after the lynching of Matthew Williams, Havel was dissecting the nature of the communist regime in Czechoslovakia. Yet a similar system of silence saturated the Salisbury community following the lynching of Matthew Williams. There was indeed a conspiracy involved in the lynching of Williams, but it operated within a more extensive system of silence that discouraged more than 130 Black and white witnesses from telling what they knew when it came time to deliver justice for Williams's murder.

In Salisbury, this silence was bred by the ideology of segregation and white supremacy. All Black and white citizens of Salisbury need not have believed all of the "mystifications" of this racist ideology; rather, it was only necessary that they "behave as though they did, or . . . at least tolerate them in silence, or get along well with those who work[ed] with them."[26] They were compelled to live within a lie, a lie that prevailed throughout all communities where lynchings took place. Using witness statements given after the events and recently uncovered from the records of the attorney general, this book tells the story of the lynching of Matthew Williams as occurring within this "system of silence" in Depression-era Salisbury, Maryland. It tells that story through the eyes of the "silent" Black and white witnesses who lived in the community, including the courageous Black voices of Dr. Arthur D. Brown, Maslin Pinkett, and Howard Purnell.

The Silent Shore is by far the most comprehensive account of the Williams lynching and the first to use recently recovered documents to uncover in detail the state of Maryland's secret investigation and subsequent cover-up of the shocking events of 1931 on the Eastern Shore.

Plan of the Book

Part I salvages the story of Matthew Williams, one of the last Black men to be lynched in Maryland, Maryland governor and US presidential hopeful Albert C. Ritchie, and the Black and white residents who risked death to bear witness to the culture of race lynching on Maryland's Eastern Shore. Part II chronicles the ten-week investigation into the Williams lynching conducted in 1931 by Patsy Johnson, an undercover investigator employed by the Pinkerton National Detective Agency. Presented as a case study, this section is more narrative reconstruction and, especially, forensic reconstruction than interpretive analysis.[27] Despite this narrative approach, interpretive analysis emerges as it relates to analyzing the structure of the mob that appeared and of the criminal conspiracy.

Historians have taken various approaches to conceptualizing the nature and structure of lynch mobs. In 1983, historian John Ross divided lynch mobs into four classes, three of them based on their organization level: the "terrorist mob" ("mob vigilantes"), consisting of members of permanent organizations such as the Ku Klux Klan; the "organized private mob" (including the "secret mob" and "private mob"), which maintained planning and cooperation elements among its leaders; and the "hue-and-cry mob," or "mass mob," an unplanned mob formed in response to the hue and cry against alleged injustice or violation of racial taboos.[28]

Building on the work of scholars such as Ross, William Fitzhugh Brundage, in his groundbreaking text Lynching in the New South: Georgia and Virginia, 1880–1930 (1988), introduced a more detailed description of four types of lynch mobs in the United States. Like Ross, Brundage first identified the terrorist mob and private mob; however, he extended his definition of the private mob to emphasize that it was less organized than the terrorist mob, and that its members sought out victims of alleged criminal offenses and kept their act of lynching cloaked in secrecy.[29]

Brundage describes two additional categories: posses—groups, often legally supported, that acted beyond the scope of their authority as they murdered unarmed victims—and mass mobs, which, Brundage claims, watched ritual lynchings and consisted of thousands of citizens who were not content with merely killing the victims but went beyond the practices of most civilized societies that consecrate the dead. Instead, these mobs defiled the body of the lynch victim and memorialized the lynched corpse and the lynching site. Considering these categories, the mob responsible for lynching Williams represented a fusion of the organized private mob and the hue-and-cry, or mass, mob. Such characterizations can be deduced from the analysis of newspaper accounts without identifying who was behind the lynching. That identification can only be done with access to the records of departments that conducted legitimate investigations. Because law enforcement officers were often involved, or at least complicit, in lynchings, we very seldom gain insight into who made up the mysterious mob—local business owners, police officers, firefighters, and laborers—due to administrative cover-ups and the status of local, state, and national archives.[30] Luckily, thanks to Governor Ritchie's secret investigation, we do have access to some of this information in the Williams case.

In writing this book, I wrestled with what framework to use in telling the story of the lynching of Matthew Williams. Scholars have employed several frameworks in analyzing racial violence. In the past, the standard framework for presenting such cases was mostly sociological, centering mainly on the background of the local area where the particular incident occurred, the immediate effects of the violence, the impact that the lynching has had on the community over time, and perhaps an account of the actual details of the incident. More recently, historians such as Benjamin Madley have moved away from this approach and adopted investigative methods similar to those of a prosecutor to guide their work. This book strikes a balance between the two frameworks in letting the sources guide the narrative.

The best example of such a balance is evidenced in the work of Howard Smead. In *Blood Justice* (1986), Howard Smead used newly recovered FBI records of the 1959 lynching of Mack Charles Parker in Mississippi to provide insight into how the mob was investigated and to highlight a pattern that remained consistent throughout the twentieth century. Smead recalls a similar struggle that he faced in deciding how to frame his book. All this changed after meeting with an FBI agent who provided a useful framework that could honor the magnitude of the evidence that Smead had obtained. The agent, Smead recalled, "drew it on a napkin, a paper napkin. He just said that, from their point of view, when they are investigating something like this, they work out from the center, and that would be the actual perpetrators of the crime; it doesn't have to be a murder necessarily, but it will be the actual perpetrators, who would be in the center circle."[31] Following that meeting, Smead took an investigative approach similar to that used by the FBI.

In laying out its case into Parker's lynching, Smead shows, the FBI developed a "sound conspiracy case" against those involved. This conspiracy, he argues, was developed "as a system of concentric circles, expanding outward toward lesser involvement."[32] The first, or innermost, circle encompassed those at the core of the conspiracy who planned and carried out the abduction and murder. These men led the planning of the lynching, went to get Parker from the jail, and took him to the Bogalusa Bridge to be executed. This circle also included local law enforcement officers who were implicated. The second circle was made up of the coconspirators who helped plan the lynching and served as lookouts around the courthouse. This circle also included those law enforcement officers who avoided the scene of the lynching. The third circle was made up of people who knew about the plan to lynch Parker and approximately when the crime would occur but played no direct role. This circle included the town officials, prominent men, some law enforcement officers, friends and relatives of the conspirators, and other area men and women.

The fourth circle included those with ex post facto knowledge of the lynching, including people who had witnessed part of the abduction but claimed not to have recognized any of the men. The fifth and final circle consisted of those who had a passing knowledge of the conspiracy, of the parties

First Circle
The very core of the conspiracy: the group of conspirators who actually planned and carried out the abduction and murder

Second Circle
The men who helped plan the lynching and served as lookouts

Third Circle
The people who knew of the conspiracy and approximately when the crime would occur but played no direct role in the lynching

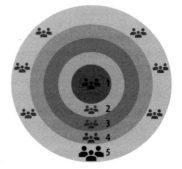

Fourth Circle
The people with direct knowledge of the lynching but ex post facto

Fifth Circle
Those who had passing knowledge of the conspiracy, of the parties involved, and of the likelihood that a lynching would take place

Participants in a conspiracy, grouped in five "circles" from those most directly involved to those most indirectly involved. Based on Smead, Blood Justice, 8, 152.

involved, and the probability that something would happen to Parker. Parker's lynching took place twenty-eight years after Matthew Williams's, in the so-called Magnolia State, which maintained a gruesome legacy in the nature of and conspiracy surrounding race lynchings.

The chapters in part II utilize this same investigative framework proposed by Smead to offer insight into the class-based structure of white supremacy and local power on the Eastern Shore. It also provides further evidence that pushes back against the myth of white uniformity and the desire for elite whites to be seen as homogenous, and explores the relationship between silence and socioeconomic status, as well as the inner workings of a mob in the context of local society.[33] By employing this investigative framework, this book determines degrees of culpability and responsibility, allowing the reader to consider what was truly carried out, to unearth and map out the specific operation of the mob and its enablers, and to view the particular operations associated with the 1931 lynching of Matthew Williams.

In part III, the book's final two chapters explore the impact that such events play in shaping our understanding of Maryland memory and explore what Matthew Williams's lynching tells us about what some have described as "modern-day lynchings," the murder of unarmed Black men and women by law enforcement. Police in their official capacity shot unarmed Black people in the nineteenth and twentieth centuries. Although many "modern-day" lynchings have occurred outside the South and differ from their nineteenth- and early-twentieth-century counterparts, several elements are the same, including African American communities' social, economic, and political vulnerability. The Black people of Salisbury on Maryland's Eastern Shore in the 1930s formed one such vulnerable community.

[Part I]

Matthew Williams, when he first
went to work for Daniel "D.J." Elliott,
c. 1915. *Baltimore Afro-American*,
December 12, 1931.

[1]

Matthew Williams

His Family, His Community, His Humanity

*Every Sunday morning, without fail, he would attend some
church, John Wesley being his favorite. He never missed
Sunday morning services.*

Mrs. Addie Black, aunt of Matthew Williams,
December 5, 1931

Annie Handy, Matthew Williams's mother, was born in Dover, Delaware, in 1867, two years after the Civil War ended, to Thomas and Mary Handy. Thomas's birthdate is unknown, but Mary was born in 1850. Annie was the oldest of the couple's five children; they had three sons and one daughter between 1891 and 1910.[1] By 1870 Annie Handy was living in nearby Barren Creek, Maryland, and in 1880 she was living in Quantico, Maryland. The earliest Handy family residence for which we have an address was on River Road in Salisbury, Maryland. The 1910 census listed Thomas and Mary in this residence with their four younger children, Benjamin, George, Minnie, and Shelie. That same year, Minnie became one of the earliest graduates of Salisbury Colored High School.[2]

In 1892, Annie bore her first child, Olivia, by Frederick Moody, whom she would marry just two years later, on May 21, 1894 in Norfolk, Virginia. This marriage was short-lived as Fredrick would not live to see the new year, dying in December of that same year. It is not clear whether Annie ever remarried; however, in 1908 she was living in Norfolk with Harry Williams. On February 8, 1908, Annie and Harry welcomed a son, Matthew Williams Handy, Annie's second child. By 1910 Annie and Harry were still living in Norfolk. Annie died of pneumonia at the age of forty-five in 1912, Harry Williams died in 1915, and Matthew and his sister, Olivia, moved to Salisbury, Maryland, to start school and live with their grandmother, their grandfather having died some years before.[3] By then, one of Matthew's aunts and two of his uncles were no longer living with Mary.

Matthew attended school until he was fourteen, when his grandmother died and he had to drop out to get a job and help his Aunt Minnie pay the bills.[4] Around this time, Williams began working at the Elliott Box and Crate Factory, a local business owned by Daniel "D.J." Elliott. Williams was a dedicated worker and was able to maintain consistent employment. He

Mrs. Olivia Simmons, the only sister of Matthew Williams, c. 1931. *Baltimore Afro-American,* December 12, 1931.

worked during the winter tending furnaces at the factory and doing odd jobs at the homes of Mr. Elliott and his son James.

After Williams's lynching, the *Baltimore Afro-American* published an exclusive interview with Holland Walters, one of Williams's coworkers. Walters provided a detailed account of Williams's tenure with Elliott, beginning in 1922 when Williams first started working at the box factory as a young man earning ten cents an hour. Walters described Williams as a "very quiet fellow" who "never engaged in any quarrels with the others," a "good reliable worker" who "worked from starting whistle to closing whistle."[5] While working his way up to earning fifteen cents an hour in 1931, Williams often encouraged younger workers to save their money. The day before the lynching, Williams had $56 in his pocket. This was a remarkable amount for a laborer during the Depression, let alone a Black laborer. In addition to the $56 in cash, Williams also maintained two savings accounts. After hearing about Depression-era bank failures, Williams had quickly taken his savings out of the bank he had been using and deposited half in the Farmers' and Merchants' Bank of Salisbury and the other half in the Prudential Bank, hoping to hedge his bets.[6]

Although Williams was successful at his job, he was often perceived by others as strange or even to have an intellectual disability. In an interview with the *Afro-American's* Levi Jolly, Williams's aunt Addie Black commented on this perception: "Some people have been saying that Buddie [Matthew Williams] was crazy and never had a sane mind." Black refuted such talk, insisting that Williams "wasn't crazy" and that "just because he didn't do the things that other people did for enjoyment that is no sign that he had a mental illness. He liked movies and reading. Occasionally he would play baseball with the boys. He also planned on joining the Elks lodge the next month."[7] Olivia Simmons, Williams's sister (who had married and moved to Philadelphia by the time of the lynching) told the *Afro-American* that she, too, thought the idea that her brother was "mentally unbalanced" was unwarranted and untrue. Matthew, she insisted, "was of good mind and seldom associated with the others who lived in this neighborhood."[8] She described her brother as a loving person who was "fond of motion pictures, baseball, and church" and regularly attended John Wesley Methodist Church in Salisbury.[9]

Finding Georgetown

This chapter provides much-needed background on the history of Salisbury's African American community as it relates to Matthew Williams. The black community that Williams was a part of consisted of two neighborhoods—Georgetown and Cuba—though, locally, the two were known collectively as Georgetown.[10] In many ways, Black Eastern Shore communities such as Georgetown were targets of white hatred long before the 1930s because they amplified Black success through early manifestations of Black leadership. As far back as the early nineteenth century, free African Americans began establishing Black churches, which became the epicenters for educational, social,

Salisbury High School graduating class, one year following
the lynching of Matthew Williams, 1932. Courtesy of
Edward H. Nabb Research Center for Delmarva History and
Culture, Linda Duyer African-American History Collection,
Salisbury University, Salisbury, Maryland.

and political advocacy crucial to the Black freedom struggle from the nineteenth through the twenty-first century. The lynching of Matthew Williams
represented an assault on the Black community as a whole.

Maryland as a Border State

Described by historian Barbara Jeanne Fields as the "Middle Ground,"
Maryland's unique position as a border state complicates traditional per-
spectives on racial violence.[11] Although Maryland is located on the US
South's northern periphery, next door to our nation's capital, it has historically maintained a distinctly southern identity, especially along the East-

ern Shore. Historically, the phrase "the Eastern Shore" has been used as a catchall term to describe the area beyond the Chesapeake Bay, "the nation's largest bay."[12] Nonetheless, like "Mississippi Delta," the name "Eastern Shore" refers to an actual geographical location and a distinct culture and history directly connected to those of the entire state. To understand Eastern Shore geography, it is important first to understand the geography of the entire state. Maryland encompasses an area of 12,192.97 square miles, of which 623.5 square miles are inland water and 9,842.62 land. The lower Eastern Shore counties of Somerset, Wicomico, and Worcester cover 1,325.62 square miles, almost 10 percent of the state's entire area.[13]

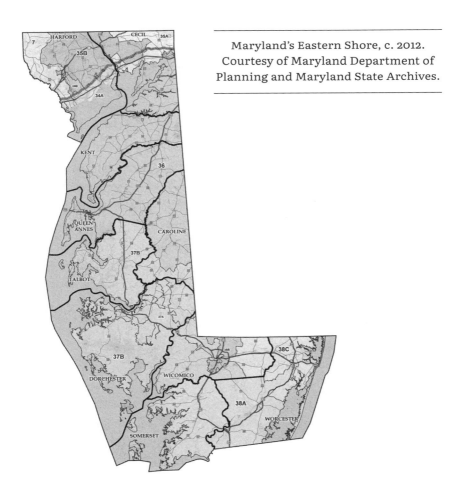

Maryland's Eastern Shore, c. 2012. Courtesy of Maryland Department of Planning and Maryland State Archives.

Matthew Williams: His Family, His Community, His Humanity

In this chapter, I focus on the Black community of the largest of those three counties, Wicomico. Covering 379.10 square miles, Wicomico County was not established until 1867, two years after the end of the Civil War. It consists of former portions of Worcester and Somerset Counties.[14] The climate and geography of all three counties made them ideal for agriculture. For more than three centuries, Somerset County has maintained an agriculture-based economy. From the outset, enslaved labor provided the workforce to support tobacco cultivation, an international enterprise. By the late nineteenth century, Worcester County had become a major producer of fruits, vegetables, grains, and lumber. Wicomico County followed suit and also emerged as a significant producer of fruits and vegetables. However, as the twentieth century approached, Wicomico County emerged as the state's preeminent livestock and poultry producer.[15]

Salisbury, Maryland, is the seat of Wicomico County. The county was named after the Wicomico River, whose name derives from the Algonquian word wicki mekee, which translates as "a place where houses are built."[16] Because it was not established until 1867, there are no census data on the slave population specific to Wicomico County; however, in 1860, out of a total Somerset County population of almost 25,000, just over 5,000 were enslaved persons, and in Worcester County, more than 3,500 of the 20,661 inhabitants were enslaved. In 1932, local historian and journalist Charles J. Truitt provided colorful insight into slavery as it existed in Salisbury before the Civil War:

> When credit is given for the development of this vast farming region, the role taken by slaves cannot be omitted. Slave labor was a potent factor, without which progress would have been slower. Planters found themselves in possession of extensive acreage of woodland, which had to be converted into tillable fields. Here was a character of work requiring able-bodied laborers. And once the soil was tillable, more labor was needed to cultivate and harvest the crops.... The average plantation was [about] 500 acres. Every farmer had his quota of slaves. Of at least two manors in the county, it was said the slave population at times was as large as two hundred.[17]

One of those large plantations, that of Major Levin Handy, dated back to the earliest years of the town of Salisbury. Construction of Poplar Hill Mansion, as Handy called it, began in 1795–96, sixty years after Salisbury's founding, and was likely carried out by its enslaved residents, some of whom probably remained after the state of Maryland forced the sale of Handy's 357-acre plantation to satisfy his outstanding debt. In 1805, following Handy's death, Poplar Hill was purchased by local Salisbury physician John Huston. In 1828, when Dr. Huston died, the plantation was thriving from the agricultural benefits of the Eastern Shore, maintaining fruit trees, vegetable crops, sheep, cattle, and keeping eighteen African Americans enslaved on the property, including one Levin Huston, who was born on Poplar Hill before construction began on the main house. Levin Huston would not be granted his freedom until 1829.[18]

In 1931, Matthew Williams lived on Isabella Street near the historic Poplar Hill Mansion, the oldest standing structure in Salisbury. Located at 117 Elizabeth Street, dating to 1795, this oldest structure was directly connected to the history of the Black community in Salisbury. Like Poplar Hill, the Black community predated Wicomico County.

Most African American communities at the time had a church at their center. At the center of the Georgetown neighborhood was Matthew Williams's church, John Wesley Methodist Episcopal Church. The original congregation traced its founding back to 1837, when a small group of free Blacks began meeting in a "red-painted slab pine building" on land described in Poplar Hill's deed as "Race Grounds."[19] The congregation's earliest leaders included Levin Huston, George Pollitt, Major Toadvine, George James, and Elijah Pinkett. They secured the purchase of the lot in August 1838 and constructed a single-story frame church the same year. This building would serve the congregation for fifty years, until the church members decided to expand the facility to two stories. By 1910, when Matthew Williams was two years old, the church had been restyled further to include a two-story apse.[20]

Georgetown and Cuba: The "Negro Section" of Salisbury

It is often said that every city in America has a Black neighborhood. Following the end of the Civil War, African Americans began to settle into the

Georgetown community of Salisbury. Its two subcommunities, Georgetown and Cuba, surrounded Humphreys Lake, created by a dam located on Division Street. By 1907 Salisbury's population totaled 5,655, of which 4,393 residents were white and 1,262 residents were listed as "colored." These individuals formed 869 white families and 239 "colored" families.[21]

In 1909, after the dam broke, the lake was drained and the dam was removed. Following the lake's destruction, the former lake bottom was sold off and became known as Cuba, which sat alongside Georgetown.[22]

Many historic Black communities in the South had boundaries that identified "white" from "Black" areas. As local Eastern Shore historian Linda Duyer notes, Salisbury's racial borders were not so clear-cut:

> Even before the pond's demise, Georgetown may have lived at the edge of town, but it enjoyed an intimate proximity to much of Salisbury. . . . Georgetown had a close working relationship with the town. Where in other communities, some black neighborhoods would be segregated to quite separate locations, Georgetown experienced a closer proximity. Georgetown residences and businesses were located on the same street as white residences and businesses. White and black properties were adjacent or occupied opposite sides of the street.[23]

Blacks in Salisbury, including Matthew Williams and his family, lived both inside and outside the Georgetown community. However, for all African Americans in Salisbury, Georgetown was a place of safety and community. Even those African Americans who lived two streets outside the boundaries of the Black community proper were still within walking distance of their church and Black-owned businesses.

Georgetown was much less wealthy than, and not as renowned as, Greenwood, the predominantly Black neighborhood in Tulsa, Oklahoma, that was thriving by the early twentieth century. Yet Georgetown embraced one of the most prominent concentrations of Black businesses in Wicomico County, if not throughout the lower Eastern Shore. By 1931, it boasted several successful Black businesses and social institutions that Williams no doubt frequented.

The Lynching of the "Negro" King

By 1870, according to the US Census, African Americans made up almost 28 percent of Salisbury's population. On March 31 of that year, the *Baltimore Sun* reported, President Ulysses S. Grant announced the ratification of the Fifteenth Amendment to the United States Constitution, guaranteeing African American men the right to vote. Salisbury, like many other southern communities, resisted abiding by the new guarantee.[24] By April, Salisbury's Black community witnessed the full effects of Jim Crow segregation and Black Codes. As in most post–Civil War southern communities, once Reconstruction ended and the Freedmen's Bureau officials pulled out, Wicomico County became solidly Democratic due to that party's support for the disenfranchisement of Blacks and its former support for secession.[25]

Reflecting on Matthew Williams's case decades later sheds light on the culture and racial climate of the Eastern Shore. Williams's brutal ritual murder was not the first in Salisbury. Thirty-three years before, Garfield King was one of more than one hundred Black lynching victims in the United States in 1898, including Wright Smith, lynched in the state capital of Annapolis on October 5.[26] Like the vast majority of lynching cases, in the end, the coroner's jury returned a verdict that "Garfield King came to his death at the hands of parties unknown."[27]

On May 21, 1898, a twenty-two-year-old white man named Herman Kenney was shot near Twigg's Store in the Trappe district in Wicomico County near Salisbury. Sheriff John Dashiell arrested Garfield King, who was about eighteen, and put him in the county jail, to remain in limbo while Kenney's wounds were treated in Peninsula General Hospital. Seventy-two hours later, Kenney succumbed to his injuries. Shortly thereafter, his remains were transported to Stansbury Short's home in nearby California, Maryland. On the afternoon of May 25, Wicomico County state's attorney Thomas F. J. Rider gave King what he called a preliminary hearing at Short's residence, just before Kenney's burial in nearby White Haven. King was then held in custody to await the grand jury proceedings, scheduled for the following September. King did not live to stand before a grand jury.

The day before his scheduled appearance, the streets of Salisbury were already swirling with rumors of a potential lynching. It seems that for a particular element of the Salisbury community, justice was not swift enough. As night descended, squads of "invisible" men gathered on the courthouse green in front of the jail where King was being held, preparing for a ritual that the town of Salisbury had never before witnessed, an act that historian Donald Matthews later called "the Southern rite of human sacrifice."[28]

The growing mob put out the electric lights that hung on nearby poles. Just before the clock struck midnight, shots rang out in the direction of the jail. It had rained earlier, and the crowd of more than 150, waiting patiently for their leader so that the ritual could begin, wore what amounted to a uniform of gummed boots, oilskin coats, and oilskin hats. A hurrah rang out from the mob as their leader arrived. He wasted no time. The leader approached Sheriff Dashiell and demanded that he hand over the keys to King's jail cell. Dashiell refused to give up the keys, so the leader ordered his men to find a telephone pole. Shortly thereafter, thirty men approached the jail carrying a telephone pole and used it to batter their way inside. They headed up the stairs to King's cell. Out of nowhere, a masked ruffian emerged with an ax and broke the lock holding King in the cell, and he was dragged out into the street. As the prisoner was pulled from his cell, the mob cried, "A rope, a rope."[29]

Presently, local attorney and former state senator Edward Stanley Toadvine, accompanied by other citizens, appeared on the scene, begging the mob to return King to the sheriff's custody. The crowd ignored Toadvine and the other residents and began preparing a noose. As they did so, King kicked and pleaded for the mob to let him loose.

King was beaten, kicked, and dragged from the foot of the jailhouse stairs to its side yard. Members of the mob fixed the rope to his neck and lifted him over the branch of a young maple tree. Immediately the rope snapped, and King fell to the ground. As he lay there, still alive, someone fired a shot into him. The mob quickly adjusted the rope, and King was once again lifted into the tree. As King hung suspended in the air, the leader yelled, "Line up, boys," to the crowd at the side of the jail. The men formed a firing squad, shooting more than one hundred bullets into King's suspended body. The mob cheered with excitement as they participated in this southern amusement. Then, like troops, the men fell into formation and marched away.[30]

Among the witnesses to King's murder was Salisbury local A. F. Benjamin, who arrived just as the ritual began, between 12:35 and 12:50 a.m. While engaged in this community affair, the mob wore no masks and called one another by name. Among the emboldened crowd were fishermen who worked along the Wicomico River and other leading citizens of the community. The *Baltimore Sun* had been given notice that the lynching was going to occur and sent a correspondent to the scene, where he spoke to the mob leaders. Expressing their devotion, they told the reporter, "We would have accomplished it had we waded through blood to our necks."[31]

Holland, the local judge, was suddenly awakened by the shots fired. When he arrived at the scene, King's lifeless, bullet-ridden body was still dangling in the air. Tragically, the spectacle would continue. Holland ordered King's body to be taken down and placed in the nearby fire engine house for protection until burial arrangements were made. By morning this makeshift mortuary had transformed into a gallery, and King's mutilated body was the featured exhibit. Hundreds of people made their way to the Fire Department to view the work of southern savagery. They marveled at the sight of the young, well-built "mulatto" teenager, a recent graduate of Princess Anne Academy (now the University of Maryland Eastern Shore), whose bloodied and mangled body seemed held together by only a thin shirt and a pair of black stockings. The gunshots had cut holes in King's chest and face, blowing away the upper part of his shirt. By afternoon, the exhibition had ended, and the town undertaker, George C. Hill, wrapped King's exploited body in a winding sheet and placed him in a coffin. King was finally laid to rest in a Potters Field, near Georgetown, just beyond the New York, Philadelphia, and Norfolk Railroad line.[32]

The Community Responds

On May 31, the "Negro" community of Salisbury and Wicomico County packed into the John Wesley Methodist Episcopal Church to condemn the lynching of Garfield King. The meeting was attended by Black leaders from across the state, including prominent banker Solomon T. Huston of Salisbury, who was chosen as chairman.[33] Those who addressed the assembly included the church's senior pastor, Reverend F. C. Wright, and Reverend A. R.

Stokley, F. N. Butler, James O. Pinkett, and Huston. Each of the speakers condemned the deplorable act while cautioning the Black citizens to keep calm and to remain law abiding. Before the meeting closed, a select committee was appointed to call upon Maryland Republican governor Lloyd Lowndes Jr. to offer a $1,000 award to anyone who could identify those involved in the lynching.[34] This committee included notable Baltimore civil rights attorney William Ashby Hawkins; Robert Patterson Graham, a Salisbury native and future secretary of state; Huston; and J. F. Gaddis of Wicomico County.[35]

The Wicomico County state's attorney soon summoned more than fifty witnesses before a coroner's jury to testify as to the lynching of Garfield King. Among the witnesses was attorney Edward Stanley Toadvine, the former Democratic state senator from Wicomico County.[36] Toadvine, an eyewitness, claimed that he entered the jail as soon as the mob broke in, hoping to reason with them and also to protect four of his other Black clients who were in the cell with King. In the end, Toadvine claimed that he was unable to identify any member of the mob due to the dim lighting and the fact that many of the men had their faces blacked and covered with red paint. The attorney described a scene similar to those of other lynchings, on and off Maryland's Eastern Shore, in which mobs' faces were remembered as being painted black.[37]

Other witnesses confirmed Toadvine's testimony; with one exception, they identified the leader of the mob as a tall, slender man who allegedly fit the description of the mob leader identified in previous lynchings in nearby Somerset and Caroline counties.[38] Another vital detail, obtained from an eyewitness quoted in a Maryland newspaper, is the level of organization exemplified in the act. The witness noted the "promptness and business-like way in which the tall leader directed things in Salisbury Wednesday night," suggesting "that he has had experience in such things before." The reporter raised the question "Have we a gang of organized Lynchers on the Eastern Shore?"[39]

Shortly after the coroner's jury's investigation, the interracial select committee made its way to Annapolis to confront the governor. On Friday, June 18 around 9 o'clock, Governor Lloyd Lowndes Jr. arrived at his offices accompanied by Major-General Lemuel Allison Wilmer and Secretary of State Richard Dallam, only to find a delegation of Black men along with Robert Patterson Graham, waiting to confront him regarding the lynching of King.[40] In addition to the original members of the delegation, the group was joined by several Black religious leaders, including Reverend Dr. Ernest Lyon of John Wesley Methodist Church in Baltimore (later US ambassador to Liberia), who served as the group's spokesman; Reverend John William Norris of Ebenezer African Methodist Episcopal Church; Reverend E. F. Eggleston of Grace Presbyterian Church; and Hiram Watty, a future Baltimore city councilman.

Collectively, the group urged Governor Lowndes to offer a reward for information leading to the arrest of those responsible for lynching King.[41] Huston then made an astonishing statement, that "many of the lynchers were from the Trappe district in Wicomico County."[42] Graham took it a step further, confessing that King's lynching was "deprecated by the better class of citizens."[43] To no one's surprise, Governor Lowndes expressed his reluctance to offer an award to assist in identifying the mob, noting that such a measure had been ineffective in the past. Nonetheless, he said that he would consider the request and expressed confidence that at least some of those responsible for King's lynching would be brought to justice.

That Governor Lowndes was willing to meet with Black civil rights and religious leaders from Salisbury and elsewhere in the state suggests that vestiges of Reconstruction-era Republican politics still seemed present in state and local government at the turn of the twentieth century. To no surprise, the delegation's effort was futile, and as in the thousands of other lynching cases, the perpetrators were never apprehended.

James E. Stewart

The signature Black institution on Broad Street in Georgetown was John Wesley United Methodist Church, the church where Matthew Williams was a member. Today, it is the only remaining building from the original Georgetown neighborhood. Across the street from the church were the home and business of James E. Stewart, the area's Black undertaker and funeral home director. He had started his company in 1919. It was in Stewart's home business that Williams's body was hidden following the lynching and where his funeral services were held. The Black Masonic Hall that Williams had planned on joining was located on Broad Street, next to the white-owned Benedict's Florist.

Stewart, a native of the Eastern Shore, provided funeral services for the Black community. He was born in 1909 in the Quantico area of Wicomico County to the late James F. and Harriet Stewart. By sixteen, he began working as a steward of the Baltimore, Chesapeake & Atlantic Railway and as a boat operator between Claiborne and Baltimore. Shortly after that, he graduated from the Eckels School of Embalming in Philadelphia and returned to Salisbury, where he developed the reputation of being a political leader, businessman, and churchman. Little is known about Stewart's stance on racial justice; however, we do know that he served as a member of the state interracial commission and that he was quite active in regional Republican politics, serving as president of the (Negro) Eastern Shore District Voter League. In addition, he promoted and supported the establishment of local educational institutions for African Americans throughout the Eastern Shore and hosted an annual fair in Salisbury for the Black community.[44]

At the same time, Stewart seemed to have had an unusual connection to white political leaders, several of whom served as honorary pallbearers at his funeral in 1949, including such prominent local and state leaders as Circuit Court Judge Levin Claude Bailey, state senator Wallace H. White, and US Congressman Edward T. Miller of Easton, one of whom (Bailey) would play a significant role in covering up the lynching of Matthew Williams.[45]

Such a connection is further complicated when one considers the statement that Stewart made with Reverend J. N. Dickerson and James L. Johnson in 1933, in which they held attorney Bernard Ades "fully responsible for the events which have happened on the peninsula during the past two years."[46] By "the events" Stewart and the others were referring to the cases of Euel Lee (1931), Matthew Williams (1931), and George Armwood (1933). Ades, a Baltimore native, was an American communist lawyer who gained national notoriety after representing Euel Lee, an African American accused of murdering a white family in Maryland in 1931 following a dispute concerning his pay.

Ades worked for the Baltimore offices of the International Labor Defense (ILD), the organization that provided defense counsel for the Scottsboro Boys in Alabama in 1931–34. Ades was able to secure a venue change for Lee's trial to Baltimore by arguing that Lee could not get a fair trial on the Eastern Shore. Despite losing the case in the ensuing trial, Ades was able to drag the case out and expose the judicial system's injustice in Salisbury and throughout the South toward African Americans. Indeed, his success made him a marked man on the Eastern Shore; he received death threats and, in one instance, was attacked by an angry white mob and beaten.[47]

Stewart, Dickerson, and Johnson's statement is relatively straightforward and fits neatly into the anti-communist "outside agitator" trope used consistently in Salisbury and throughout the United States in the 1920s and 1930s.[48] Indeed, Stewart's thoughts echoed sentiments, pushed by the white community of Salisbury and published in the *Salisbury Daily Times*, suggesting that communist agitators from New York and Baltimore had descended on the Eastern Shore and "were holding secret meetings with black residents in Salisbury and other Eastern Shore towns."[49]

Stewart's thoughts concerning the communist movement reflected a broader debate during the time concerning who represented the Black community. Indeed, the relationship between the Black community and the Communist Party USA was evident in the competition between the ILD and the NAACP (National Association for the Advancement of Colored People) as the two organizations sought to speak for and defend those suffering under Jim Crowism and the reality of racial violence.[50]

Although the communist outside agitator theory was eventually debunked, at least in Williams's case, by the local court, Stewart and others continued to use Ades as a scapegoat, providing cover for the white racist establishment that was responsible for the lynching of Williams and Armwood. Indeed, one of the most revealing statements, among many, is that in which Stewart, Dickerson, and Johnson argue that Ades was not needed and that they "had confidence in the justice of the local Courts and, so far as the Courts were concerned, believe that he could have received a fair and impartial trial. There was no reason to presume otherwise. We had seen the orderly process of law carried out for so many, many years here that it would have been foolish and unfair to make any other presumption about the people of the peninsula."[51]

Stewart's role as a leader in the Salisbury Black community was further exemplified when he said that his statement was given "on behalf of our local people" and that it represented "their attitude on such matters."[52] In closing, Stewart and the leaders doubled down: "We state, without fear of contradiction, that it was the tactics he [Ades] employed in that case which caused the death of Matthew Williams and George Armwood."[53]

Aside from the question of whether Stewart actually spoke on behalf of the Black community of Salisbury, it is quite clear that the white press saw no problem in Stewart speaking for the "Negro" community on the Eastern Shore. Indeed, this assumption is evidenced in the title of the *Daily Times* article: "Colored People of Salisbury Protest Interference of Ades." Stewart maintained a prominent leadership role in the Black community and garnered the support of white political and community leaders in Salisbury, a clear distinction between him and Dr. Brown.

Church Street

The highest percentage of Black-owned businesses in Salisbury was on Church Street. The property between Church and Broad streets included residences and stores and a narrow structure known as the Flat Iron Building. The First Baptist Church (previously the Colored Missionary Baptist Church) was located on the corner of Church Street and Poplar Avenue. Demonstrating the lack of fluidity across racial boundaries, the Old School Baptist Church, a white church, was also located at the corner of Church and Baptist streets. As in most Black neighborhoods, there was also a local dry goods store. Langston Store was located east of First Baptist Church and Pollitt's Alley and was operated by Ulysses S. Grant Langston and his wife, Julia. They had previously operated a livery as well as a dry goods store. Georgetown also had its own bicycle shop, owned by Joseph Cornish Sr., located on Church Street to the east of Langston Store. Bob Toulson was another successful business owner in the Georgetown community. Toulson's Shop, a tailor and shoe shine business, was a community fixture in Georgetown during the late 1920s and 1930s.[54]

Beyond Broad and Church streets, the community extended to Boulden, Cathell, Cemetery, Chestnut, Ellen, Happy, Pollitt, Popular Hill, and Water streets. But Broad and Church were the most popular and frequented areas in Georgetown. It is essential to see how Matthew Williams's lynching would have affected Salisbury's Black community. In lynching Mat-

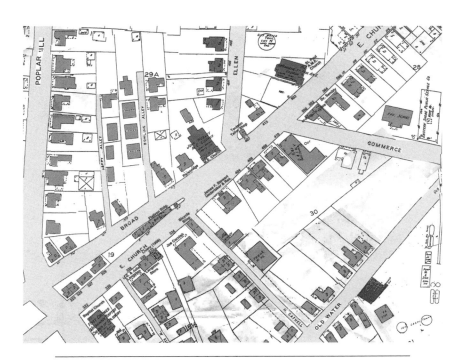

Annotated Sanborn map of the Georgetown community,
c. 1931. Courtesy of the Library of Congress,
Geography & Map Division.

thew Williams, the whites in the city were warning the Georgetown community's Black men and women that no matter how successful they were, they were still inferior and subject to Judge Lynch. Matthew Williams should be seen not only as a victim but also as a loving Black community member. In lynching Williams, the mob was terrorizing the entire Black community.

[2]

"The Blood Lust of the Eastern Shore"

The Crime, the Kidnapping,

and the Spectacle

The blood lust of the Eastern Shore has claimed a victim. Lynch law has prevailed. The mob has had its way. It has wreaked its vengeance. It has made its kill, and upon the altar of its cruelty it has immolated not merely the Negro, Matthew Williams, but the justice and decency which are the foundation of a civilized community.

Baltimore Post, December 5, 1931

The editorial from which this chapter's epigraph is taken was published not in the 1890s during the height of the lynching crisis in the United States, but more than thirty years into the twentieth century. Lost in these dramatic words is the human story not just of the community but, more important, of the victim, Matthew Williams. Williams was just one of four men targeted by racial terror on Maryland's Eastern Shore in 1929–31.

Before the lynching of Williams, three African American laborers in Maryland, Richard Ford of Delmar, Euel Lee (aka Orphan Jones, the name given to him by his foster parents) of Berlin, and George Davis of Chestertown had slipped out of the hands of three bloodthirsty mobs after allegedly committing violent crimes against local whites. These near lynchings occurred at the beginning of the Great Depression when racial tensions had grown inflamed as whites were forced to compete for jobs that had historically been reserved for African Americans.[1]

Setting the Stage for What Was to Come

Richard Ford

On September 15, 1929, Dallas M. Ellis, a thirty-four-year-old white railroad worker, was found dead at the home of a local African American laborer, John C. K. Trader, just two miles from Delmar, Maryland.[2] According to the local newspaper, Trader was said by Maryland police to have an "unsavory reputation." Those who claimed to have seen the shooting reported that, after arriving at Trader's home, Marion Wooton, Oscar Phillips, Frank Lowe, and Ellis got out of his car and began walking to Trader's back porch. As Ellis approached, Richard Ford, a local African American mechanic, allegedly appeared in the doorway and shouted, "I will kill the first man who comes on this porch."[3] After issuing this warning, it was said, Ford went back in the house, returned with a gun, and shot Ellis after the latter stepped onto the porch. Witnesses said that Ford had a grudge against Ellis and that the murder was connected to this dispute. From the outset, however, this account was shaky, as Wicomico County sheriff Ralph Duffy and Maryland State Police sergeant E. M. Mills admitted that all of the individuals they questioned were too drunk to "give a coherent story."[4] Following the shooting Ford vanished.

In reaction to the killing, a group of white citizens descended on the Delmar community, searching for Richard Ford to no avail. The mob activity following Ellis's murder was not surprising as the Ku Klux Klan maintained an active presence in Wicomico County throughout the 1920s. Among the centers for Klan activities on the Eastern Shore was Delmar, a small community on the border of Maryland and Delaware, just six miles from Salisbury. By the 1920s Maryland's Eastern Shore saw a small rise in Klan activities, and in 1923 the Wicomico County Chapter of the Ku Klux Klan had 250 members.[5] Following the lynching of Matthew Williams, some Salisbury residents speculated that the perpetrators had come from Delmar.

Euel Lee

On October 12, 1931, Green K. Davis, his two daughters, and his wife were found murdered in their home near Taylorville, Maryland, in Worcester County (less than forty miles from Salisbury), where Green Davis operated

A Ku Klux Klan rally held sometime in the 1920s in Delmar, Maryland, approximately eight miles from Salisbury. Courtesy of Harold W. T. Purnell Collection, Delaware Public Archives.

a produce stand. The next day Euel Lee, a sixty-year-old farm laborer from the Carolinas whom Davis had fired just three days before the murder, was identified as the main suspect. According to the reports, Lee was arrested at his home in Ocean City, where investigators allegedly found jewelry and other personal property from Davis's house. Shortly after his arrest Lee was taken to Berlin and then to Snow Hill, the county seat, where his statements were taken after hours of interrogation. According to investigators, the murder happened after Davis refused to pay Lee for working on a rainy day, and Lee had wanted to get even. As news spread of the Davis family murder, a lynch mob began to form and Lee was quickly smuggled out of Worcester County to Baltimore for his safety.[6]

On October 17, with Lee away from the Eastern Shore, a mob of more than fifty local white citizens terrorized the Black community of Berlin for nearly two hours. After Raymond T. Quillen, Berlin's mayor, denied reports of the mob violence, African American reporters conducted their own investigation into the riots by interviewing members of the Black community. The truth was subsequently revealed, and reporters relayed an announcement that went out to all Black citizens, who "were warned to stay off the streets Saturday night [October 17] after more than 50 whites began beating Purnell Leonard (30) and his wife, Mrs. Mattie Leonard (24)."[7] As the mob descended on Berlin, Black citizens were forced to find cover in nearby stores. Others were unable to escape and were hit with "brickbats," including Earl Douglass, who was attacked while attempting to fetch a doctor for his sick wife. Five of the citizens who were able to find shelter in local stores were subsequently escorted to their homes by the police. Eventually, Benjamin Parsons (a white man whose name would reappear in the future) was arrested along with six others. An additional thirteen white men were issued arrest warrants for terrorizing the African American citizens.[8]

George Davis

On November 21, 1931, George Davis, a twenty-eight-year-old Black man, was accused of attempted assault of Elizabeth Lusby, the twenty-five-year-old white wife of his previous employer, farmer Edgar Lusby, near Kennedyville, in Kent County, Maryland, less than ninety miles from Salisbury. Following the incident, Davis fled to Wilmington, Delaware, where he was captured three days later, on November 24. Sheriff John T. Vickers then transported Davis to the Kent County jail in Chestertown. Shortly thereafter, Sheriff Vickers was informed that a mob was en route to the prison and was preparing to lynch Davis. Immediately the sheriff decided to relocate Davis to Easton County jail, thirty miles away.

Just after Sheriff Vickers left with Davis, the mob arrived at the jail, with one of the leaders carrying a coiled rope, only to find State's Attorney Stephen R. Collins, who pleaded with the men to "let the law take its course," promising that "every effort would be made" to bring the "negro" to a speedy trial.[9] Upon receiving Davis in Easton, authorities learned that the mob was headed there, intending to storm the jail and retrieve the prisoner, so they sent him on to Baltimore. Just missing Davis by thirty minutes, the mob of hundreds of men demanded that Sheriff A. Ray Carroll deliver Davis to them.

After searching the jail, the mob split up with one group heading to the Queen Anne County jail in Centerville and another two hundred making their way to Elkton to the Cecil County jail, hoping to find Davis.[10]

Clarence Bell Pays the Penalty under the Lash

In September 1931, Clarence Bell, a forty-year-old African American carpenter, went to court after he was accused of beating his wife. Presiding at the trial was circuit court judge Joseph L. Bailey, who invoked a law dating back to 1789 and sentenced Bell to receive thirty lashes.[11] Bailey justified this form of penalty based on the precedent set forth in Foote v. Maryland (1883), which upheld flogging as punishment for assault since the practice was permitted at the nation's founding. Also on the bench in Somerset County courts was Judge Robert F. Duer, another notable Eastern Shore jurist, who would play an important role in the events leading up to the lynching of George Armwood two years later in 1933.[12] Sheriff Murray G. Phillips was to administer the flogging. Having never carried out this form of punishment before, Sheriff Phillips sought advice from officers in Delaware, a state where the whipping post was still being used openly.[13]

According to a local reporter in the courtroom, Bailey's sentence sent shockwaves through the crowd, even surprising his nephew, Levin C. Bailey, the Wicomico County state's attorney, who prosecuted Bell. Judge Bailey concluded his remarks by saying directly to Bell—in open court: "This is something that you will remember for 30 years, if you live that long."[14]

The next morning, word had spread throughout the community, and a crowd of nearly three hundred descended on the courthouse. However, the people assembled would soon learn that Judge Bailey had decided to have the whipping administered in private in the presence of a select group of Wicomico County leaders, including State's Attorney Bailey, the deputy sheriff, newspapermen, and Herman Phillips, brother of the sheriff.[15] Around 8:55 p.m., the beating commenced on the second floor of the jail. With whip in hand, Sheriff Phillips began beating Bell. A local reporter in the room grippingly described the flogging:

[While] Bell stood outside the locked cell door, Sheriff Phillips, whip in hand, took a position to the prisoner's left. Bell's face was not visible to the spectators. The solid wooden doors to the cells on either side of the corridor were closed, denying the thirty inmates a view of the scene being enacted a few feet away. Not a voice or a sound were heard from behind the doors. Sheriff Phillips and a spectator counted the lashes as they were given. Several times Bell winced as more red welts appeared on the exposed portions of the flesh. Three whips, about one-half inch in diameter at the largest end, were used. Each lasted for ten lashes.[16]

In enacting this outdated law for the first time in the county's recent history, Judge Bailey was putting a Black man and the Black community on notice—evoking repressed memories of the master-overseer-slave relationship. Judge Bailey represented the master, the sheriff represented the overseer, using the whip to keep Bell (and by transference, the entire Black community) in line, as overseers had once kept enslaved people in line.

The Great Depression in Black and White

Before delving into the statements of eyewitnesses to the lynching of Williams, it is necessary to highlight the economic climate in which his lynching took place. Racial terror lynchings directly correlated with economic strife, strife to which whites have historically responded with racial violence. This correlation can be traced by examining the rise in racial terror lynchings during the economic depressions of the 1890s and the 1930s.[17]

While the economic climate helped produce an environment conducive to lynching in the early 1930s, the intersections of race and class in Salisbury are also crucial to understanding people's responses to and perceptions of the lynching.

President Herbert Hoover took a minimalist approach to using his office to address the Great Depression. Although he offered a number of remedies, including the establishment of the Reconstruction Finance Corporation (RFC) and various public works projects, he avidly opposed involving the federal government in direct relief efforts.[18] He believed that African Americans should look first to their own communities for economic relief, and then to their municipal and state governments. Yet he did not consider

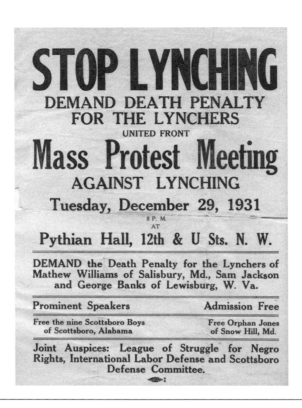

A flyer, c. 1931, advertising a meeting hosted by the International Labor Defense in Washington, DC, and demanding the death penalty for the murderers of Williams in Salisbury, Maryland, and Sam Jackson and George Banks in Lewisburg, West Virginia. Courtesy of Moorland-Spingarn Research Center, Howard University, Washington, DC.

their especially difficult circumstances. On April 1, 1929, he wrote to Eugene Kinckle Jones, the executive secretary of the National Urban League: "The first step toward being a good citizen is to achieve economic independence. It is the soil in which self-respect takes root, and from which may then grow all the moral and spiritual enrichments of life. The work of the National Urban League to train Negroes in the city to find new lines of occupation is fundamental to the progress of the race."[19] By 1930, there were more than 5.5 million gainfully employed African Americans in the United

States, representing 59 percent of the African American population.[20] However, in Wicomico County the level of unemployment for Blacks differed considerably from that of the rest of Maryland and the nation. According to some sources, the unemployment rate in Wicomico County was 2.3 percent.[21] Upon further analysis, this number does not match up with what was taking place on the ground. If unemployment was so low in Salisbury, why was there such a demand in the community to assist struggling citizens in Salisbury?

Like most of the Deep South, Wicomico County and much of the Eastern Shore depended for their economic well-being on agriculture, a natural extension of the plantation economy that had controlled much of the nineteenth century. Eastern Shore farms began showing signs of distress as early as 1927. When depression came, agriculture took the most significant hit, affecting Black and white relations on the Eastern Shore. Among the signs of decline were the low market prices for crops and increased production costs. In many ways, these issues resulted from the Eastern Shore's failure in the 1920s to take advantage of technological advances in agriculture. Whites in Salisbury and Wicomico counties blamed worsening business conditions on the region's growing Black population. By the 1930s, this population increase would be further complicated when considering that both Wicomico County and Somerset County had a Black population two times the state average.[22] (See tables A.1 and A.2 in the appendix.)

By February 1931, the *Salisbury Times* began publishing advertisements sponsored by President Hoover's Emergency Committee for Employment, which begged citizens to put their neighbors to work. These advertisements admonished citizens of Salisbury to join the scores of citizens all over America who had taken significant steps in "the war against Unemployment."[23] Despite such calls to voluntarism, by year's end, one-third of African Americans in southern cities were unable to find employment. During the following year, the unemployment rate rose to more than 50 percent.[24]

Traditionally when we consider the Great Depression, the image of white men and women standing in bread lines comes to mind. The national media neglected to capture images of African American men and women who were suffering in exponential numbers. Both sets of images, the seen and the unseen, exposed the American Dream as crumbling. The Great Depression was a national economic crisis that affected millions of Americans. However, as the banks failed, so too did the financial hopes and dreams of African Americans, who had to deal not only with the same economic calamity their white counterparts faced, but also with Jim Crow segregation. As historian Harvard Sitkoff argues, "The depression dealt a staggering blow to blacks. It magnified all their traditional economic liabilities. It created newer and harsher ones. No group could less afford the precipitous decline that followed the stock market crash of 1929. None suffered more from it."[25]

When it came to relief, African Americans for the most part were left out. Any aid they did receive came mostly from private sources. By 1930, 142,106 African Americans in Baltimore received relief and assistance from private agencies.[26] The next year, 1931, 42.8 percent of African Americans were among the caseloads of private welfare agencies in Baltimore. Wherever public relief was extended to Black people, they formed a disproportionate part of the rolls. In 1931 African Americans in Akron, Ohio, accounted for only 4.5 percent of the population, but they made up 25 percent of the total number of relief cases. In Baltimore, African Americans represented 17 percent of the city's population and made up 34 percent of the full relief rolls.[27]

In Salisbury, the plight of African Americans was not much different, and they were not represented in any of the local unemployment commissions. The twelve-member all-white Emergency Committee for Employment included a number of Salisbury's leading public figures, including A. T. Grier of the Lion's Club and editors Charles Truitt and Sheldon Jones, who represented the local press. Indeed, their strategy for obtaining data concerning the unemployment rate in the county was problematic as they did not go door to door. Instead, they expected people who were struggling to find jobs to travel to the Chamber of Commerce to register as unemployed residents of Salisbury.[28]

Sociologist Ira De Augustine Reid argues that several problems led to high "Negro" unemployment during the Depression, among them local legislation that targeted Black employees and increased competition between Blacks and whites for jobs that heretofore were ordinarily held by African Americans.[29] The Great Depression fueled a mob spirit on Maryland's Eastern Shore in which disenfranchised whites took to racial violence to keep "Negroes" in their place. After failing to lynch Euel Lee and George Davis, this element finally was successful in its attempt to make an example of Matthew Williams.

The lynching of Williams, then, needs to be understood as a message crime designed to stoke fear in Salisbury's African American community and to enforce white supremacy on Maryland's Eastern Shore. To understand the argument that I propose, it is useful to look back at antebellum southern plantations, whose success was predicated on maintaining a racial hierarchy in which both enslaved Blacks and poor whites were exploited. The economic success of white plantation and business owners was not the success of the entire white community. This is where class becomes vital in the history that I recount. Poor Black and white laborers shared a common poverty; however, as historian Grace Elizabeth Hale argues, the system of segregation kept the two from joining efforts by maintaining the racial hierarchy.[30] This racial hierarchy distracted whites from seeing their commonalities with Blacks, particularly the shared experience of being exploited for their labor.

Feeling that they were failing to maintain social control, Eastern Shore whites took to violence in hopes of reinforcing the racial hierarchy that had seemed less noticeable during the gaudy Roaring Twenties.

A. D. Brown

It was probably the commotion that prompted Dr. Arthur D. Brown to look out of the window of the house where he was treating two patients on December 4, 1931, and see Matthew Williams stagger out of the office of his employer, Daniel "D.J." Elliott, a prominent manufacturer, banker, and native of Wicomico County.[31] By 1931, the forty-five-year-old Brown, known as the area's leading "colored" physician, had garnered a reputation for being militant and outspoken against the maltreatment of African Americans on the Eastern Shore and the injustices they experienced.[32] His status as a physician somehow allowed him to transcend the system of silence in the community and to become one of the state's leading witnesses after Williams's lynching. How was Brown able to do what other Black people could not?

The white community of Salisbury was fine with Black professionals like Dr. Brown thriving, but for the entire Black community to do so posed a problem to whites. The Wilmington Massacre (North Carolina, 1898), Atlanta Race Riots (1906), Tulsa Race Massacre (1921), and Rosewood Massacre (Florida, 1923), during each of which an entire Black community was burned to the ground, provide examples of what happened when Black success or survival rivaled that of whites.[33]

Unlike other Black professionals, Brown did more than just treat his patients, take their money, and go home. Brown's agency and actions shed light on local manifestations of Black power during the early civil rights movement. His case is indeed unique, as recent arrivals such as Dr. Brown, the product of the Great Migration, were often more susceptible to lynching due to their lack of connections. However, Dr. Brown, who had spent time in Baltimore, was part of a broader strata of Black elites in Maryland and perhaps the Upper South who somehow lived to tell the tale.[34] In the end, Brown's protected status was maintained not solely because of his wealth but also because of his social profile throughout the state.

Brown was born December 16, 1887, in Salisbury, North Carolina. He graduated with a bachelor of arts from Livingston College and completed his medical training at Shaw University's Leonard Medical School in Raleigh, before being drafted into the army during World War I. After the war, in 1920, he moved to Baltimore before eventually making his way to Salisbury, Maryland, where he set up a private practice on the west side of town. While in Salisbury, Brown was active in a number of social and civic organizations, including the Methodist Episcopal Church, the Elks, the Independent Order of Odd Fellows, the Knights of Pythias, and the Masons.[35]

Unlike working-poor African Americans, but like Williams and the majority of Salisbury's African American community, Brown, as the area's only Black physician, did not depend on the traditional white establishment for his income. Like the city's Black morticians and clergy, Brown provided a necessary alternative service that allowed "separate but equal" segregation to function. It was during the era of spectacle lynchings, Grace Elizabeth Hale argues, that segregation created space in society for Black doctors such as Brown, as well as for "black colleges and increasingly black business districts" throughout the South, in which to thrive and expand "as southern African Americans moved into growing southern cities."[36]

Segregation provided the same protected status afforded Brown to other prominent African Americans during the height of spectacle lynchings and the economic turmoil of the 1890s, and during the first thirty years of the twentieth century.[37] In many ways, Dr. Brown fits the profile of such notable Black leaders, including Colbert "Buck" Franklin, a civil rights attorney and the father of pioneering Black historian John Hope Franklin. Like Dr. Brown, the elder Franklin lived to tell the tale after bearing witness to anti-Black terror in Tulsa's Greenwood community.[38]

328 Lake Street

Around 1 p.m. on December 4, 1931, Brown received a request from two patients to make a house call. It must have taken him some time to get to their rented house, because Matthew Williams's aunt would later say that her nephew was still safe at her house, playing with his cousins, at around 2 p.m., and that he had told her when he left that he was heading to Elliott's factory to do some work.[39] Brown's patients were at 328 Lake Street, directly across the street from the Elliott Box and Crate Factory. He tended only the first patient, who was upstairs, before he looked outside and spotted Williams staggering out of the factory office.[40] He saw James Elliott, D.J.'s son, immediately behind Williams. Brown then observed James chase Williams down the street while pointing a gun directly at Williams's head and shooting.[41] Brown later recalled James yelling "son of a bitch, damn son of a bitch," as he pursued Williams.[42] Brown also remembered hearing a woman scream at this point.

Brown left the home and headed to the scene. Williams, struggling to keep his footing, ran across a field, only to stumble over some lumber as if he were blind. Blood was spewing from his mouth, but he could walk, and Brown led him to an older Black man whom he asked to assist Williams in getting to the hospital. The man refused, as did several others, but a "good Samaritan" who was visiting from New York finally agreed to give Williams a ride to the hospital.[43] D.J. Elliott had already been taken to the hospital in an ambulance. He later died there of his wounds.

Office where Daniel J. Elliott was shot, c. 1931. On the right is the lumber yard where Matthew Williams was shot by Daniel's son, James Elliott. Courtesy of Baltimore News American (Hearst Corporation).

After Williams was taken away, Brown walked into D.J. Elliott's office and confronted an elderly white man who worked at the mill. When he asked him why Elliott had shot Williams, the man responded, "He [Williams] had no business grabbing that white girl."[44] Brown quickly replied, "Suppose he did grab a white girl, he didn't have any business to shot [sic] him" over such a minimal offense.[45]

The exchange between Brown and the elderly laborer sheds light on the distinctly southern attitude toward justice, specifically as it was served on Blacks. This worker's response is left out of all known accounts.[46] This exchange presents a hallmark example of how white sexual anxieties and rape fantasies were used to rationalize segregation, disenfranchisement, and lynching.[47] Extending Ida B. Wells-Barnett's work, Walter Francis White, in his groundbreaking text *Rope and Faggot*, sees this lie not as based on seeking equality and justice for white womanhood but rather as "a symptom of malodorous economic and social conditions within the American South."[48] White aptly describes the social and economic factors that made lynching prevalent in the twentieth century at the onset of the Great Depression. The exchange between Brown and the elderly laborer suggests whites' perception that they had failed to keep Blacks in line, an understanding rooted in post-Reconstruction ideologies concerning race.

While walking through the crime scene alongside the elderly white worker, Brown noticed a revolver lying on a table. It held two cartridges, three having been discharged. Just as Brown finished scanning the room, a number of men walked into the office. Henry Chatman, who had been on the phone with D.J. Elliott when he heard a gun go off, was one of these men. Following the gunfire, Chatman also heard a typewriter on the other end of the line. After Elliott went silent, Chatman phoned the hospital to urge the staff to send an ambulance to Elliott's office. Chatman told Brown all of this, and then Sheriff Murray Phillips walked in and asked Brown what had happened.[49]

Brown responded that "a Negro [Williams] shot Mr. Elliott and then shot himself and then Jim Elliott shot him [Williams]."[50] Shortly thereafter, Maryland state policeman J. C. Peroutka arrived on the scene and noticed about ten people standing outside the office. Moving through the crowd, Officer Peroutka recalled, he walked into the office and saw a pool of blood near D.J. Elliott's desk. Hoping to secure the scene, he walked out, closed the door behind him, and sent word to Sheriff Phillips. Officer Peroutka then told the onlookers that they had better get away from the office.[51] Shortly thereafter, Sheriff Phillips, Officer William W. "Will" White, Salisbury attorney Curtis Long, and two other men arrived. Sheriff Phillips walked around the office a few times, then called Wicomico County state's attorney Levin C. Bailey before heading to Peninsula Hospital to interrogate Williams.[52]

Officer Will White and a few concerned white citizens entered the office next as Brown walked outside and addressed the crowd gathering at the scene of the shooting, near Willow and Lake streets. He told them that Williams would not live ten minutes; he would be dead, Brown said, before he made it to the hospital. Brown hoped that this prediction would calm the growing crowd. Among them Brown recognized attorney Curtis Long, a state police officer, and a number of Salisbury locals, including Herman Townsend and Pap Hitchen, who owned a garage at Lake and Main streets; Marion Smith, a mechanic at Bill Larf Garage; Norman Purdue, who ran a tire store on West Lake Street; and Bill Windsor, who ran a local trucking business.[53]

Around this time a number of rowdy men in the crowd began plotting retaliation for Elliott's murder. In their view, they "ought to run every damn Negro out of Salisbury tonight."[54] Alarmed by their threat, Brown headed to his car. The words from the crowd represented the prevailing demand that racial segregation be enforced whenever white supremacy was threatened. Brown was quite familiar with the mob spirit and could guess what was eventually going to happen. On August 6, 1906, when Brown was only nine-teen years old, he had witnessed the lynching of three African American men, Jack Dillingham, John Gillespie, and George Irwin.[55]

Marion Smith came out from among the crowd and began talking to one of the other men. Brown broke into their conversation to inquire what they were discussing. Smith responded, "Oh nothing, this fellow Purdue says that the fellow that shot D.J. Elliott he should be strung up."[56] Smith was speaking of Norman Purdue, who was drinking alcohol at the time. Lee Harris, a Salisbury local, later lamented to an undercover detective investi-gating the lynching what he perceived as the social and cultural circum-stances that produced this mob spirit: "Why, Dan Elliott was one of the fin-est men who lived in Salisbury. He fed that nigger and took good care of him, and it was a shame not to hang the nigger because the niggers were starting to run wild and it came right after the killings that Yuel [sic] Lee and the other nigger had done."[57] Lee Harris concluded, "Boy, you can't let these niggers run wild, as they will run you out of town."[58]

Did James Elliott Shoot His Father and Williams?

Several accounts from both African American and white witnesses offer a different narrative altogether from individuals who were more familiar with the community, suggesting that it was D.J. Elliott's son James who did all the shooting. According to their versions of the incident, it seems that Matthew Williams had agreed to lend James Elliott a sum of money on condition that it would be returned. When Williams's attempts to get repaid by the younger Elliott failed, Williams took the matter up with his friend D.J. Elliott, and that was when James walked into the office and shot both Williams and his father.[59]

In a report presented to the attorney general's office, Maryland State Police sergeants Walter Martin and Graydon Ware recorded an interview with a "Negress" identified only as Jones, who lived on Ward Street in south Salisbury. Her son, who was working at the factory the day of the shooting, had told her that Williams did not kill Elliott and that James Elliott and his father had been arguing on the day of the murder and during the days leading up to it. According to the investigation conducted by Martin and Ware, "[James] Elliott is supposed to have had difficulties with his father about desiring money to go to Florida this winter, and his father due to hard times, is supposed to have refused him this money. Within the last week, Elliott has returned from Florida."[60] Following the shooting, James Elliott was said to have gone to the hospital to see if Williams was still alive, leaving shortly thereafter.[61] According to the report, Ware and Martin were unable to locate Jones or her son for a second interview.[62] In addition to the above direct reference to James Elliott in the reports of Martin and Ware, investigators would later also conduct a search for additional evidence, possibly suggesting a potential motive, which included contacting several life insurance companies to determine if any insurance policies had been taken out on Daniel Elliott. In the end, investigators found no existing policies. However, they did identify policies dating back to 1919 that had been terminated.[63]

Joseph Sutton was an African American farm laborer and waterman from the Eastern Shore born in a former slave community in 1885. Shepard Krech III, in his biography of Sutton, *Praise the Bridge That Carries You Over*, quotes a conversation Sutton had in Easton with a friend who stated that James Elliott was the one who killed both Williams and his own father. According to Sutton,

> I heard a white man from down there was telling it. He said, "He didn't shoot that man."... Didn't nobody shoot him but his son and put it on this colored fellow. And the colored fellow had been workin'

for this man, the man had some kind of lumberyard, I think. "Well," he say, "he'd been workin' for him ever since a boy. . . . We know he didn't shoot him. And they always give him [Williams] everything he wanted." And [James Elliott] was spoiled! And he was the only one that killed his father.[64]

Sutton continued with this version of the story, which was widely known in the Salisbury community:

And after they had lynched this fellow, well, they say the majority of them down there spoke of it, they said the same thing, said, "Wasn't nobody but his son." He killed his father and then shot this colored fellow so he wouldn't be there to be against him. Then he said this colored fellow had killed his father and he took the gun away from him and shoot [sic] him.[65]

Salisbury native Reverend Asbury Smith recalled a similar story communicated to him a few days following the lynching by a local African American high school teacher, Milton Hearne, who had passed by the site of the lynching as it was happening. Hearne told Smith that "Daniel [D.J.] Elliott was not killed by Matthew Williams but by his son James."[66] The aforementioned accounts are a few among the many that strayed dramatically from accounts widely believed by whites.[67]

According to family lore related to Elliott Neal White, the great nephew of James Elliott, "[James] . . . came onto the scene and discovered his father slumped over the desk, shot and apparently dead."[68] White's statement is in line with the official account reported to the state's attorney by Sheriff Phillips and the local press, and with the only known statements given by James Elliott.[69] The day of the lynching, the Salisbury Times quoted James as telling its reporter: "The man [Williams] must have been drunk. . . . There had been no quarrel between father and him. He had been working for us for 7 or 8 years. We gave him work whenever we had it. He has even worked here this week, but we did not have work for him today."[70]

By 1902, D.J. Elliott had made his way back to Salisbury, starting a milling company and eventually expanding his business interests to include canning and the crate and box factory on Lake Street. Elliott developed a

Daniel "D.J." Elliott. Steel
engraving, c. 1931. Courtesy
of Elliott Neal White.

reputation for providing jobs to laborers throughout the county. While in
Salisbury, Elliott was also active in several social and civic organizations,
including the Methodist Episcopal Church, Free and Accepted Masons,
and the Ancient Arabic Order of the Nobles of the Mystic Shrine. By the end
of his life, Elliott had also become a prominent banker, serving as a director
and vice president of the Farmers and Mechanic Bank of Salisbury.[71] Elliott's
wealth was indeed remarkable, and by September 1929, an advertisement
for the opening of his bank listed it as having $1.7 million dollars in assets.[72]

Until now, little has been known about the extent of Elliott's finances.
However, his will offers insight into his economic prowess and his relationship with his son James. On July 23, 1929, Elliott registered his last will and
testament with the Wicomico County government. The first and second
sections of the will list his wife, Lottie, as receiving all of his real properties
(amounting to more than 390 acres) in addition to all of the household and
kitchen furniture. In section three of the will, Elliott directs his executors—

F. Leonard Wailes, a dear friend, and James M. Elliott, his son—to operate his "manufacturing plant and the equipment connected therewith situated on the East side of and binding upon Lake Street, in the City of Salisbury, Wicomico County, Maryland."[73] The will allows additional time for Wailes and Elliott to "manufacture all materials" on hand at the factory. Once said materials were manufactured, the manufacturing plant was to be sold, including the company, real estate, and factory equipment. It is clause four that can aid in understanding the relationship between Daniel Elliott and his son. This section obligated the estate's executors to pay James Elliott $10,000 to be used for construction of a home, and if the son made any claim against the estate, say, for a debt the father owed him, payment of the claim was to come out of that $10,000.[74]

At the very least, D.J. Elliott's will seems to indicate that the father did not trust his son with the company. It was named D.J. Elliott and Son, and yet for some reason, D.J., in the event of his death, did not want his son to carry on the business.

F. Leonard Wailes died in 1936, leaving James Elliott to execute the wishes of his father's will. James filed a petition to begin selling off the machinery and personal property. It is within this petition that we gain clarity as to the vast portfolio that Elliott maintained during the Great Depression, detailing his shares of various stocks, the sale of over 390 acres of property throughout Maryland totaling $16,925 (the modern-day equivalent of $317,255.45), the amounts "received from the sales of merchandise manufactured at the mill," totaling $120,095.53 (the equivalent today of $2,251,164.60), and the amounts received from insurance companies for fire loss at the mill totaling $9,086.84 (today worth $170,330.84).[75]

Williams's "Confession"

When Williams arrived at the hospital—half dead and semiconscious—he was immediately put in a straitjacket by a "Negro" orderly to prevent his making further attacks, because he was under suspicion for a violent crime. Upon arriving at the "Negro" ward of the hospital, Sheriff Phillips found State's Attorney Bailey, ward physician Randolph M. Nock, nurse Helen Wise, and Deputy Sheriff Donald Anthony Parks all surrounding Williams's bed.[76] Phillips and Nock were standing to the right of Williams. Having gained confirmation of Elliott's death, Phillips supposedly instructed Dr. Nock to ask Williams, who was going in and out of consciousness, if he knew who had killed Elliott. According to Phillips, Williams responded, "I did it and I am glad of it, he worked us for 15 cents an hour, starvation wages."[77] Williams allegedly continued: "He is not all that are going to get it, there are others that are going to get it, and he'll never rob anymore."[78] In Phillips's account, Nock then proceeded to ask Williams who had shot him (Williams). According to the sheriff, Williams replied, "I guess I shot myself first, later I was shot twice, but I can't say who shot me."[79] Williams lapsed back into unconsciousness as if he were dead. To wake him up, Dr. Nock took a sharp instrument and pierced Williams's cheek about two inches. Williams came to and stated, "You better let me alone I am going to die anyhow."[80] That was the last that Phillips would hear from Williams; thirty minutes later he left the "Negro" ward, leaving Bailey behind, but not before charging Deputy Sheriff Parks to guard Williams.

The above account of Williams's confession is the so-called official story told by Bailey, Phillips, and the local press. Although the supposed confession took place in the presence of other witnesses, the statements of those witnesses make no mention of it. Indeed, it is essential to understand that this story was eventually passed along as the story, the only story. It became a historicized memory for many people, many white people. This narrative violence is part of the psychological trauma that has caused irrefutable damage to the Black and the broader Salisbury community.[81]

Peninsula General Hospital: "First, do no harm"

At the time of Williams's kidnapping from Peninsula General Hospital, a number of the hospital's founding staff were present and witnessed the incident firsthand. Their statements shed light on the complexity of class struggle within the Salisbury community. These statements expose the system of silence, as well as the ways anti-Blackness complicated the age-old pledge of medical practitioners "First, do no harm."[82] Indeed, the hospital remains one of the central scenes surrounding the death of Matthew Williams, as it is the place of his alleged confession and the place of his abduction.

Peninsula General Hospital in Salisbury, Maryland, where Williams was abducted by members of the mob. Postcard, c. 1930. Courtesy of Washington Area Spark.

The southern Eastern Shore's first hospital was established in 1897, following the economic depression of the 1890s, by Dr. George W. Todd with the help of Senator William P. Jackson and other prominent citizens. The hospital's first surgeon joined the staff in 1898, and in 1907 Peninsula General graduated its first nursing class. In 1922 the hospital expanded, adding one hundred beds. By the 1930s, Peninsula General had both "Negro" cooks and orderlies in its employ who worked throughout the hospital. Aside from the cooks and orderlies, the hospital's staff was all white. By 1932 the Great Depression had arrived in Salisbury, and the hospital was battling a massive increase in the number of tuberculosis cases, which the staff argued was the result of rising malnourishment in the surrounding population.[83]

When Sheriff Phillips left Williams in the hospital, he headed back to his office until suppertime, at around 7:00 p.m. He made sure to tell Deputy Truitt to relieve Parks so that he could get dinner as well. After supper,

Phillips performed his standard routine of four nights a week, writing reports and letters. While Phillips was completing his paperwork, Salisbury chief of police Nicholas H. Holland entered the office and offered some of his men to relieve Parks. Phillips assured him that Parks would be fine, but Holland wouldn't take no for an answer and left to assist Parks in guarding Williams. Next, a tenant on a farm Phillips owned in the nearby town of Hebron stopped by with his son-in-law to let Philipps know of some difficulties they were having on the farm.[84]

After this meeting Phillips was approached by state senator David Jenkins Ward, a native of Salisbury.[85] Word of Williams's condition had spread quickly and Senator Ward asked Phillips for an update, saying, "I heard the colored man is getting better."[86] Phillips replied, "The last report I have he was recovering."[87] Ward said, "Try and take care of him the best you can."[88] Phillips assured Ward that he would take care of Williams, but that he was going to die: "A man hurt as badly as he was couldn't live."[89] After this brief exchange, Phillips headed around the courthouse, down to the post office, then back to his office. He then decided to return to the hospital to check on Williams. By the time Phillips reached the hospital, he was unable to drive up to the front gate as cars were blocking the entrance and the adjoining streets.[90]

Inside the Hospital: The Nurses on Duty

Inside the hospital, Mary Massey was the white nurse in charge of the "Negro" ward where Williams was hospitalized. She later remembered four men entering the hospital looking for Williams; two of them came within two feet of her. Although she saw the culprits, Massey, like other witnesses, insisted she had not recognized them. She was not on the ward when Williams was taken. On her way back to the ward, however, she passed one man and saw another man talking to another patient, Rufus Jernigan, who was hysterical.[91] In the ward, Williams was surrounded by a screen, and an officer was there on duty, watching over him. Around 7:30, Florence S. Smith, the hospital's dietician, warned Massey that a group of men were coming to take Williams.[92]

Hospital superintendent Helen V. Wise received a call from Chief Holland and was approached by another, unidentified officer in plain clothes

Helen V. Wise, Peninsula
General Hospital's
superintendent. Courtesy
of Peninsula Regional
Medical Center.

Dr. James McFaddin Dick,
Peninsula General Hospital's
first surgeon, who was working
the day of the lynching.
Courtesy of Peninsula Regional
Medical Center.

around 7:40 p.m., just before leaving for the day.[93] As she headed out the front door, she did not see a crowd approaching; however, she sensed something in the atmosphere, almost a calm before the storm.[94]

Helen E. Fisher was another of the nurses on duty that night. Born in Worcester County in 1906, she had graduated from the Peninsula General Hospital School of Nursing in 1923. Between her graduation and 1931, she had emerged as a supervisor and hospital manager and a pillar of both the medical and local communities. Shortly after her graduation she organized and headed the hospital's accident ward; she was thus familiar with a number of the accident victims in the "Negro" ward, including Jernigan and Jacob Conquest, who were both in the room with Williams. However, according to Fisher, she was upstairs attending a case when Williams was removed through the window. She did not learn of the kidnapping until she came downstairs, after receiving word from hospital dietitian Florence Smith that four men had entered the hospital and that Smith had referred them to the officer on duty.[95]

Florence Smith, a native of Westover, Maryland, had worked at the hospital for a number of years.[96] As in most accounts, Smith placed the kidnapping at around 8:00 p.m. A little before then, a young man approached Smith, warning of the crowd that was coming to get Williams. She immediately summoned Chief Holland, who had come over to the hospital against the advice of Sheriff Phillips.

Nursing school graduation photo of Mary Johnson Waller (seated to left of trophy) and her classmates, Peninsula General Hospital, 1934. Waller tended to Williams's fellow patients in the "Negro Ward" after the mob abducted him. Courtesy of Peninsula Regional Medical Center.

Smith then tried to call Phillips. When he did not answer, she contacted Mary Massey, the first-floor charge nurse, to tell her that the crowd was coming to get Williams. Massey told Smith not to be frightened and confirmed that the crowd was coming. Massey then closed all the doors to the ward and returned to her office, where the phone rang. When Massey answered, a man warned her that a crowd was coming to get Williams. She hung up the phone and headed back to the entrance of the hospital just in time to come face to face with the mob. "There they were coming in the front door," she testified later; "it was a quiet crowd not making any noise and the ones in the lead were beckoning the others to come in."[97] A select few of the men told her, "Yes, we came to get him and we are going to get him."[98] Massey said to the crowd, "Well, I can't stop you if you have to come in, but respect the other patients and you must keep as quiet as possible in this house."[99] One of the mob leaders promised that they would abide by her requests. As the men entered, they walked up to Chief Holland.

When later asked by Maryland attorney general Preston Lane about the identity of the mob members, Smith, unlike other witnesses, simply stated that she did not know them "well." She then described each of the men. The first was a tall, slender white man around thirty years old and weighing between 140 and 150 pounds. She remembered that the men wore both sweaters and coats, a detail confirmed in the other statements. The second man was younger, around nineteen or twenty years old. He stood right beside her. She noticed that he was shorter than her, around five feet, seven inches tall.

The Orderlies on Duty

John Williams Easton was one of the "colored" orderlies at Salisbury Hospital. Residents of Salisbury since September 1928, he and his wife, Jennie V. Easton, were boarders in the Salisbury home of Joshua Cooper and his wife, Bertie E. Cooper.[100] Easton understood that, as a married man who shared a home with another family, if he decided to take a stand and name the leaders of the mob, he would risk not just his own life but also the lives of his wife and the Cooper family. Nonetheless he decided to give a statement the same evening as patient Rufus Jernigan gave his, Friday, December 18, 1931.

On December 4, Easton had been on duty since 7 p.m. He did not see the mob come in and was with a white orderly, Harry Palmer, just thirty-five minutes before the men took Williams. According to Easton, at about three minutes before 7, he fired up the furnace and asked the patients how they were feeling. According to Easton, Williams was on "the second bed from the end," near the window, but he did not see anyone come in and take him.[101]

He followed his daily routine and checked on all of his patients. Shortly after his interview on December 18 began, Easton was called away by Miss Helen Fisher, the nurse on duty asking if he could be used on the second floor. When he returned to the interview, Easton stuck to his story and insisted that he was in another wing of the hospital and that he knew nothing. Helen Fisher told the story a little differently, remembering that Easton actually hid in a nearby room as soon as the mob came in to take Williams.

William Handy, another "colored" orderly who was working that night, overheard Leah Brewington, a "colored" cook in the hospital, telling someone that she knew at least one of the men who had entered the hospital, and had seen him "down town lying around drunk again."[102] After his initial statement, Handy refused to give any further information. When the attorney general contacted Brewington, her story changed and she now denied having any information.

The Other Patients

Alongside Williams in the "Negro" wing of the hospital were five other patients: Rufus Jernigan, Jacob Thomas Conquest, Charles Jenkins, Albert Bell, and William Beckett.[103] All were in the same ward, as was common in hospitals in the 1930s. Of these five, only two, Jernigan and Conquest, gave statements to the attorney general. Their statements are essential in understanding who was responsible for kidnapping Matthew Williams from Peninsula General Hospital.

The question "Why me?" must have been going through Rufus Jernigan's mind the evening of December 4, 1931. Somehow he had ended up in the hospital bed beside Matthew Williams, the target of a bloodthirsty lynch mob in Salisbury, Maryland, a town that Jernigan was only visiting. Nursing a broken leg when he was interviewed a few days later by Assistant Attorney General G. C. A. Anderson of Baltimore, Jernigan was still rattled from the experience of witnessing white men take Williams from his bed and throw him from the first-floor window, which was one story above ground on this side of the hospital. "When they came in," Jernigan recalled, "I went right to crying, the minute that they opened the door." He continued, "I was afraid, because I had never been in anything like that before. I pulled the sheet over my head."[104]

It became clear during Jernigan's interview that he was not going to admit to seeing anything. However, he did point a finger at two of the ward's other patients, Jacob Conquest and Albert Bell: "Conquest and that Bell was the only ones that I know with their eyes open and seen everything."[105] Jernigan, almost hysterical with fear, was mocked and ridiculed by Conquest and Bell for crying and hiding under the sheets. "They said they were not afraid," Jernigan told Anderson. "They said that they knowed them and saw them and they wasn't afraid, and they didn't cover up their eyes."[106]

Jacob Thomas Conquest of 418 Davis Street was another of Williams's fellow patients in the "Negro" ward, fearing for his life. According to Conquest's account, he and Jernigan where the only patients awake. The officer who was guarding Williams left the ward, Conquest testified, and two minutes later four men entered the room and asked Conquest, Jernigan, and others, "Is this the man?" Then they went directly behind the screen or curtain that shielded Williams.[107] This happened very quickly, in no more than two or three minutes—"I could snap my fingers" Conquest said.[108] When pressed to describe the men, Conquest said he did not know any of them, but they looked like "common men, just poor, common men."[109]

As Conquest watched in fear, he could hear the growing crowd outside. After throwing Williams out the window, one of the men walked up to Jernigan, who was still crying, and told him to be quiet. Conquest remembered that the hollering outside increased as the crowd got their hands on Williams. Conquest said that the trauma and fear from his experience on December 4 had caused him to forget a number of details concerning that night, but that he could recognize the one who had approached Jernigan. He was a "heavy talking small fellow" wearing a black overcoat and weighing around 135 pounds.[110]

Like most of the other witnesses, Conquest was not able to provide information concerning the role of local and state police officers. Conquest's silence was almost certainly the product of intimidation and threats by the men who took Williams. However, unlike the others, he did share some information while indicating to the attorney general that the people in the hospital were not talking. Conquest was one of the few individuals to see the four men delegated to remove Williams from the hospital face to face. Based on Conquest's statement, it seems likely that his life had been threatened. Later, when he was to be called to testify before the grand jury, he was found dead in Salisbury. He was one of two Black witnesses, the other being Rufus Jernigan, who went missing or wound up dead shortly after giving their statements to the attorney general.

Marie Johnson

Twenty-year-old nursing student Marie Johnson was working in the "Negro" ward that day. Earlier in the day she had decided to take her weekly half-day break. Williams was admitted while she was at home resting before returning to the hospital to finish her shift. While there, her brother (and ride into town) came to tell her that they would be leaving for the hospital a little earlier than usual as he had heard that a "Negro" was to be lynched in Salisbury. Johnson soon found out that the man was one of the patients in the ward where she had just been working. Later she recounted: "A posse came into the hospital, picked the man out the bed and threw him out a window. In view of all of the nine or ten patients, which ever it was and it was two floors because the hospital was built on the hillside so he was thrown out the window and landed on the cement floor."[111]

After arriving at the hospital after her break, Johnson returned to the ward, where she saw blood at the foot of the bed from which Williams had been snatched just moments earlier. Many years later, Johnson remembered that when she approached the nurse who was on duty and asked, "What did you do to stop the posse?" the other woman said, "I ran in the bathroom and locked the door."[112] Johnson was enraged by the nurse's cowardly response, possibly mindful of the oath that they had made to care for their patients.

It was Johnson who tended to Williams's fellow patients Jernigan, Conquest, Charles Jenkins, Albert Bell, and William Beckett after they witnessed the horrific episode. She recalls their state of mind: "It was the most pitiful bunch of men that were patients. There was no sound, you could hear a pin drop in that ward and I don't think many of them slept that night. I used all the compassion that I knew how to use, but it didn't do the trick."[113] As Johnson surveyed the room, she noticed that the bloodstains went from the foot of Williams's bed to the place where he had landed outside, down the hospital's back driveway, and all the way to the scene of the spectacle on the downtown courthouse lawn.

To See the Bloody Spectacle

Directly following the taking of Williams from the hospital, onlookers witnessed the traditional conclusion to such rituals. A parade marched Williams from the hospital to the lynching tree at the bustling town center. Along the path to the courthouse green stood Salisbury's pillars of industry, modernization, and community that had thus far survived the crash of 1929, including the Wicomico Hotel and Barber Shop, Cinno's cigar store, the *Salisbury Times* building, Red Star Garage, the Arcade Theatre, Red Star Lines bus terminal, Lankford's Sporting Goods store, the Salisbury Fire Department, Read's Drug and Chemical Store, and Preston Economy Store.

Newspapermen

Alfred T. Truitt, editor of the *Salisbury Times* and coach of the Wicomico High School football team, had attended a game that afternoon against Delmar High School. Around 4:30 p.m. he returned to Salisbury and joined the post-game festivities, including a banquet for both teams held at the famous Wicomico Hotel. Around 7:30 p.m., following the banquet, Truitt headed directly to his office at the newspaper. He noticed a crowd forming on Main Street by the Arcade Theatre. Truitt pushed his way through the crowd. When asked later, he said he did not remember hearing any talk of a lynching.

Around 7:45, he called the state editor of the *Baltimore Sun*, Peter C. Chambliss, informing him that there would be no lynching. (Chambliss had apparently been waiting on word from Truitt.) In the office beside Alfred was Charles J. Truitt, his business partner (relation unknown). At around 8:10 p.m., Alfred Truitt noticed the crowd leaving Main Street and heading in the direction of the hospital. Spotting a member of the Maryland state legislature and E. Sheldon Jones, editor of the *Salisbury Advertiser*, Truitt left his office and joined them as they followed behind the crowd that was marching toward the hospital.

They soon arrived at the hospital, and Truitt stood nearby on a porch located on the east side of South Division Street with Salisbury native W. Denwood Mitchell. Several minutes later he watched some 150 people "come through the main entrance from the hospital property bringing with them a colored man," Matthew Williams.[114] Truitt watched as the mob traveled down South Division Street to its intersection with Main Street, then made its way to the courthouse green. Possibly hoping for a closer view, Truitt headed to the northwest corner of the Wicomico Hotel less than forty yards away from the lawn and watched as Williams was hanged the first time. His unconscious body was suspended in the air in front of the mob, which by this point had grown to one thousand onlookers and spectators. With the image of the lynching burned into his mind, Truitt headed back to his office and began working on a story to distribute to the local papers. He identified fellow spectators but claimed not to recognize any participants, reflecting the system of silence that had saturated the community: "There was not a single individual in the lynching party whose face was at all familiar to me."[115]

Police Officers on Duty

Carl William Wilson, a Salisbury police officer, was also on duty the night of the lynching. Wilson's twelve-hour shift began about 6:00 p.m., and he worked alongside Officer Burton, Officer John M. Goslee, and Chief Holland. Wilson patrolled the lower end of downtown Salisbury, near the docks along Camden Street on the west end of town. His district did not cover the courthouse plaza, where Williams was hanged, but when he walked up

Main Street, he saw a large mob rushing to the courthouse lawn near the Arcade Theatre.[116] By the time he arrived at the scene, there were nearly one thousand people watching the lynching; the mass of people was so tightly packed that Wilson was unable to get through. He did not see Chief Holland emerge from the crowd until after Williams was hanging from the tree.[117]

By the time Holland saw him, Wilson stated, "they had hung the nigger . . . and taken him down from the tree."[118] Overwhelmed by the size of the crowd, Wilson decided to direct traffic near the Wicomico Hotel and keep people moving along: "They already had the man up the tree, and it looked to me like he was dead by the time I got anywhere near the crowd, and they commenced blocking up the streets there with cars and people walking, and everything; and the only thing I seen I could do right there—I could not get in nowhere near—was to try to keep some of them from moving on, and try to keep as many away as possible."[119] As Williams was lowered from the tree, Chief Holland directed Wilson to proceed across the bridge to protect the "Negro quarters" of Salisbury.[120] Like many other witnesses who later gave testimony, Holland suggested that the perpetrators of the lynching were vigilantes from outside the state. When asked by the attorney general shortly after the lynching if he had been directed to conduct an investigation into the lynching, Wilson replied that this was the first time he had talked about it since it occurred.

Officers Wilson and Goslee were the only police officers to identify anyone in the mob. They later provided Chief Holland with a list of the names of eight men whom they had identified within the mob. At a minimum, this suggests that the members of the mob were identifiable as local people and that other witnesses could have known them. Regrettably, this list of eight men has never been located; however, as the attorney general's investigation continued, their identities would become clearer and it would become evident that Holland himself knew them quite well.

Local police officer Samuel C. Broughton was also working the evening of the lynching. Later (on December 19) he remembered seeing members of the lynch mob "marching like soldiers."[121] One may conclude, at the very least, that the police showed a lack of interest in what was going on down-

Downtown Salisbury during its bicentennial celebration, 1932. The Wicomico Hotel is the corner building on the left, and Read's drugstore is on the right. Courtesy of Edward H. Nabb Research Center for Delmarva History and Culture.

town, as they did not cover the areas where the lynching took place. Broughton first found out about the lynching after hearing someone yell in the street, "They have got the nigger."[122] Like Officer Wilson, Broughton decided to direct traffic at the intersections of Main and Division streets while Williams was being lynched. "When I got to Division and Main Street," he recalled, "there was lots of women and children in the street, and automobiles racing and blowing their horns, and I thought I better stay there and save lives rather than go up there. I thought that was the most humane thing to do."[123] Broughton also identified Chief Holland in the crowd, just as the mob took Williams down from the tree. After seeing this, Broughton decided to head back to his regular patrol.

Wicomico Hotel Employees

Walter Muller Dashields was a Black waiter working at the Wicomico Hotel the evening of the lynching. From the hotel dining room, Dashields saw the mob drag Williams up Division Street. Howard Leonard, Landon Morris, and headwaiter Talley were also on duty. After stepping out the back door of the hotel and preparing to head home, Dashields noticed a large crowd marching up the street from the direction of the hospital. He went back into the hotel and called for a taxi. When it came, he quickly headed home with his coworkers.[124]

Around a quarter to 8, Randolph Ralph, a "Negro" bootblack at the Wicomico Hotel Barber Shop, noticed the crowd after hearing a fire engine outside. He went out the front entrance and walked up the street where he observed the crowd preparing to hang Williams. He then "saw them carry him up the tree."[125] Ralph described a young white man around twenty or twenty-two years of age, who tied the noosed rope to the tree and began preparing Williams for the lynching. Ralph identified a ringleader of the mob as a big fellow wearing a brown and black lumber jacket who led the crowd as they dragged Williams through the street. Ralph is the only witness known to have even hinted that he could identify the members of the lynch mob, telling Assistant Attorney General Anderson, "I guess I do know the gang, although I don't know them personally."[126] Ralph's statement suggests that he knew the men behind the lynching, possibly having seen them around town. Unfortunately, he did not provide further details as to the culprits' identity.

Immolation

After leaving Salisbury Hospital, Chief Holland made his way downtown with Mrs. Heath, the jailer's wife, and another woman. After parking his car right "in front of the Court House on Division Street," he saw Williams hanging from the tree in the middle of the courthouse lawn, with "the rope . . . stretched across the tree" to a lamppost. Holland attempted to get through the crowd but had no luck. From his vantage, twenty-five or thirty feet away, he watched as the men took Williams down from the tree. He noticed several men grab Williams's body as soon as it touched the earth and then drag it behind the courthouse.[127]

Holland now followed the bloodthirsty crowd to the Red Star Garage, near the Black community of Georgetown.[128] By the time he arrived at the garage, the mob had already begun burning Williams's body. "I didn't get close enough to see how big the fire was," he testified, "but I thought it best to [get] a fire engine in case the garage or anything should catch fire[.] I went

Courthouse yard where Matthew Williams was hanged before his body was burned, c. December 5, 1931. The arrow points to the tree limb from which he was hanged, directly in front of the Wicomico County Courthouse and next door to the city jail. Collection of Maryland State Archives.

in the [Wimbrow's] garage and tried to get the operator but she didn't answer, so I went up to the fire hall and told them to send one of the engines down there and I got on the engine."[129] About this time, Holland identified a man named Heister who drove up and joined the mob, and once the crowd moved on, Holland got back in his car and drove away.[130]

Most historical accounts credit the "Wi-Hi" (Wicomico County High School) football game audience as having contributed to the lynch mob of hundreds. However, these accounts fail to also consider the likely contribution of the concurrent boxing match audience.[131] Also in town the night of the lynching were Ed Brockman, a well-known boxing referee from Baltimore, and two Baltimore boxers, Andy Kelly and Heinie Welch. The day after the lynching, Brockman recounted what he had witnessed:

> We were in the fight club and several hundred persons were waiting for the first bout. I was weighing in Red Shreves and Bud Crosby, who were to fight. . . . Suddenly the word came that they were lynching Williams. There was a stampede for the doors. I drove my car a distance of about a mile and a half to the courthouse green and they had just cut the Negro down. As I walked around the courthouse here came the leaders, carrying the body along. As they stepped out into the street they let it drop and then dragged it by the rope down through the Negro part of town. . . . Later I saw the fire, but didn't want to go down there. We went back to the fight and the bouts didn't get started until after 10 o'clock. And some of the fighters didn't show up and only about half of the crowd. It was a quiet and orderly mob. I saw no drunks. There were many women.[132]

Years later one of those women who was present among the mob recalled a story similar to Brockman's:

> Then they tied him with a rope and dragged him to the courthouse lawn. His buttocks did not have a God's bit of skin left on them. They were raw from being dragged down South Division Street. When they got to the courthouse lawn, they threw a rope on the highest limb. Then they hoisted him up and let him drop to the ground, hard as they could. They did this at least three times. I think this is

really what killed him. Then they dragged him to the filling station on East Main and Market Street. There they carried bucket after bucket of gasoline and poured on him and then set him afire. He was burned to a crisp charcoal. Then they dragged his burned body back up to Pat Doody's Wholesale Grocery Store and hung him up a post in front of this store.[133]

After burning Williams's body, the crowd proceeded to hang it yet again, this time from a nearby guy wire as about a thousand people looked on.[134] Around this time Maryland State Police officer J. C. Peroutka, along with Officer John J. Thompson arrived on the scene. Peroutka was ordered by Officer M. D. Brubaker to protect the garage.

After ten to fifteen minutes of watching the desecration of Williams's corpse, Chief Nicholas Holland decided it was time to put a stop to this and began looking for a truck in which to take the body away. It was almost as if Holland had deliberately waited in order to give the lynchers just enough time to quench their thirst for Williams's blood. The police chief now headed over to the Victor-Lynn Garage to get a truck. He then saw Officer Thompson backing up to the body in a Chevy truck. But Thompson was prevented by the mob from reaching Williams's corpse, and Holland was finally able to borrow a Ford truck from a local man named Roy B. Wilson. Driving the truck himself, Holland backed it up to Williams's body, telling the crowd, "Fellows, you have done enough to him."[135] Among the mob, standing right next to Williams's body and Holland, was a "big fellow" in blue overalls, weighing between 215 and 225 pounds and standing almost six feet tall. According to Holland, this man was said to have turned to the mob and told them, "Let them have him."[136]

Chief Holland stood next to the body as a group of at least four men attempted to drag it away. Wanting to make an example of Williams, the mob planned on taking him through Jersey Heights, one of Salisbury's "colored" settlements. This was a common practice in spectacle and racial terror lynchings throughout the United States during this nadir of race relations. The mob hoped the act would spread fear and terror throughout Salisbury's Black community, hoping to maintain the social control enforced through Jim Crowism.[137]

Holland then got on the truck bed with Deputy Sheriff Charles Truitt, who had cut Williams down from the guy wire. After putting Williams's remains on the truck, Holland and Truitt drove up Market Street, passing the Fire Department. As they made their way down East Main Street, two cars approached from the rear and began following them. They turned down East Salisbury and lost one of the cars. The officers contemplated taking the body directly to the "colored" undertaker, James Stewart, but didn't want to put him in harm's way, so they headed out into the country about a mile and a half. Holland and Truitt stayed with the body for about an hour and a half until Stewart, the town's only Black mortician, arrived to pick it up.

Where Were the State Police?

State police officer J. C. Peroutka, after leaving the scene of Elliott's shooting that afternoon, had made his way back to his station in Pittsville, where he wrote some reports. Around 7:00 p.m. he and Officer Thompson left the substation and headed back to Salisbury. Traveling down Ocean City Road they came up to the intersection of Main and Division streets, where they saw a mob of some fifty people hanging around the corner.

Shortly thereafter, Peroutka and Thompson left downtown and headed out Delmar Road to patrol the town of Delmar. There, they stopped for a Coca-Cola. While they were at the store, someone came in and told them that "they" were lynching a "Negro" in Salisbury. Dropping everything, Thompson and Peroutka headed back to Salisbury, arriving around 8:30 or 8:45 p.m. While pulling up into the jail yard, Peroutka saw a city policeman and said to him, "I hear there is a lynching going on down here."[138] The policeman responded, "You came too late to see it, to see him hanging, they took him down and are burning him."[139] That is when Peroutka and Thompson proceeded to the scene of the burning and ran into Chief Holland, asking if they could assist in any way. Holland told Thompson and Peroutka to direct traffic. After doing so for a while, they decided to head into the Red Star Garage, where they saw the clerk, Ralph Wimbrow, distributing to the mob members and spectators sections of the fifteen-foot rope that had been used in the lynching, as keepsakes.

Selling Souvenirs

After the mob pulled Williams up by the rope strung over the tree at the courthouse, Officer Will White headed up the street and ran into a white photographer who wanted to capitalize on this spectacle. White stated that the man said that he could collect up to $25.00 for any photograph of the lynching. Someone alongside them said, "He could ask $200 to $300 for it."[140] Like most of the other witnesses, White claimed not to have recognized anyone in the mob, as it was made up of outsiders.[141] Paul S. Henderson, a photojournalist for the *Baltimore Afro-American*, was also on the scene directly following the lynching of Williams and collected a piece of the rope.[142] With a note, now preserved in the National Museum of African American History and Culture in Washington, DC, Henderson included a remnant of the rope that he described as follows: "Rope 'souvenir' which was used by Salisbury, MD mob to hang Matthew Williams, 23-year-old citizen. It is soaked with oil which was poured on his body before the blood-thirsty shoreman [sic] burned the body beyond recognition. Thousands of white ["white" has been added and then partially erased] women and children carried these souvenirs home to keep."[143]

Ropes were among the many prized souvenirs of spectacle lynchings. Often cut into pieces and taken home by spectators, these souvenirs suggest how lynching was considered a sport. Just as a mounted deer head reminds the hunter of his dominance over a lower species, trophies such as these collected during lynchings served as visual reminders of white "superiority" over African Americans. Many such prized rope sections, like mounted deer heads, eventually ended up displayed on the wall at Campbell and Perry's Sporting Goods store.[144]

Following the journey that this rope took to get to Campbell and Perry's store provides insight into the system of silence that reigned in Salisbury. According to Campbell and Perry, the store's proprietors, it was mounted on the wall by one of the men who participated in the lynching. Although the store owners had no direct connection to the lynching, the fact that they allowed this piece of evidence to be mounted in their store suggests their complicity in the lynching, a fact they were of course unwilling to admit.

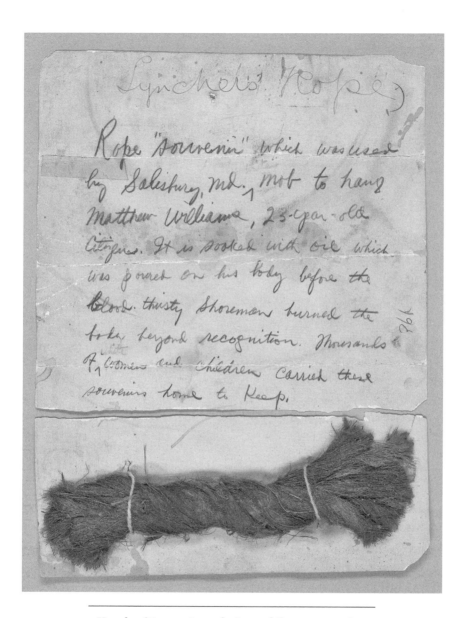

Handwritten note and piece of the rope used to lynch Matthew Williams. Collection of the Smithsonian National Museum of African American History and Culture, Gift of The Estate of Paul S. Henderson. 2013.50abc.

The Silent Shore

The rope is symbolic in a number of ways. Whether the store owners had participated in the lynching or not, their silence afterward made them complicit, even though they might not have cared less about the ideology or the acts that led to the rope being theirs. The rope's display in their store fed the ideology of anti-Blackness and white supremacy. Like the sign placed in Havel's greengrocer store, the rope was a sign that "contains a subliminal but very definite message."[145] Even if they had not witnessed or participated in the lynching, for all the white customers who entered into Campbell and Perry's store and saw the rope section on display as a reassertion of white power over Black bodies, the souvenir functioned as a means of inclusion in the dominant race. Like Williams's "confession," the rope souvenir also functioned as evidence—of Black criminality and white justice done.[146]

Sheriff Phillips

After leaving the hospital, Sheriff Phillips headed downtown. As he drove up South Division Street, from the corner of the Wicomico Hotel he saw Williams's lifeless body hanging before the courthouse. He quickly called Judge Joseph L. Bailey. Coming around the south side of the courthouse, he saw the rope that they were hanging Williams with thrown over a lamppost some nine feet in the air. As the crowd grew, Phillips heard someone from within it shout, "Let's take him down and burn him," and another yell, "Let's pull him apart."[147] Salisbury natives John Downing and Wesley W. Nibblett came up to Phillips from the crowd and asked if they could help him take charge of the body. Meanwhile the mob continued hollering, "Let's Burn him."[148] Just ten minutes after he got to the courthouse scene, the crowd took Williams down and dragged him by the rope out toward Division Street. While they dragged his body, Phillips and Downing grabbed the rope and cut it about six feet from Williams's head. Phillips then took the rope from around Williams's neck; at this point, Salisbury resident Alex Pollitt came to the sheriff's aid and rebuked the crowd, "You have done all you can to it, let the Sheriff have it."[149]

According to Phillips, Pollitt grabbed the left side of Williams's body while the sheriff grabbed the right and others held his feet and they started to carry him across the gas station lot to the jail. Getting as far as the cement walk that leads to the jail, the sheriff was shoved by the intervening crowd and he fell over Williams's lifeless corpse. Dazed, he stayed on the ground for two to three minutes, during which time the crowd took the body down the hill on the north side of the jail on Water Street.

As Phillips stood up, a member of the mob, a big fellow, over two hundred pounds and age forty-five to fifty, said, "Sheriff I didn't know that was you, I wouldn't hurt a hair of your head."[150] As the mob took the body down to the vacant lot, Deputy Sheriff Anthony Parks walked up to let Phillips know that Judge Bailey was on the phone and wanted to meet with him. Not long after, Phillips headed to Judge Bailey's home and stayed there for around twenty minutes.

Officer Thompson

Maryland State Police officer John J. Thompson recalled arriving with Officer Peroutka at the scene of the lynching around 8:15 p.m. (earlier than Peroutka remembered), as the mob was burning the body in front of the Red Star Bus Terminal. Thompson later described the crowd as mysteriously quiet, almost as if they were in a trance. He noticed Chief Nicholas Holland at the scene directing traffic, and he walked up to him and asked him if he could be of any assistance. Next Officer Brubaker walked up to him and he directed Officer Peroutka to head into the Red Star Bus Terminal and assist him in monitoring the crowd.

As more people joined the mob, Thompson remembered, someone yelled, "Here comes the gas."[151] Around 8:45 p.m. men in the crowd dragged the body directly past Thompson, who was standing in the middle of the street, at the corner where the bus terminal sat. Thompson and Holland followed directly behind the crowd as it moved to Main Street. When they arrived at the corner of Lake and Main, they were met by Deputy Sheriff Truitt, and they found the corpse of Williams hanging a second time, this time from a guy wire. Thompson suggested to Holland that this had gone far enough and that they should try to wrest the body from the mob. Thompson went six cars deep into the mob, he recalled, and found a truck. Around this time, a "Colored" boy was seen heading east on the south side of Main

Salisbury police officers with Mayor Wade W. Insley, c. 1925. Some of these officers were present during the lynching. *Left to right*: Sidney O. Furness, Officer Polk, Samuel C. Broughton, Officer Anderson, Officer Will W. White, Officer Williams, Mayor Insley, and Officer Roslee. Courtesy of Edward H. Nabb Research Center for Delmarva History and Culture, Salisbury University, Salisbury, Maryland.

Street, and someone in the mob shouted, "There's another one of those Sons of Bitches, let's get him."[152]

Thompson held out his arm trying to stop the crowd as the young "Negro" man ran. He told the crowd shouting, "'Let him alone, he hasn't done anything'—they were just blood thirsty—then they went back to where the body was hanging and I went to the truck to move the body."[153] Just as Thompson reached the truck, a large man leading the mob called the truck driver by name and told him, "Don't you dare do that, don't put that damn thing in your truck." Upon hearing this, the driver quickly changed his mind.[154] That the leader called the driver by name suggests that this large man was someone whom people would have been able to identify. Thompson then began pleading with the mob to turn over the body, saying that

"The Blood Lust of the Eastern Shore"

they had gone far enough. A leader came out from among the mob and asked Thompson what the officers wanted him to do? Officer Thompson asked the leader to take the crowd away so that he and other members of law enforcement could remove the body. At this point, a short fellow in the mob yelled out, "What the hell you got to do with it?"[155] The leader of the mob rebuked the young man and directed the crowd up the street. Forty to fifty people stayed surrounding the body.

Wallace H. White

At about 7:45 p.m. Wallace H. White, manager of the *Salisbury Advertiser*, was heading out of a Lions Club meeting at the Wicomico Hotel. As the Lions members filed out of the clubroom, someone said that a crowd was heading over to get Williams. As the Lions stepped onto Division Street, they saw the mob carrying Williams their way. White later described the whole crowd as composed of boys who were "16–20 years of age," all of them, he further claimed, working-class people.[156]

As White came around the side of the hotel along Main Street, he recognized a number of the mob leaders who were standing near him. He stood within a foot of the mob as they dragged Williams up the street, "holding his arms and walking him entirely on his own feet."[157] They dragged Williams right up to the edge of the sidewalk. Standing next to White was S. H. Hurdle, a state health officer. White and his colleague just stood there and watched as a young man climbed the tree on the courthouse lawn and Williams was pulled up by a rope.

Alex Pollitt got word of the lynching while driving up Camden Street when someone came up to his car and told them that there was a lynching downtown. By the time Pollitt made it to the courthouse, Williams was hanging from the tree and the rope had been tied to the lamppost. By this time he must have been dead, as Pollitt remembered "he wasn't kicking."[158] Then, Pollitt testified, Deputy Sheriff Parks came up, seemingly out of nowhere, and pushed his way into the mob, stopping near the tree. Pollitt recalled the deputy sheriff then shouting to the mob, "Boys, don't do that."[159] Concerned about the women and children among the crowd, Holland yelled, "Boys, let me have him you shouldn't be letting him hang up there nude before all the women, it is bad."[160] According to Pollitt, Holland demanded that the mob untie Williams from the tree. After failing to acknowledge Holland's request, the mob seems to have had a change of heart, and Pollitt and the sheriff decided to cut the rope from the pole and bring Williams back down to earth. Pollitt then grabbed the body along with Sheriff Phillips and proceeded to carry it to the jail. They carried him as far as they could until the mob descended upon them and took the body from their hands.

Dr. Brown Returns to Salisbury

As the mob toyed with remnants of the rope, Dr. Arthur D. Brown was tending to a patient in nearby Jesterville, just eighteen miles outside Salisbury. Around 8:30 p.m., after Brown had returned to his office, Walter Dashields, one of his patients, arrived for treatment, saying "Doc, they got him."[161] Upon hearing Dashields's news, Brown canceled his appointment and told him to head home safely. Brown then got a call from a patient in Delaware and, following that, another call, this one from his wife's brother, Andrew Derritt, who was downtown in the midst of the lynch mob at West Main and Lake streets. He said, "Doc, they are burning the body in the open lot on the other side of the Red Star, a fellow just came up and told me."[162] Derritt was trying to get close enough to the crowd so that he could identify some members of the mob. In case someone had noticed him and his life was threatened, he decided to leave the scene and accompany Brown to Delaware. Brown sent his wife to stay with a friend of the family, while he and Derritt headed to treat his patient in Delaware. When Brown arrived at the corner of Lake and West Main streets to pick up Derritt, he saw the mob dragging Williams's body down the street, preparing to hang him for the second time after burning him.

Unable to get through the mass of people and automobiles, Brown noticed two officers, including Will White, directing traffic while the mob dragged Williams's lifeless corpse up the street. After they passed with Williams's body, officers refused to let any cars go through, so Brown turned back onto Lake Street, heading north of town. After he finally arrived at Broad Street, he picked up his brother-in-law, and they headed across the

Scene where Matthew Williams's body was burned,
December 5, 1931. Courtesy of Baltimore News American
(Hearst Corporation).

state line into Delaware. Dr. Brown and Derritt remained there for two to three hours tending to the patient. Several hours later, at around 11:30 p.m., he drove toward the Love Point Ferry, considering going to Baltimore to get help from his friends among the city's civil rights attorneys. Deciding that he could not make it in time, Dr. Brown and Derritt arrived in Salisbury around 1:30 in the morning and circled around the "colored" settlement, where the final hanging had occurred, and then headed down to the Red Star Garage, where the mob had burned the body, just two blocks from the courthouse lawn.

Brown then got out of his car and gathered some of Williams's ashes to put in a receptacle. Shortly thereafter, the men headed to Reese Gordon's garage to get some gas. As soon as Brown pulled up, Reese asked, "Did you see it?"[163] Brown did not respond. According to Reese, the mob had rushed into the garage and taken the gasoline that they used to burn Williams's body. Brown and Derritt stayed around the garage for a little while, making small talk and hoping to get some information as to who had led the lynching.

Brown's fearlessness is further evidence of his protected status and his ability to transcend the system of silence. This gave him the ability to openly criticize policies levied on the Black community, and to drive to the edge of a lynching while it was taking place and live to tell the story. Moreover, this protected status allowed him to advocate for social justice and openly drive through the mob with a shotgun on his car dashboard, without being murdered or run out of town. Brown, a militant who dared to defend himself, did not fit the traditional racist stereotypes of Black men that the white citizens were used to. He also was connected to the elite Black class of NAACP leaders in Baltimore, having lived there briefly before moving to Salisbury.[164]

The Examination

After Brown was unable to get any information at the garage, he and Derritt headed home. As soon as the doctor entered his house, his phone rang. It was Jim Stewart, the area's "colored" undertaker. Stewart had been trying to reach Dr. Brown for hours after picking up Williams's body from the country where it had been abandoned. Brown was shocked to learn that Stewart was now hiding Williams's corpse at his home, which also happened to be his place of business. Brown requested that he be allowed to examine the body and headed over to Stewart's place. He wished to see if he had bullet wounds in his brain and if he had wounded himself in the chest.

In examining the body, Brown was unable to find any bullet wounds in Williams's chest, but he found one in the back of the head that "just grazed the scalp" and one in the front of Williams's skull. The bullet had not passed through the brain, but had traveled "from the right temple and just grazed the skull and [come] out about the left eye."[165] Thus, the bullets were no longer in Williams's head: "One passed just on the outer side of the skull and came out about the eye."[166] Williams's skin was burned, but still retained

The death certificate issued for Matthew Williams in which the coroner stated the cause of death as "hung by mob," December 6, 1931. Collection of Maryland State Archives.

---

some color. His neck was stiff, indicating that it had been broken. The burned rope was twisted around his neck and cut off at the end with pliers, and the skin was drawn up tight around his neck and chest.

◇◇◇

The witness statements recounted in this chapter make clear that Matthew Williams was the victim of a racial terror lynching. The Equal Justice Initiative describes *racial terror lynchings* as a tool used "to enforce Jim Crow laws and racial segregation—a tactic for maintaining racial control by victimizing the entire African American community, not merely punishment for a crime."[167] The lynching of Williams and the attitudes of witnesses in the community are consistent with this definition, and yet they diverged from traditional cases throughout the South.

We know that local law enforcement failed in their duty to keep Matthew Williams safe; one officer, for example, was supposed to be guarding Williams in the hospital at all times. However, as noted, the police knew where to be when the mob entered the room to take Williams. This is evidence of the system of silence that was common throughout local communities where lynchings occurred.[168] In giving their testimony later, it was almost as if whites who witnessed lynchings throughout the South were reading from a script; they were often unable to identify anyone in the mobs, arguing that the participants were masked or were "outside agitators" who had no relationship to their own, "civilized" communities. Myths of the "Negro" rapist and murderer served their traditional purposes for justifying and gaining support for putting innocent men to death.

Economic factors cannot be overlooked in analyzing Williams's lynching in 1931. Under the surface of all the unfounded accusations concerning lynching is the economic threat African Americans posed when white citizens' lives were interrupted during economic downturns. Forced to compete with African American laborers during the Depression much as they had following the Civil War, white laborers became resentful of African American laborers such as Williams, who were often willing to work for wages that whites would not accept.

Williams's lynching strayed from the majority of lynching cases in one respect: the response of the state government and the role that it would play in demanding an investigation into the mob actions and the death of the victims. Governor Albert Ritchie would make this demand, joining a small group of governors who decided to take action concerning the lynchings that had taken place in their states the same year. As honorable and groundbreaking as this stance was, the economic considerations that motivated it should not be overlooked. Ritchie saw lynching as a disruptive expression of social instability, a disruption that could potentially scare away investments, destabilize the labor pool, and inflame racial tension. Likewise, the system of silence that prevailed is also part of this response to lynching, specifically related to the perceived need to protect the local reputations of businesses, officials, and local law enforcement politicians. The prevailing myth that lynchings were the work of outside agitators, too, was nothing more than a strategy designed to safeguard the reputations of towns and cities for the sake of business and tourism throughout the South, protecting them from legal, economic, and political consequences, all of which became more heightened during the Great Depression.

[3]

Governor Albert C. Ritchie
Confronts Judge Lynch
The Politics of Anti-Black Racism
in the Free State and Beyond

I will leave New York in the midnight train for Baltimore tomorrow.
I want to ascertain the facts regarding this case before making
any statement. If they are reported briefly to me tonight,
I will have something to say, and something very emphatic to say.

Governor Albert C. Ritchie, December 5, 1931

The following day, December 5, 1931, word of Williams's lynching made its way to Governor Albert Ritchie, who was visiting New York City. He rushed back to Baltimore on the midnight train, disgusted at the prospect of the disgrace that the lynching would bring to Maryland. Ritchie was again becoming a major Democratic contender for the presidency and was among the governors that the national media was calling the "Big Four of presidential possibilities," the other three being Gifford Pinchot of Pennsylvania, Franklin D. Roosevelt of New York, and George White of Ohio.[1]

Ritchie had been in New York preparing for his presidential campaign. He was bold in the first statement that he released to the press concerning the tragic lynching of Matthew Williams. Ritchie not only spoke out against the lynching but would also take an active role in the investigation. To understand Ritchie's response, it is important to comprehend his stance from a national political standpoint during the Great Depression. Ritchie's was just one of a number of responses that governors took regarding lynchings during a time when their numbers rose in the United States, particularly in the South. Taking this fact into consideration, this chapter charts and analyzes what Governor Albert Ritchie said and did after the lynching of Matthew Williams and how his political aspirations factored into the strategies he adopted for dealing with racial issues and lynching.

Ritchie was attempting to wrestle with changes within the Democratic Party in the early 1930s that would eventually led to a split within the party in 1948, when the Dixiecrats walked out of the national convention. Ritchie was caught between urban Democratic and conservative southern Democratic forces within the party, seeking to appeal to both. For the latter faction, he vigorously pushed for states' rights, helping reawaken the faith of the progenitors of the southern rebellion that had led to the Civil War.[2]

Urban Democrats may not have supported Ritchie's call for states' rights in general, but his adamant support for the repeal of Prohibition appealed to them. Southerners who favored anti-liquor laws could tolerate Ritchie's appeal to home rule when it came to ending Prohibition because they wanted to end the Volstead Act's federal overreach. But they also wanted home rule when it came to racial issues, and that included opposing federal anti-lynching legislation. By 1932, as Ritchie spoke out against the Solid South's fading political and social weapon, Judge Lynch, and attempted to openly investigate the lynching of Matthew Williams, he ran up against the mores of the Eastern Shore, which was in many ways a focus group representing the southern conservative Democrats to whom his states' rights approach had once appealed. In the end, choosing to investigate the lynching would threaten Ritchie with the loss of not only the Eastern Shore but also the Deep South in his bid for the White House.[3] In January 1932, the *Baltimore Afro-American* referenced the political quagmire that Ritchie found himself in as it related to his decision to investigate the lynching: "Some of Governor Ritchie's friends if not himself, fear the effect any real effort to bring the lynchers to justice would have on his political support in the South where in some states lynchings are condoned. On the other hand, some of the Democrats in Pennsylvania have rapped him for his lack of action."[4] As time would tell, the most successful Democrats, such as Huey Long and Franklin D. Roosevelt, would find a way to appeal to this racist element while at the same time gaining support from African American constituents. In a secret poll of the 123 Republican members of Congress in 1932, *Cosmopolitan* magazine reported that Roosevelt got 59 votes, Ritchie 37, and Owen Young 27. Ritchie's chances in a contest with FDR for the presidency seemed slim.

The African American vote in the South could give him an edge. His failure to bring the lynching culprits to justice would cause him to lose the already tepid support that he had maintained among these voters since the mid-1920s, when he established the Maryland Interracial Commission. Ritchie recognized that the African American community was beginning to move away from the Republican Party after remaining loyal since the 1870s, following the Civil War. Herbert Hoover failed to advocate for African Americans during the Depression, even avoiding any public statement against lynchings. In many ways, Hoover was the last straw for African American voters, and they began looking to the moderate Democratic Party to improve their economic well-being and to end the scourge of lynching.[5] Ultimately, Ritchie was one Democrat the African American community rejected after its members realized that his interest in Black issues was nothing but smoke and mirrors.[6] This chapter connects Ritchie to the rise of progressive Democratic governors, a rise that would be stifled decades later by the white backlash against *Brown v. Board of Education* in the late 1950s.[7]

"King" Ritchie and the "Free State"

Albert Cabell Ritchie was born on August 29, 1876, in Richmond, Virginia, to political royalty on both sides of his family. His father, Albert Ritchie (1834–1903), served as associate judge for Baltimore City (1892–1903) and was professor of law at the University of Maryland Law School. His mother, Elizabeth Caskie Cabell (1851–1931), was a Virginia native who claimed Virginia governor William H. Cabell and Joseph Cabell, a close friend of Thomas Jefferson, among her ancestors. The Ritchies moved to Baltimore when the young Ritchie was just three months old. During his early years, he attended private school in Baltimore and lived in Maryland all his life.[8]

In 1896, Ritchie graduated from Johns Hopkins University with a bachelor of arts. Two years later he followed in his father's footsteps, graduating from the University of Maryland Law School and passing the bar. In 1900, he joined one of the most powerful law firms in the city, Steele, Semmes, Carey, and Bond, but left three years later to start his own practice. Yet, still in his father's shadow, he was appointed assistant city solicitor of Baltimore (1903–10), then formed a law firm with Stuart S. Janney where he worked until he was elected governor in 1919. In 1907, he was appointed professor of law at the University of Maryland Law School and married Elizabeth Catherine Baker of Catonsville, Maryland. However, his marriage was short-lived, and Ritchie abandoned his wife after just three years when he left to go live with his mother. He and Elizabeth officially divorced in 1916, and Ritchie would never remarry nor have any children; instead, he would become married to politics.[9]

Albert Ritchie began the first of what became four terms as Maryland's chief executive on January 14, 1920. To ultimately gain national and presidential traction, Ritchie knew that he had to appeal to the African American voters, who had been tied to the Republican Party since Reconstruction.[10] Ritchie saw the Republicans' weakness as the party in power at the beginning of the Depression as an opportunity to begin courting the Black vote. In considering how he might appeal to African American voters on the national stage in 1931–32, Ritchie looked first to secure the Black vote in Maryland—not an easy task, even for a progressive. Yet he was able to do so despite the recent division between supporters and opponents of Black disenfranchisement. Conservative politicians led three attempts through referendums between 1905 and 1910 to bar African Americans from voting: the Poe Amendment (1904–5), the Strauss Amendment (1908–9), and the Digges Amendment (1910–11). Each of these proposed amendments to the state constitution sought to disenfranchise Black citizens by means of a grandfather clause or an "understanding" clause.[11] The failure of disenfranchisement efforts in the Free State can be attributed to the growing immigrant population and increasing Black political power, strengthened by the sizable pre–Civil War free Black population and the educated Black community in the state's most populous city, Baltimore.[12]

By 1923, the key to achieving the Black vote became evident when Black Marylanders, largely concentrated in Baltimore, began to break away from the Republican Party. This was evident in October of that year, less than a month before the gubernatorial election, when the *Baltimore Afro-American* broke precedent and officially endorsed Ritchie for the first and only time during his tenure as governor of the state. Among the reasons for this dramatic shift were the improvements to Black education during Ritchie's tenure resulting from increased teacher salaries and establishment of six new Black high schools throughout the state. Also, he saw to the opening of a new hospital for Black tuberculosis patients and supported a hospital for mentally ill African Americans, the Crownsville Hospital for the Negro Insane of Maryland.[13]

Most important was Ritchie's denunciation of one of the driving forces behind the Democratic Party, the Ku Klux Klan. Ritchie distanced himself from the Klan by barring the organization from leasing meeting space at the state armory. Instead, he found space for the Colored YMCA and the Knights of Columbus to meet. In reaction, the Klan verbally attacked Ritchie, prompting a rally led by J. H. Hawkins of Newport, Virginia, a representative of the Imperial Wizard. By July 1923 Hawkins had made his way to the Eastern Shore, seeking to increase membership. Frank H. Beall, chief of the Inspection Division of the Highway Department, replaced Hawkins as the Grand Dragon of the Realm of the Ku Klux Klan for the state of Maryland. At this time Klan membership in Maryland had grown to 33,000 members, with seventy-two individual chapters throughout the state. The discontent with Ritchie among whites on Maryland's Eastern Shore also can be traced to this period, when Ritchie began distancing himself from the Klan. This created a unique situation for the Ku Klux Klan in Maryland, where it would end up supporting a prominent Republican, Alexander Armstrong, the incumbent in the race for attorney general.[14]

During the 1923 election, Ritchie broke a long-standing record by winning nearly 15,000 of the more than 40,000 African American votes cast—making him the first Democratic gubernatorial candidate to receive so many Black votes.[15] Shortly after the election, Ritchie sought to repay and solidify the loyalty shown him by the Black community by appointing an interracial commission, comprising thirteen white members and eight Black members, to "consider legislation concerning the welfare of the colored people of Maryland and report legislative recommendations to the Governor and General Assembly."[16]

Governor Albert C. Ritchie Confronts Judge Lynch

WHY THE "AFRO" IS FOR RITCHIE

Political cartoon showing Governor Albert Ritchie shutting the door on the Ku Klux Klan. *Baltimore Afro-American*, November 2, 1923.

By 1925, however, the *Baltimore Afro-American* was regretting its earlier endorsement, as the governor seemed to turn his back on the African American community. He appointed a Baltimore police commissioner who then failed to hire any African American officers. The newspaper also called out the contradictions in Ritchie's philosophy toward African American education: he advocated for so-called equal schools but did not work for equal pay for Black teachers.[17]

The Dyer Anti-Lynching Bill

The following year, Ritchie continued to waffle on issues important to African Americans, specifically in arguing against the Dyer Anti-Lynching Bill. This bill, sponsored by Leonidas C. Dyer, a Republican US representative from Missouri, was Congress's effort in 1922 to make lynching a federal crime that required federal prosecution.[18] Ritchie remarked that the bill "illustrated the invasion of states' rights. It is called the anti-lynching bill—an illustration of the tendency in American politics to attach labels to measures which divert attention from their realities."[19] Ritchie's comment made clear that for him Maryland was indeed the South: "I resent any suggestion that the South does not deplore mob violence or that it will not exert its full power to prevent it. I resent any suggestion, too, that instances of this violence which unhappily now and then occur, are in the South alone. And I resent any proposed remedy which does not come clean and straight."[20] He concluded, "[The] Dyer Bill in truth is a political measure designed to capture the colored bloc vote, and it extends Federal sovereignty and jurisdiction over every State official from constable to governor."[21] In the end, Ritchie saw the Dyer bill as an attempt to suppress the power of the states to exercise their police powers or to choose inaction.

Ritchie's belief that a strong-willed governor like him could end lynching simply by enforcing state laws was arguable in the early 1920s given that the number of lynchings nationwide dropped through the decade. By 1922, it had been more than twenty-five years since the last lynching in Maryland, and Ritchie saw law enforcement in his state as a success story and a model for the rest of the United States.

Among the Republican leaders whom Ritchie accused of exploiting the Black vote and trampling on states' rights was one of Maryland's US senators, Joseph Irwin France. On December 9, 1920, two years before Ritchie's scathing criticism of the Republican Party and the Dyer Anti-Lynching Bill, Senator France traveled to Brooklyn, New York, to join NAACP executive secretary James Weldon Johnson, assistant secretary Walter White, and Leonidas Dyer in pushing for support of the federal anti-lynching law. The rally they headed came after forty-six individuals had been lynched in the nation in the preceding eleven months, a number that would rise to sixty-one before year's end, with fifteen lynchings taking place between December 9 and 31 alone.[22] Before a crowd of more than two thousand African American men and women, France, who had coauthored the Dyer bill, proclaimed:

> The race problem will never be solved with consistent and concerted efforts to keep the colored races in ignorance and degradation by depriving them of schools and sanitary surroundings, by recriminations, hatred, prejudice, vengeance, violence, lynching and burning at the stake. It must be solved by fearless facing of the facts, with recognition that the unchanging principles of liberty and justice are

everywhere and at all times applicable, with an acknowledgment of the fact, recognized by all the great anthropologists, that the colored races have great mental and moral capacity, and that they were created to fulfill a great destiny. I believe that the time is at hand when the party of Abraham Lincoln will deal with this problem in his spirit.[23]

Two months later Senator France had little hope that the Dyer bill would pass in 1921 but saw better prospects for 1922–24:

I believe that this Congress should pass stringent legislation to prevent lynching and I would be in favor of the Tinkham resolution in the states where disfranchisement exists. I do not feel that with our present very slender majority in the Senate we can pass this session anti-lynching legislation, but I hope that in the next session we can be able to enact legislation which will put an end to this inhuman practice, which is such a disgrace in certain sections of our country, which is indeed a lynching of the law, and the setting up of irresponsible, mad, mob rule in place of even-handed justice.[24]

Senator Joseph Irwin France, c. 1917–23. Photograph by Harris & Ewing. Courtesy of the Library of Congress, Prints & Photographs Division, LC-DIG-hec-19257.

The Silent Shore

On December 6, 1921, Senator France introduced his own anti-lynching bill (S. 2791), which he authored to "assure to persons within the jurisdiction of every State the equal protection of the laws and to punish the crime of lynching."[25] France and Dyer were hardly the only lawmakers to introduce anti-lynching legislation or to see it defeated. The first anti-lynching bill had been proposed in 1901, by Representative William H. Moody of Massachusetts, after more than 130 victims had been lynched in the United States that year. Moody's bill, like subsequent ones, was based on the Equal Protection Clause of the Fourteenth Amendment to the Constitution. Eleven years later Dyer joined Moody in introducing a bill in every session of the House until it was passed by a vote of 236 to 119 on January 26, 1922.[26]

Endorsed by the NAACP, the Dyer Anti-Lynching Bill stipulated that the phrase "mob or riotous assemblage, when used in this act, shall mean an assemblage composed of three or more persons acting in concert for the purpose of depriving any person of his life without authority of law as a punishment for or to prevent the commission of some actual or supposed public offense."[27] To understand the opportunism motivating Ritchie's opposition to this bill, it is necessary to break down this crime bill's interrelated components. The first element of the proposed act punished state and local police officers who failed to protect the life of the lynching victim from the vigilantes. In the case of the lynching of Matthew Williams, and in the majority of all lynching cases, this was one of the more common occurrences. The narrative that witnesses and law enforcement officers often presented was that the mob of hundreds, sometimes thousands, of individuals overpowered state and local officials. In many ways, this section of the bill acknowledged that the silence of local and, in some cases, state police, if not their outright complicity, made them just as guilty as the perpetrators. The second element of the act required federal prosecution for those who carried out the crime. The third, most crucial element, which speaks to the value placed on Black life in the United States of the 1920s, required the county where the lynching had taken place to compensate the family of the victim $10,000.

For whatever reason, in the end, Ritchie saw the anti-lynching legislation as a nonstarter. He doubtless knew that the racist southern Democrats would never buy into the bill, as any such law violated the norms that had been established during slavery and perpetuated in Jim Crow segregation, according to which African Americans were captives, commodities, and people who, even if freed from slavery, must be socially controlled. In this case, the fear that lynchings instilled throughout Black communities and throughout the nation helped enforce the racist ideas legalized by Jim Crow segregation.

Ritchie, and eventually FDR (who also never supported an anti-lynching bill), took a hyperpartisan approach to combating the bill. The governor politicized the suffering of African Americans by evoking the traditional Democratic appeal, making the bill about states' rights rather than about bringing justice to the victims of these thousands of crimes against humanity. To Governor Ritchie's point, by the time of the next election, in 1924, it was clear that Senator France was indeed attempting to secure the African American vote, gaining the endorsement of the *Baltimore Afro-American* and publishing advertisements that labeled him "Colored Peoples' Strong Defender."[28] However, by then France would suffer defeat by the Democratic establishment, losing to William Campbell Bruce. The Dyer Anti-Lynching Bill was also halted in the Senate when southern Democrats filibustered it on January 26, 1922.

Regarding the strength of the Black vote in Maryland during the 1920s, very few statistics survive that can help determine the number of registered Black voters in Maryland. In 1920, however, the year the Nineteenth Amendment was ratified, the NAACP tabulated the probable increase in Black voters in eight pivotal states, including Maryland, as a result of allowing women to vote. This survey estimated 150,000 likely Black voters; besides the recent enfranchisement of women, the NAACP attributed this increase to a rise in immigration from the Caribbean and other areas of the Black Diaspora.[29] By 1930 in Baltimore, Maryland's most populous city, eligible "colored" voters (men and women over age twenty-one) increased to 92,610 and "colored voters" increased to 37,209.[30]

By 1927, Ritchie saw an excellent opportunity to court the black vote for his presidential run in 1928, and he thought his Maryland Interracial Commission (MIC) the perfect vehicle. Formed three years prior, the MIC was billed as a platform to investigate "Negro welfare throughout the State." The Commission also fostered interracial dialogue concerning civil rights

The Silent Shore

[90]

Albert Ritchie, forty-ninth governor of Maryland, c. 1926. Courtesy of the Library of Congress, Prints & Photographs Division.

policies and investigated such issues as "housing, the improvement of farm life, educational betterment and [Black] representation on the police force."[31] The original white and Black members included politicians, attorneys, educators, activists, and religious leaders.

The MIC was a pioneering force in the Maryland civil rights movement during the earliest years of the Great Depression and, in fact, helped lay the foundation for the Maryland anti-lynching movement of the 1930s. Among its first members were prominent white and Black leaders from Baltimore and Maryland's Eastern Shore. By 1927, the Commission had drafted several bills that proposed to repeal Jim Crow laws, equalize county teachers' salaries, establish the House of Reformation for Colored Children in Cheltenham, and provide the MIC with a salaried secretary. To the Commission's surprise, Ritchie declined to endorse their proposals, though he did encourage the commissioners to submit their recommendations to the General Assembly.[32]

Behind the scenes, Ritchie monitored racially charged criminal cases to a degree unusual for Maryland governors. In January 1925, eighteen-year-old Carroll Gibson, a Black man, was accused of raping Clara E. Baker, a white woman with whom he had previously maintained an intimate relationship. Shortly after Gibson's arrest, trial, conviction, and sentencing, Ritchie met with Walter White and a delegation of thirty-five African American NAACP members, who asked for thirty additional days to collect evidence in the case. Ritchie declined this request. Having visited Gibson in his cell, he insisted that Gibson had recanted his original statement that he "had gone to her room at her invitation." On February 13, 1925, the state executed Gibson by hanging.[33]

Capital punishment, particularly executions by hanging, were meted out on African Americans in Maryland—and in the nation—at a disproportionate rate compared to whites or other ethnic groups. Between 1876 and 1930, ninety-three men were executed in Maryland. Of those ninety-three men, all but twelve were Black—in other words, nearly 90 percent of those executed during that time were Black men. In 1899, in Kent County, Maryland, following the murder of Dr. James Heighe Hill in Millington, a little over eighty miles from Salisbury, nine Black males, some of them boys, were accused of killing him. A mob nearly lynched the nine. At the completion of the trials, four of the "Kent County Nine"—Cornelius Gardiner, Charles James, John Myers, and Joseph Bryan—received death sentences. (The nine would come to be known as "Maryland's Scottsboro Boys" after nine African American young men were falsely accused of raping two white women in Scottsboro, Alabama, in 1931, a case that received national and international attention.) The Kent County executions would have resonated on the Eastern Shore, leaving a lasting impression and precedent of how the Sho' would and should handle justice.[34]

"A Credit to the Democratic Party"

In 1927 American journalist and political theorist Frank Kent lifted up Ritchie as the ideal presidential candidate, based on his record of accomplishment in Maryland. In reporting on the growing national support for Ritchie as a presidential contender, Kent claimed the governor "would make the sort of President for the country that he has made as governor for Maryland—a highly intelligent, extraordinarily capable, amazing, industrious, extremely effective, absolutely upright, and very popular president. . . . If ever he does get to the White House Ritchie will look more as if he belonged there than any President we have had in a considerable time."[35]

Four years later, in 1931, the Williams lynching again focused national attention on Governor Ritchie, who was preparing to run for his third term after unsuccessful presidential campaigns in 1924 and 1928.[36] On December 6, two days after the lynching, Maryland state attorney general Preston Lane Jr. sent a telegram to Ritchie at the Sherman Hotel in Chicago, assuring him that the investigation was under way and that he had received complete cooperation from the local authorities thus far.[37] Ritchie was in Chicago to discuss his putative presidential campaign with leaders of the Illinois Democratic Party.[38] Hundreds had flocked to Grand Central Station to meet Ritchie's train on the Baltimore and Ohio and to congratulate him on his progressive stance toward stamping out Jim Crowism and racial violence. As Ritchie prepared to leave the train station, however, a delegation of Black citizens approached and presented him with a resolution endorsed by the Ten-Year Progress Plan and Program for the Colored Citizens of Chicago:

> The decent, peace-pursuing, law abiding American citizenry is justly encouraged by the immediate and sweeping investigation ordered by you yesterday of the lynching of Matthew Williams a resident of Salisbury, Maryland. . . . On behalf of the 246,000 colored citizens of Chicago we add our genuine welcome to another of the nation's executives whose oath to uphold the majesty of the law and to protect all citizens regardless of creed, color or previous condition [of servitude] has meant more than empty lip service. More power to the Governor of Maryland, who meets every challenge of leadership for the whole citizenry.[39]

Mayor Anton Joseph Cermak and Michael L. Igoe, an Illinois delegate to the Democratic National Committee, also welcomed Ritchie. "We are glad," said Cermak, "to greet and entertain a man who is such a credit to the Democratic Party as Governor Ritchie and who is so prominently and acceptably spoken of as the possible Democratic nominee for President, which means the Presidency itself. We hope everybody will avail themselves of the opportunity Tuesday night to listen on the radio to the Governor's speech."[40]

Three days after Williams's lynching, the Ritchie for President Committee of Maryland wrote Attorney General Lane attributing the intensified hopes for a Ritchie presidency to the investigation into Williams's death. The leaders of the committee got straight to the point:

> Being a great admirer of Governor Ritchie, and wishing to see him in the White House as the next president of the United States with you as his Attorney General, I feel sure you agree that the successful bringing to Justice of the perpetrators of the Eastern Shore Lynching will depend on Governor Ritchie's nomination and election. . . . It is a reasonable deduction that if a man can bring criminals in his own state to Justice, he will be able to do the same thing in the larger national field, and will impress voters with his forcible personality.[41]

Committee leaders realized that Lane's and Ritchie's standing in the press after they spoke out against the lynching was groundbreaking. At the same time, they raised issues pertaining mostly to the role of the police officers and hospital attendants who had watched the lynching take place and done nothing, and they asked whether the nurses in the hospital were "aiding and abetting the mob by criminal negligence or conspiracy."[42] The letter also posed another, central question: "Can or cannot the local authorities be expected to prosecute mob leaders and members and other persons working in a hospital who may have aided in a crime if the authorities belong to some secret organization to which the mob members, etc. also belong?" The committee headers concluded by wishing Ritchie and Lane "success in this difficult task, and hoping to see" Ritchie "elevated to the highest office in the land."[43]

Courting the Black Vote

On December 11, 1931, while still in Chicago, Governor Ritchie took an interview with Theodore Holmes of the Negro Associated Press. Having covered a lynching in Little Rock, Arkansas, three years earlier, and having read the news of Williams's recent lynching, Holmes wasted no time, asking Ritchie, "Well now governor, I understand that you are in line to become a candidate for President. What would be your position in respect to a national anti-lynching law if you should become a candidate?"

Holmes recalls that the question caught Ritchie, seasoned politician though he was, off guard, in part because he had been challenged by a "colored" reporter. The tension in the air cleared after Ritchie and Holmes shook hands at the behest of Michael Igoe, the Democratic National Committee delegate from Illinois, who informed Holmes that he was shaking hands with "the next President of the United States." Baltimore mayor Howard W. Jackson was among the group, and Holmes overheard Igoe telling Jackson about the "four or five 'darky' newspapers in town."[44]

Appealing to Ritchie's need for the Black vote, Igoe, who was considered to be "the angel" of urban "Negro" Democrats, most likely was greasing the wheels to secure some role in a future Ritchie White House. As the conversation continued, Ritchie quickly deflected Holmes's question, expressing surprise: "Good gracious! That's too blamed far off to talk about now."

"But, Governor," Holmes persisted, "surely you have some position in respect to lynching. You can say whether you favor or do not favor an anti-lynching bill, can you not?"

Ritchie hesitated and Holmes followed up: "Would you prefer then for me to report you as not being willing to be quoted on the subject?"

"Well, yes," Ritchie replied. "You see, I am an advocate of states' rights. I believe that the states should take care of those things."

Holmes next asked Ritchie about the lynching of Matthew Williams: "What are you going to do about Friday's lynching in Maryland?"

Ritchie quickly responded, repeating what had already been printed in the local newspapers: as soon as he had heard about the lynching, he had placed Attorney General Preston Lane on the case.

Holmes began challenging Ritchie about the details of the case: "Where was the sheriff when the lynching occurred?" hinting that he had obtained word that the sheriff was possibly involved. Holmes was trying to expose the fact that Ritchie was either in over his head or was using the lynching of Williams to further his campaign while having no real intention of holding the perpetrators accountable. "The Maryland governor and presidential aspirant," Holmes later wrote, "did not know where the sheriff was, nor what he was going to be able to do to the sheriff if that official had been negligent in the performance of his duty."

The newspaperman concluded the interview by asking Ritchie, "Will any of the mob members be punished?" Reluctantly, Ritchie responded, "We are going to try to get them . . . but I doubt that we shall have much success. It is very difficult to get grand juries to indict in such cases." By the end of the interview, it had become clear to Holmes that Ritchie, a presidential aspirant, "was not very hopeful about [ending] mob violence in his state and had no encouraging position in respect to lynching as a national crime."[45]

Baltimore's 800,000 citizens constituted half the state population.[46] Considering this fact, it is very clear that Ritchie's motives for initiating the investigation were linked to his political aspirations. Ritchie's decision to investigate the lynching was an attempt to secure the Black vote through an action that might also appeal to white urban progressives, whose votes he needed to secure the presidential bid. A full understanding of the political climate in which Ritchie's response to the lynching was born requires an examination of how other state governors responded to lynchings in 1931.

Gubernatorial Responses to Lynching

Given the Republican Party's support of anti-lynching legislation since the beginning of the twentieth century, it is perhaps not surprising that the Republican governors of West Virginia, North Dakota, and Missouri spoke out against and vigorously investigated lynchings. By 1931, the vast majority of southern governors did not investigate lynchings or make statements condemning them. In pursuing the investigation into Williams's lynching, Ritchie joined a small group of Democratic governors who showed at least a remote interest in ending lynchings of Black men, including Robert Glenn of North Carolina and Doyle E. Carlton of Florida.[47]

In the Deep South, there were the race-baiting or silent Democratic governors such as Theodore Bilbo and Huey Long, who were showing signs during the 1920s and '30s of their future split from the party.

By the end of 1931, the national lynching toll had reached its highest point since 1923. After lambasting Republican anti-lynching legislation earlier in his political career, Ritchie joined governors throughout the nation who were forced to confront Judge Lynch. Up until this point, Ritchie had somehow been able to maintain African American voters' support. But Matthew Williams's fate reminded them that the Free State was not immune to Judge Lynch. The lynching of Williams caused Ritchie to draw an even more precise distinction between himself and his fellow southern Democrats. Days after the ugly deed, Ritchie set a plan in motion that we have come to fully understand only recently: he launched two investigations, both of them private and secret, into the lynching of Matthew Williams.

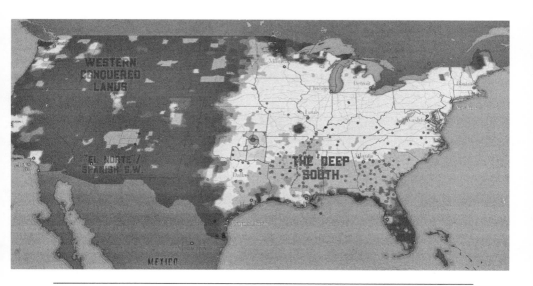

Map of lynchings in the United States, 1921–1931. This map is based on the traditional definition of lynching proposed by Monroe Work in 1940 as the basis of his Tuskegee Institute study. It does not include larger attacks on whole communities of color such as the 1921 Tulsa Race Massacre. Light gray dots represent African American victims, medium gray dots represent Latinx victims, and dark gray dots represent white victims. Monroe & Florence Work Today. Accessed June 21, 2020. https://plaintalkhistory.com/monroeandflorencework.

Governor Albert C. Ritchie Confronts Judge Lynch

Governor Ritchie's Investigations

Charged by Governor Ritchie to lead the inquiry into the Williams lynching was the heretofore obscure Attorney General Preston Lane. Lane had risen to the post a little more than year earlier. On October 12, 1930, state attorney general Thomas H. Robinson died of a heart attack during his re-election campaign. In Robinson's place the Democratic Party's central committee put Lane on the ballot. Lane was a native of Washington County, and his success was credited to the tremendous support he garnered from western Maryland Democrats. He also carried eight of the nine Eastern Shore counties, losing only Somerset.

On December 5, one day after the lynching of Williams, State's Attorney Levin C. Bailey summoned a coroner's jury composed of leading citizens. Bailey was adamant about quickly beginning the investigation. "There will be no more delay than is necessary for the identification of those who took part in the crime," he declared in a statement published in the *Baltimore Evening Sun*. "I plan to prosecute this case vigorously, stopping not at the leaders, but carrying it to fix responsibility for the death of Williams."[48] The same day, Ritchie telegrammed Bailey at his Baltimore office to express his pleasure with the statement and thanking him for his "vigorous prosecution of the perpetrators of the Williams lynching." He added, "I feel it is my duty to render all the assistance I can, and so I am requesting the Attorney General to cooperate with you in every way he can."[49]

Another Murder

Following Williams's lynching, rumors circulated that Williams was not the only "Negro" to have been killed in Salisbury in early December. On December 7, Bailey told Attorney General Lane "that there had been a careful investigation of the facts and circumstances surrounding the death of a negro whose body was found on the railroad tracks yesterday."[50] According to Lane's contemporaneous notes of the conversation, Bailey told him more about the as yet unpublicized case: "The negro had a broken arm and his skull was fractured. There were blood marks on the railroad track for approximately 25 feet from the place where the body was found. The conclu-

Death certificate issued for the unknown victim (John Smith) of a "railroad accident," December 8, 1931. Collection of Maryland State Archives.

sion is irresistible that this man was struck by a railroad train and killed, and Mr. Bailey and the Coroner said that in their opinion there is no occasion for a formal inquest."[51] Lane stated that he agreed with Bailey's assessment of the situation. However, he suggested that Bailey "obtain a written statement from the witnesses to the above facts, and reserve for future reference in case of necessity."[52] The Baltimore Afro-American was the only newspaper that reported the death. "There are many mysterious elements surrounding the man's death," the article suggested. "The identity and finding of the man's body at College Avenue and Railroad Street have caused beliefs and rumors that the man was attacked and fatally injured by a group of bloodthirsty whites who were out to get any unprotected colored person seen on the streets Saturday night."[53]

The same article quoted Salisbury mayor Wade W. Insley's comment on the investigation and race relations in Salisbury: "A careful investigation shows that everything is quiet and no further trouble is anticipated. There never has been any trouble between the races here and there is not going to be now."[54]

Clearly, Mayor Insley was ready for the cloud over the Eastern Shore to lift. Just four days after Williams's lynching, Baltimore police commissioner Charles D. Gaither offered his detectives to assist the Wicomico County authorities in identifying members of the mob. The attorney general and the governor supported this offer, which indicates the unique relationship that Governor Ritchie had with Baltimore, particularly regarding race relations in the state. Ritchie recognized that he was governor of a southern state whose politics and power resided in its largest city, Baltimore, where in 1931 half of Maryland's population resided. A state's control of its largest city's police force is definitely rare. Historically, only New Hampshire, Maine, and Missouri maintained a similar relationship with their largest cities. Ritchie vaguely explained the relationship between the state and the Baltimore City Police in discussing the state's appointment of the Baltimore police commissioner: "This provision was made a great many years ago for reasons which have now passed into history, but the law has never been changed, because it has worked excellently. I think the people prefer it to any other method of appointment."[55]

The arrangement between the state and Baltimore City Police that Ritchie spoke of dated back to 1862, when Union military commanders turned the Baltimore City Police over to the state of Maryland after Union forces occupied the city on June 27, 1861. The state Board of Police Commissioners was established in 1867, and from then until 1920 the board was appointed by the governor.[56] After 1920, during Ritchie's tenure, a single police commissioner for Baltimore City was appointed and served at the pleasure of the governor, in addition to serving on the governor's advisory board. In 1971, *Baltimore Sun* reporter Turner Catledge exposed contradictions within Ritchie's politics and problems with the power that he wielded over the Baltimore City Police:

Baltimore was a cultivated city, but it was also wide open. Prohibition was the law then, but Maryland's aristocratic governor, Albert Cabell Ritchie, wouldn't let the state police enforce it, or the Baltimore city police, over whom be had control. When federal officials would try to raid in Baltimore, the local officials would often tip off the speakeasy owners, and sometimes Governor Ritchie's men would arrest the federal officers. The governor, as you might guess, was himself a man who liked to drink. I got to know him well and I admired him for his candor. In those days he was highly regarded as a future prospect for the White House.[57]

According to the *Cumberland Evening Times*, the officers sent by Baltimore police commissioner Gaither to help with the investigation into Williams's lynching were Sergeants Walter Martin and Graydon Ware. Martin and Ware arrived in Salisbury on December 7, 1931, to conduct a weeklong investigation.[58] On December 8, Police Commissioner Gaither also offered Bailey and Wicomico County authorities the services of the Baltimore detective bureau in the search for and identification of members of the Salisbury mob. The coroner's jury had already examined Williams's body.

At 4:10 p.m. on December 11, 1931, State's Attorney Bailey called Attorney General Lane to ask Lane when he thought the Baltimore detectives in Salisbury would complete their investigation. According to Bailey's assistant, Bailey "said he didn't wish to hold the Coroner's inquest until the investigation had been completed, and he had thought about holding it on Wednesday of next week."[59] It is this nod that, I argue, prompted Lane to question Bailey's motives in investigating the case. Responding to this pressure from the prosecutor, Lane seemed to have suggested to Bailey that the Baltimore detectives would be close to completing their investigation by the end of December and would submit their final report in January of the following year. However, this was not to be the case, and the Baltimore detectives would continue with their investigation.

By December 10, nongovernment officials had started to weigh in on the investigation. F. C. Bandal of the Baltimore Federation of Labor demanded an investigation not only of the lynching but also into labor conditions for Black workers on Maryland's Eastern Shore. From Scottsboro to Salisbury, the Black laborer was under attack. It was at this time that the state, county, and local police forces reported that they would conduct separate investigations into the lynching, not presenting their evidence to the grand jury until they had ironclad evidence sufficient for indictment.[60]

Attorney General Lane and Assistant Attorney General G. C. A. Anderson went to Peninsula General Hospital a few days after the lynching to interview witnesses. Next, they interviewed L. W. Selse, vice president and general manager of the Red Star Motor Coach terminal, where the mob had poured gasoline on Williams's body and set it afire. Shortly after that, Lane interviewed Chief Nicholas H. Holland. Before leaving Salisbury, Lane also met with Bailey. Per the *Cumberland Evening Times*, Lane was traveling with the reports of the Baltimore detectives.[61]

By January 1932, Governor Ritchie and Attorney General Lane knew that they could not trust Salisbury's local law enforcement or the state's attorney to find out who was behind the lynching. While working with local authorities in Salisbury, Lane initiated a separate and secret investigation led by the Pinkerton National Detective Agency (PNDA), using an undercover informant from Trenton, New Jersey, a former professional boxer named "Patsy" Johnson.[62]

In his campaigns for the presidency in the 1920s and in 1931, Governor Albert Ritchie insisted on tying his progressive stance on racial problems to the traditional Democratic concept of states' rights, a strategy that prevented him from ever supporting a federal attempt to combat lynching and mob violence. Clearly, he saw African American support for his candidacy and his opposition to lynching solely as a source of political capital. African Americans were looking for a candidate who would ease their economic plight during the Depression and stamp out Jim Crowism.[63] Ritchie had been good to his word in encouraging a state investigation into the Williams lynching. But his actions, or lack thereof, in the wake of the investigation's finding showed his commitment to ending lynching to be weak, at best. Whatever his original intentions in authorizing the investigation, his timid follow-up would leave the system that supported white supremacy intact.

[Part II]

[4]

From Pugilist to Private Eye

A Former Prizefighter Infiltrates the Mob

*Governor Albert C. Ritchie is sitting quietly on a political munitions heap
and . . . the lynching of Matthew Williams on December 5
may be a big factor in deciding who the next
President of the United States will be.*

Baltimore Afro-American, January 2, 1932

Two days into the new year the *Baltimore Afro-American* newspaper reprinted *Chicago Tribune* staff writer Tom Petty's report into what he described as "Lynchland, Maryland." Petty's investigation and the *Afro-American's* own reporting fed into the narrative that Ritchie and his supporters wanted to sell to the citizens of Maryland, and also to the citizens of the South. To progressives the investigation into the lynching of Williams marked a step forward. However, to whites on the Eastern Shore, and to the Democratic-controlled South, the investigation was nothing more than a ploy to get votes, one that would lead to no arrests or convictions and would succumb to the savage ideal. This ideal emerged in the Unites States after Reconstruction, was revived in the 1920s, and was not confined to the Deep South. Subscribers to this faith enforced conformity, honor, and intolerance through lynching and other forms of racial violence and saw such violence as the only way to solve the so-called Negro problem.[1] Little did the progressives or the southern Democrats know, Ritchie was aware of the almost certain failure of any local investigation into the lynching and had already set another, secret investigation in motion, led by the Pinkerton National Detective Agency.

Meanwhile, race relations and the upcoming elections continued to make front-page news. As the Williams investigation was just getting started, the mob element of the Eastern Shore continued to grow enraged. To make matters worse Richard Ford, Euel Lee, and George Davis had somehow evaded Judge Lynch, as Lee's trial was moved to Towson, Maryland, away from the shore, and Davis eluded execution after being sentenced to sixteen years in prison. These events provided a pretext for the disgruntled white community in and around Salisbury to vow to make an example out of the next "Negro" who stepped out of line.

Not only was the lynching of Matthew Williams consistent with the spectacle lynchings of the 1890s in its public brutality and exhibitionism, but the mob element behind Williams's lynching had the structure of lynch mobs laid out by historians, intellectuals, and criminal justice experts in the nineteenth and twentieth centuries.[2] There is no way to know whether this structure factored into Ritchie's response to the lynching of Williams; however, the fact that it had occurred at all gave the lie to Ritchie's states' rights argument against a federal anti-lynching law, as the state's chief executive appeared unable to control the backward mob element.

The first three months of the secret investigation of the lynching of Matthew Williams began with a strategic infiltration by Pinkerton detective Patsy Johnson and continued with revealing the secrecy employed to cover it up. In considering the historic nature of the lynch mob dating back to the 1890s, in most cases those behind the lynching were sworn to secrecy. This secrecy, or system of silence, was not only directed at protecting the men behind the lynching, but it was also invoked to protect the whiteness of communities. In exploring this issue, the next three chapters will expand upon the case study approach, leaning on the contemporaneous journal entries of an undercover Pinkerton detective. In addition, the frameworks of historians John Ross and William Fitzhugh will be utilized to shed light on the organizational structure of the mob responsible for the lynching of Williams. Using historian Howard Smead's concentric circle approach, I analyze the various circles of the conspiracy behind the lynching of Williams. Last, I explore the class structure of white supremacy and local power in Salisbury and the lower Eastern Shore of Maryland. Examining class structure pushes back against the myth of white uniformity and brings into the foreground elite whites' use of anti-Black racism to maintain the compliance of the white working class in the system that prolonged their exploitation.

This analysis not only describes the investigation but also reveals the secret and strategic effort of an organized criminal collective of white citizens to racially terrorize a Black community, not just in Salisbury but throughout Maryland's Eastern Shore. However, to gain access to the workings of this loosely organized mob it is important that we understand the operative who successfully infiltrated the mob. Five days into the new year of 1932, one of two secret operatives employed by the Pinkerton National Detective Agency arrived in Salisbury.

From Pugilist to Private Eye

It was a cold winter night at the Oasis Athletic Club in Portsmouth, Virginia, on December 4, 1931. As Matthew Williams was suffering at the hands of the mob, a seasoned pugilist, Patsy Johnson, won what would be his second-to-last professional match, defeating Al Reyes of Portsmouth, Virginia, going eight points in a three-one-three decision. Unbeknownst to Patsy, by January 1932 he would find himself at the center of one of Maryland's most hideous lynching crimes.[3]

Patsy was born Pasquale "Patrick" Anthony Petta in Syracuse, New York, on April 7, 1900. His parents, Anthony and Camilla "Martello" Petta, arrived in the United States from Italy around 1890, a time when anti-immigrant sentiment was emerging in America.[4] One of nine children in the Petta household, Patsy Johnson shared his parents' home with five brothers—Angelo, Florine, Nicholas, Ralph, and John—and three sisters—Rose, Olive, and Elvira.[5] Following in the footsteps of his older brother Florine "Battling" Johnson, Patsy took to boxing very early, at the young age of thirteen, and began his professional career just three years later.[6] In many ways, Patsy and his brother's dedication to the sport reflected Italian immigrants' attempt to integrate into white society.

Despite the family's southern Italian identity, they worked to transcend their immigrant status and be accepted into white society. Second-generation Italian immigrants such as Patsy took to boxing to shake off their foreign identity and more fully assimilate into white culture. In 1912, New Orleans–born Pete Herman—one of the all-time great bantamweight world champions, a second-generation Italian, and a future opponent of Patsy in the ring—adopted this strategy to his advantage. In many ways, Herman's success laid the foundation for Patsy and other Italians who sought to integrate into white society via boxing.[7] In many ways, Patsy would go in the ring as the "immigrant other," and if he won or put on a good-enough show, white men and women in the audience would, as Nelson Algren later wrote, applaud him "for being white too."[8]

In 1919, after a brief enlistment in the US Army, Patsy left New York, where boxing had been outlawed in 1917, following "Young" McDonald's death in the ring, and would remain so until 1920, when the Walker Law created the New York State Athletic Commission.[9] He relocated to Trenton in New Jersey, which legalized professional boxing for the first time in 1918 with passage of the Hurley Boxing Law.[10] Patsy joined the area's vibrant Italian American community and began to make a name for himself, following in the footsteps of famous boxer Jack Dempsey. Patsy also joined the Knights of Columbus, the world's largest Catholic fraternal service organization.[11] By 1920 he had contended against several bantamweight world champions, including Kid Williams (with whom Patsy was matched in 1914–17), Pete "Kid" Herman (1917–20, 1921), and Joe Lynch (1920–21 and 1922–24).[12] Throughout the United States, many saw boxing as the sport of vice and impurity, associated with the gambling, alcohol, and crime that ran rampant during the first thirty years of the twentieth century. The bootleggers and desperate wage laborers among the fans drew social criticism to the game. Before the Walker Law, bribes were rife in New York boxing culture, which further fueled the sort of lawlessness and criminality that would be common in the "Roaring Twenties."[13]

Patsy left Trenton in 1922 and began bouncing around the country, hoping to secure income from boxing somewhere. By 1924, he had fought from Miami, Florida to Akron, Ohio.[14] Sometime after March 1925, Patsy joined the army, serving in the Panama Canal Infantry Brigade. In 1927, he was diagnosed with third-degree bilateral "pes planus" (fallen arches), a condition quite common among boxers, whose arches are frequently under tremendous stress.[15] In 1928 Patsy was back in Trenton, where he thought he could return to his former fan base and make a comeback. This unsuccessful attempt resulted in expulsion: in September 1929, the New Jersey Boxing Commission barred Patsy from participating in any Jersey rings, deeming him "physically unfit to remain in the game."[16] One month after the Boxing Commission barred Patsy, the stock market crashed and the United States economy fell into shambles.

"Patsy" Johnson, former professional boxer, at the beginning of his career. Courtesy of the Hank Kaplan Boxing Archive, Brooklyn College Archives and Special Collections.

From Pugilist to Private Eye

Patsy found his way back to the ring on Virginia's Eastern Shore. On November 20, 1931, Patsy Johnson, billed as a "Philadelphia showman," defeated "Tuffy" Banks at the Oasis Athletic Club in Portsmouth, Virginia, a little over 130 miles from Salisbury. After he beat Banks by an eight-point decision, Patsy's comeback was official.[17] A week and a half later, on December 4—about the time Matthew Williams was dragged from Peninsula General Hospital's first-floor window—Patsy was back in Portsmouth, defeating Al Reyes, a native of the Philippines, at the Oasis Athletic Club.[18]

It is not clear how Patsy came to work for the Pinkertons. Since its inception in the 1860s, the Pinkerton National Detective Agency had maintained brawlers and pugilists in its employ. Like Patsy, Irving Hatch (the father of Academy Award–winning filmmaker Norman Hatch) began working for the agency after retiring from a boxing career.[19] Maryland native Dashiell Hammett provided insight into the recruitment strategies employed by the agency when he recalled being hired after reading an advertisement in the local newspaper in 1915, just as Patsy was beginning his boxing career. Hammett, looking for employment and adventure, responded to a blind recruitment ad printed in a local Baltimore newspaper looking for "intelligent men."[20] The Pinkerton National Detective Agency was hoping to recruit detectives for its newly established office in Baltimore. Other operatives have also described this blind advertisement, which read: "WANTED—A bright, experienced salesman to handle good line; salary and commission. Excellent opportunity for right man to connect with first class house."[21]

By 1915 similar ads soliciting "intelligent men" and offering the opportunity to earn up to $80 a month were appearing in the *Baltimore Sun*. Ads such as these encouraged those interested to respond only in writing. We may never know exactly how Patsy was recruited, but we do know that he was hired by the agency in Philadelphia, less than forty miles from his second home in Trenton, New Jersey.[22] And we know that his undercover detail in Salisbury was one stop he made in his postboxing career, along with opening an ice cream parlor in Trenton in August 1932 and fighting in an exhibition match in 1933. He moved to Detroit to work security at the Ford Motor Company in 1937, the same year the Battle of the Overpass occurred, in which Ford security guards clashed with labor organizers from the United Auto Workers.[23]

Until this point, Patsy's role in the investigation has never been mentioned in any of the scholarship surrounding the lynching of Matthew Williams. Most historical accounts suggest that the state was no match for the conspiracy of silence that saturated Maryland's Eastern Shore. These works lean on the coverage of the investigation in the *Baltimore Sun*, *Salisbury Times*, *Baltimore Afro-American*, and other newspapers, as well as oral histories from the 1970s and 1990s. The account in this book, by contrast, is based on the stenographic witness statements analyzed in chapter 2.

Secret investigations like PNDA's were not without precedent in Maryland. Following the 1911 lynching of King Johnson in Brooklyn, Maryland (today a suburb of Baltimore), the Republican governor, Phillips Lee Goldsborough, commissioned the first secret investigation by a private firm, the Burns National Detective Agency.[24] In transitioning from the previous administration of Democrat Austin Lane Crothers, Goldsborough was tasked with governing a largely Democratic state and confronting a party that would become emboldened following the Democratic National Convention held in Baltimore in 1912, the subsequent election of Woodrow Wilson, and the emerging rebirth of the Ku Klux Klan. Although the political dilemmas Goldsborough faced differed from those Ritchie would later confront, it is quite evident that Goldsborough had serious doubts about the ability of local officials to adequately investigate the King lynching.[25]

On December 31, 1931, Lane received a letter from E. L. Patterson, Pinkerton's superintendent for New York. The two had conferred on December 29 about securing PNDA'S services to investigate the lynching of Matthew Williams. Patterson wanted to solidify the agreement and detailed the price for his firm's services. "It is understood," Patterson wrote, "that our rates for this work are $15.00 per day, plus expenses, for each operative detailed for Investigation; $12.00 per day, plus expenses, for each operative detailed for Secret Work."[26] Patterson went on to lay out prices for other PNDA services and attached a carbon copy for Lane to endorse to make their arrangement official. After receiving confirmation from Lane, Patterson wrote back the same day: "We acknowledge the receipt of your guarantee securing the payment of our claim against the State Law Department of Maryland, for services and experiences of this Agency. We hereby notify that we accept your guarantee, and in consideration thereof, will perform the services required."[27]

Under this agreement Ritchie and Lane secured the services of two nonsecret and two secret operatives. The nonsecret operatives were administrators from the two regional PNDA offices, namely Assistant Superintendent "T.J.F." of Baltimore and Assistant Superintendent "H.W.M." of Philadelphia. The two secret operatives hired were identified by the code names "B.J." and "No. 301." PNDA's primary secret operative was B.J., whom I have identified as Patsy Johnson.[28] Originally, evidence suggested that Lane wanted Johnson's investigation to pick up where Sergeants Ware and Martin had left off; however, they continued to investigate alongside Johnson, focusing specifically on Black witnesses.

Week One

Establishing Cover

Patsy arrived in Salisbury in early January of 1932, about a month after the lynching of Williams. He was new in town, and everyone could tell. Shortly after arriving, he decided to stop by Thompson's Grill on East Main Street for breakfast. Thompson's was located in the same building as the Red Star Lines bus terminal, where Williams's body had been doused with gasoline and burned.[29] While eating breakfast, Patsy made the acquaintance of three young men between the ages of eighteen and twenty-three, as well as Mr. Thompson, the proprietor. As he made his way outside after eating, he noticed how busy the men were who were working across the street at Wimbrow's Garage, a large, modernized, fireproof building with a hundred-car capacity. Thirty-year-old Ralph E. Wimbrow, a Salisbury native, was the manager and owner.[30]

Around 12:30 p.m. the same day, Patsy entered the Mayflower Grill at 116 East Main Street for a bite to eat. Known for having some of the best food in town, the Mayflower Grill was the restaurant in the Mayflower Hotel.[31] While there, Patsy "ironically" ran into a fellow Italian American from

Syracuse whom he had known for twenty years. This man, Joe Fusco, was currently living in Ocean City, Maryland, just over thirty miles from Salisbury.[32] Fusco was in Salisbury conferring with his attorneys as he prepared to head north for the winter. Forty-five-year-old Fusco represented the old stock of the progressive big money of the Mafia-run northern cities. An extraordinarily wealthy man, he had recently finished construction of one of the most luxurious hotels that the Eastern Shore would ever see, the George Washington Hotel, "the GW," in Ocean City, Maryland. Billed as the best hotel south of Atlantic City, the GW was built at a cost of $200,000 (over $3.2 million today). Standing six stories, this modern marvel contained two hundred rooms, each with its own telephone, bath, and shower. The opening was an invitation-only event for 250 couples, featuring the Continental Novelty Orchestra from Paris, France.

Given the tight job supply during the Depression, it was perhaps most noteworthy that the hotel was applauded for having an all-white staff. This calculated decision to choose white labor over the cheaper alternative played well from a marketing standpoint and appealed to whites throughout the Eastern Shore. It provides evidence that working conditions may have been a little different in this part of Maryland as it relates to the early impact the Great Depression had on the Eastern Shore.[33]

Realizing that Patsy would be interested in connecting with the area boxing promoter, Fusco arranged for his pugilist friend to meet Captain William B. S. Powell, who also lived in Ocean City. Powell was a fifty-eight-year-old former United States Coast Guard warrant officer and former mayor of Ocean City. Having inherited the Atlantic Hotel from his father, Powell owned thousands of acres of beach-front property, making him the largest individual landowner in Worcester County. A prominent businessman, he also promoted all of the boxing matches in Salisbury.[34]

Fusco may have saved Patsy from being exposed as a Pinkerton early on, as he supplied him with insight into the attitude and personality of the community on the Eastern Shore, telling him, "Don't worry, if they take a liking to you, you will not have to worry. The Police give you more than an even break down on the Eastern Shore."[35]

At around 6 p.m., Patsy headed back to Thompson's Grill for dinner. Shortly after that, he went to the Arcade Bowling and Billiard Parlor, located inside the Arcade Theatre on Main Street, where young men unwound and relaxed following a long day's work. As he prepared to retire, he noticed several signs in car windows that read, "I am an East Shore man and proud of it."[36] By the end of his first day in Salisbury, Patsy had begun to develop his cover and connect with the power brokers on the Eastern Shore.

The next morning Patsy followed the same routine, eating breakfast and getting acquainted with the staff at Thompson's Grill. After finishing his meal, he headed to the barbershop to get a haircut before going to Ocean City to meet with Fusco and Captain Powell. As he walked into the shop, he noticed three or four men waiting ahead of him. While Patsy waited, the barber brought up the Euel Lee murder trial. "Do the damn Baltimore people think we cannot give a nigger a fair trial on the Eastern Shore?" he asked. "Well, they ought to hang that nigger the same as we did Williams in Salisbury." The men who were waiting agreed with the barber, suggesting that a Black person could obtain justice—through lynching. Having loosened up, the barber asked Patsy from what part of the country he hailed. After deciding that Patsy was not a threat, the barber continued, "Well, you only have to string one up and that will keep the rest of the niggers in their place for a long time."

Chronicling the development of the barber's statement offers a glimpse into the contradictions that prevented true justice and the rule of law from prevailing. At first, the barber pushed back against the backward criticism that was being focused on the Eastern Shore—most likely by a Baltimore newspaper—describing the entire region as backwards and morally bankrupt. By the end of his statement, he forgets, just for a moment, about how the Eastern Shore was perceived, and after recognizing Patsy's whiteness, he lets the mob's true motive slip out: racial terror. After spending a little time with these men, Patsy started to see that the only justice they saw fit for the "Negro" was rope justice.[37] Just a few days into the investigation, Patsy had found evidence that aligned with traditional racial terror lynchings throughout the South and observed strategies used to terrorize and socially control Black communities. Thus, the lynching of Williams provided members of the economically frustrated racist element of the Eastern Shore a means to show the Black community their "proper" place in society. Indeed, the brazenness of their statements speak to the confidence they possessed in the white supremacist power structure that undergirded not only the community of Salisbury but also other communities throughout the United States. The statements Johnson recorded provide insight into the "privileged" space afforded by whiteness, a space where anti-Black racism, Black dehumanization, and murder are nonchalantly discussed over breakfast in anti-Black spaces. Based on the casual conversation in the barbershop, it is clear that the lynching was a community affair protected by a system of silence.

Meanwhile, Patsy saw his haircut as an opportunity to tell the guys a little more about himself. He proceeded to tell the men of his successful fighting record, and that, having challenged several world champions, he planned to meet Captain Powell in Ocean City about arranging a fight. They suggested that he train twenty-three-year-old Harry "Kid" Guthrie so that he could further develop his skills. Guthrie, a southpaw and native of Salisbury, had made his professional debut on January 17, 1930. While boxing part-time, Guthrie also worked as a chauffeur. His wife, Anna, had died on July 13, 1931, just months before the lynching of Williams—leaving him to raise their daughter alone.[38]

Shortly after leaving the barbershop, Patsy went over to the site of D.J. Elliott's murder, at the Elliott Box and Crate Factory. He surveyed the plant and noticed an automobile parked in front of Elliott's office with the license plate number 298-594. Later he saw the car again, parked on Main Street near the courthouse—and this time he could see the driver. According to Patsy, the man was between forty-two and forty-six years old, six feet, one inch tall, and 210 pounds, with a long nose. He wore a leather lumber jacket. This individual fit the description, referenced in the witness statements taken following Williams's lynching, of a suspect said to be wearing a leather lumber jacket. Patsy had the Pinkerton Detective Agency run the tag on the vehicle, and it came back as belonging to one Steven W. Murray, a fifty-year-old lumber dealer living in Berlin, Maryland.[39]

Establishing the Partnership

Patsy left for Ocean City, arriving at around 1:30 p.m. He found Fusco, and the two went to meet with Powell. Having just missed Powell, Fusco decided that he and Patsy could kill time by touring the new George Washington Hotel, which was closed for the winter season. Leaving the GW, they met with several residents around town. After spending all day with Fusco, Patsy finally met with Powell at 7:30 p.m. He described Powell as being about sixty years old, five feet, two inches tall, and weighing 250 pounds. Following introductions, Powell attempted to challenge the public view concerning his financial success, arguing that he paid only $15 to $25 for his fights and that he had lost $800 last summer as a result (this amount would have equaled approximately $14,539.62 in 2018).[40]

Powell did not, however, say how much he thought Patsy would bring in for a fight. Nonetheless, he told Patsy to connect with Lee Oland Harris, as Powell had agreed with Harris only to use "his boys" on the fight cards. Harris, a native of the Eastern Shore who hailed from nearby Deals Island, was a thirty-seven-year-old boxing promoter and owner of a small gym in Salisbury.

Powell represented the robust Eastern Shore stock who chose region over everything else.[41] He saw Patsy as the perfect fit—a seasoned fighter from out of state. As Patsy prepared to leave, Powell recorded his name and weight in his book and said that he was promoting a fight in Salisbury for January 15. Powell had plans for Patsy, not only as a business partner with Lee Oland Harris but also as a fighter, and intended to match Patsy up with "Kid" Guthrie, promising that he would pay him a bonus if he knocked Guthrie out. They sealed the deal, and Patsy agreed to begin training young fighters from the surrounding areas at Harris's gym in Salisbury. Powell told Patsy he would see him in Salisbury on January 15.[42]

"It Served the Nigger Good"

After spending the past two days in Ocean City, Patsy and Fusco made their way back to Salisbury, arriving just before noon on January 7. Fusco now introduced Patsy to Lee Harris, the owner of the gym in Salisbury. Harris escorted Patsy around town, connecting him with other local people, before assigning him to be Danny Russell's training partner. Said to be Salisbury's best boxer, Russell, born Russell B. Dennis, was a twenty-four-year-old lightweight from Salisbury. He had been a teenager when he had made his fight debut in 1927.[43]

After Russell was finished training for the day, he and Patsy headed to the cigar store inside the Arcade Building on Main Street. As they approached the store, a young man in the crowd yelled out to Patsy, "Boy, you should have been here about a month ago. We sure had some excitement," and told him that he, along with other local men, had had a lynching party and strung up Williams. Patsy replied, "Perhaps it served the nigger good." Patsy made a note of this young man, sensing that he could easily get information out of him if he saw him in the gym the next afternoon.[44]

Later, Patsy accompanied Russell to the barbershop, where the lynching came up once again when a heavyset man he had met before blurted out, "Well, when are you fellows going to hang another nigger here in Salisbury?" The barber, who was working at the second chair, quickly responded, "Well, I do not know. We are ashamed of ourselves for this last job we did that I think everybody is about caught up on the whole thing." The subject quickly changed when a customer asked Russell about his upcoming fight.[45] This exchange between Patsy and the unnamed barbershop customer provides additional evidence that the men had accepted Patsy as white, and their casual comfort in discussing the lynching shows that they did not perceive him as an outsider. Without revealing any names, these two witnesses, the barber and the customer, provided Patsy with evidence that the lynching had been performed by a hue-and-cry mob, in historian John Ross's classification. The motives were tied to the death of D.J. Elliott, but this evidence did not indicate a level of organization on the part of the lynchers that enabled them to plan the lynching.

"Our Own Little Hanging Party"

Around 6:00 p.m., Governor Ritchie's name came up in conversation as Patsy was eating dinner at Thompson's Grill. One of the customers was reading the *Salisbury Times*, which featured a large photo of Ritchie announcing a banquet the Ritchie for President Committee was hosting in Baltimore.[46] Suddenly, Harry Waller, the waiter working the counter, said, "Well, Ritchie would do better if he ran through a corn field." A man eating next to Patsy, a salesman from Baltimore, responded, "What have the people down here got against Governor Ritchie?" Waller replied, "Well, the Yuel [sic] Lee case has soured us against him. But there is one case he did not beat us out of—our own little hanging party." He criticized the Baltimore detectives that Ritchie and Lane had hired, arguing that no one would talk. Patsy recorded what the counterman next said:

> Why damn it! How did they expect to find out anything when some of the leading men in Salisbury are involved in the matter? Why even the Chief of Police [Holland] would not squeal on the men and he knows who they are. Why damn it! Some good friends of Captain Greer [sic], who is at the head of the fire department, asked the captain if they could have some rope to hang the nigger with, and Captain Greer said: "Sure! Come on in. I will give you all you want." And do you think that Captain Greer is going to squeal on any of his friends? Why the whole town was like a pack of wolves after the nigger was lowered from the tree. They dragged the nigger back of the lunch car and laid him on the ground, and even women said: "Why turn that dirty nigger on the other side and burn him up some more."[47]

The captain of the fire department whom Waller mentioned was Frederick A. Grier Jr., another representative of the old stock of the Eastern Shore, one who came from a rich history of business and industrial labor.[48] Grier would not be the first or the last member of the area's law enforcement leaders found to have been complicit in the lynching of Matthew Williams. Yet Grier's role would prove to be more extensive in that he provided the rope with full knowledge that it would be used to lynch Williams.

Waller continued to open up to Patsy, stating that Thompson had received a $10 check from a New York newspaper after calling and giving a reporter play-by-play details of the lynching as it was taking place. Reporters stated they could hear screaming through their phones.[49] At the counterman's request, his conversation with Patsy and Thompson was done quietly so that other customers could not hear. Winking his eye before speaking, the counterman said, "But the boss or I, or none of us around here, saw anything; we were too busy with our work feeding people." He later told Patsy why everyone in Salisbury, including the witnesses whom Lane and others had interviewed, was keeping quiet: "You know things like this are not supposed to be discussed because the word was passed out by some big shot in Salisbury that everybody should keep still and not open their mouths to anyone."[50] Harry Waller not only identified those who par-

Chief Frederick A. Grier Jr., 1920s.
Courtesy Salisbury Fire Department
Museum.

Chief Frederick A. Grier Jr. in front of the Salisbury Fire
Department. Members of the mob claimed that Grier
provided the rope used to lynch Matthew Williams.
Edward H. Nabb Research Center for Delmarva History and
Culture, Salisbury University, Salisbury, Maryland.

ticipated or were complicit in the lynching but also indicated the reason why previous interviews and subsequent accounts depicted a conspiracy of silence. Waller attributes this call for silence to one specific leader in Salisbury who put the word out for witnesses to remain silent.

Later in the day, Patsy met up with Danny Russell, who introduced him to Ralph Wimbrow and a few other Salisbury locals. After playing a little pool and seeing a picture show, Patsy got a chance to talk with Lee Harris about becoming his partner at the gym. Harris was interested, as he knew nothing about boxing. He was worried, however, about the fairness of the deal, as the gym was in bad condition, needed repair, and lacked showers and a mat. They agreed to become partners only if Patsy consented to make some of the repairs. Seeing this as a perfect opportunity to reduce suspicion surrounding his presence in town, Patsy planned on buying a half interest in the gym. Having gathered a substantial amount of intelligence concerning the lynching that day, he headed back to his hotel around 11:30 p.m.[51]

Three days into his investigation, it was becoming clear why Ritchie had hired Patsy to conduct the secret investigation. The governor must have been aware of the discontent among the racist elements concerning his decision to launch the public investigation of the lynching of Williams. Now, the myth of outside interference began to look less and less plausible, with Harry Waller's statements placing local law enforcement officers in the first, innermost circle of the conspiracy. He revealed the role that Chief Grier had played in providing the rope used to lynch Williams. In Howard Smead's schema of concentric circles, the innermost ring is made up of those who planned and carried out the abduction and murder. Waller's statements provide a second component, one that characterizes the mob as a fusion between a single mob and a hue-and-cry mob. Those behind the lynching of Williams came from two specific groups, both intent on preserving white supremacy by seeking him out and maintaining the anonymity of the lynching's perpetrators. After a few days in Salisbury, Patsy had been able to get a handle on the daily routines of the rough element around town. Most of the sporting men in the city spent the first half of the day at Lankford's Sporting Goods, until the gym opened at 2:00 p.m.[52]

On Friday, January 8, while the men Patsy Johnson was with waited for the gym to open, Governor Ritchie's presidential run came up again in conversation. Lee Harris laughed at the governor's odds of success: "A hell of a chance Ritchie has down here on the Eastern Shore." "Well, Lee," Howard Campbell responded, "you cannot hold the lynching matter against Governor Ritchie. He is Governor of Maryland and he should come out with some kind of a statement. You know Governor Ritchie said he was neutral in the matter." Harris answered, "Well, that is all right, but that other damn fool from Baltimore [one of the Baltimore detectives] who came down here to investigate did not have to give out the statement that the nigger was alive, yet, before or while the lynchers got him out of the hospital." Harris then turned to Patsy and said, "Why, Dan Elliott was one of the finest men who lived in Salisbury. He fed that nigger and took good care of him, and it was a shame not to hang the nigger because the niggers were starting to run wild and it came right after the killings that Yuel [sic] Lee and the other nigger [George Davis] had done. Boy, you can't let these niggers run wild and they will run you out of town." Campbell asked Patsy if he had heard of the lynching. Patsy remembered that he had boxed on Virginia's Eastern Shore in Portsmouth on the night of December 4 and had heard about it at one of the gas stations on his way back north. Campbell, who had witnessed the lynching, replied, "You should have seen it. It was a sight."

Lee Harris then confirmed what Dr. Arthur Brown had stated, indicating that he was at the Elliott Box and Crate Factory fifteen minutes after Williams had allegedly killed Dan Elliott. By the end of the conversation, Patsy had gleaned substantial insight into the men's attitudes concerning the lynching; however, he had failed to obtain any names. As the day came to an end, it began to rain hard, and things slowed down. Word had spread around town that Patsy was going to fight Russell.[53]

The conversation that Patsy observed between Harris and Campbell reveals the political damage that Ritchie was suffering on the Eastern Shore as a result of his decision to investigate the lynching. It also reflected the plantation-like mindset that still saw Williams as chattel and Daniel Elliott as his faithful master who fed his "nigger" and took good care of him. Harris, like others involved in the lynching, saw Williams as a representation of the whole Black community.

That Sunday at around 11:00 a.m., while Patsy was standing near Main and Division streets, a man approached him and asked, "Do you see that tree over there?" Patsy, who recognized the man from the gym, replied, "Yes." The man said, "Well, we hanged a nigger on that tree about a month ago. And what excitement we had." Shortly after this pronouncement, the man followed Patsy to the gym to watch him train.[54]

At 3:30 p.m. or so, after training with Russell, Patsy took a long walk with Sam Preston, a Jewish businessman and owner of the Preston Economy Store at 236 West Main Street.[55] By the end of the day, Patsy had heard only one mention of the lynching; however, he had learned about a gang living in south Salisbury near the Peninsula General Hospital. After visiting several oyster places, he headed back to his hotel and decided to strengthen his pretext for buying into the gymnasium by preparing for next Friday's match, where he hoped to meet "Kid" Guthrie and the rest of the mob.

By the end of the first week, Patsy Johnson had established a cover and begun to build relationships with locals. As it happened, he had gained access to those at the top of the mob's leadership structure and was introduced to a number of individuals who identified members of the mob or admitted to participating in the lynching. It was also quite clear that a number of the local prizefighters were involved in the lynching. The pro-South sectionalism and politics of anti-Black racism throughout the state were brought out during this first week as discontent was expressed with Governor Ritchie and his demand for the investigation. The near lynching of Euel Lee and the subsequent trial seemed to have inflamed local hatred toward African Americans and contributed to the lynching of Matthew Williams. Patsy was also able to corroborate evidence obtained from the previous investigation, specifically as it related to Dr. Brown's statement.[56] Before the beginning of the second week of Patsy's investigation, he gained his first glimpse into the first circle of the conspiracy, standing face to face with a local who had played an active part in the lynching.

Week Two

Early Monday morning, Patsy traveled to the Pinkerton National Detective Agency's Philadelphia office to quickly meet with officials before hopping back on the 10:25 a.m. train to Salisbury, arriving at 1:47 p.m. News of Patsy's arrival in Salisbury had finally made it to the local press, and the Salis-

bury Times ran a short story on the training at the gym. "Lee Harris and Walter Mitchell, operators of the gymnasium in Market Street" the article said, "have secured for their boxing students the services of Patsy Dalarngro, from Syracuse, N.Y. Dalarngro, who fought all comers in his class throughout the country, will train the fighters who are members of the gym's club."[57] Patsy had taken the alias "Dalarngro." The article continued highlighting the improvements that Patsy had already brought to the performance of local favorite Danny Russell, who was preparing to fight Red Journey (sometimes spelled "Journee") of Norfolk, Virginia, on the upcoming Friday. The fight was billed as "The Battle for the Eastern Shore."[58]

Once Patsy was back in Salisbury, he headed straight to the gym, where between fifty and sixty residents were waiting for him to spar with Russell. After the training session had ended, Patsy met a man by the name of Buck Johnson, a fighter from nearby Parsonsburg. They left the gymnasium together and took a walk.[59] Patsy quickly realized that the man walking next to him was one of the those who had lynched Matthew Williams. The first clue came when Buck told Patsy that five years ago, he had killed a "Negro" in Baltimore. After some "nigger" had bothered his girl, Buck said, he had pulled out a 38-caliber revolver and shot him.[60] Facing up to eighteen years in prison, Buck was able to get off because of his uncle, who was a Baltimore sheriff; even so, he had had to promise never to return to the city.[61]

Next, Buck shocked Patsy when he said that he had helped lynch a "nigger" in Salisbury. He had been in the mob that had dragged Williams out of Peninsula Hospital, he said, and had participated in Williams's lynching. He warned Patsy that another "Negro" was soon to be lynched like Williams if the "nigger" failed to "change his tactics." After this conversation Patsy decided to head home, as it was getting dark and he had to walk back two or three miles from outside Salisbury. Buck had provided further evidence to suggest that the lynching of Matthew Williams was a racial terror lynching.

Rope Hanging on That Nail

After seeing Buck off, Patsy realized that this was someone he should get to know, someone who could provide information about the identities of the other men who had participated in the lynching.[62] And, indeed, after his conversation with Buck Johnson, the floodgates opened.

Changing up his routine, Patsy headed over to Lankford's Sporting Goods, where co-owner Rufus Perry asked him, "Do you see that piece of rope hanging on that nail?" Patsy turned and saw a piece of rope that looked about four inches long and a half inch in diameter. "Well," Perry continued, "that is a piece of the rope that hung Williams, the nigger." Patsy jokingly responded, "Gosh, I would not save a remembrance like that if I committed anything."

Perry assured Patsy that the relic had been brought in by someone else, who had participated in the lynching. Patsy was starting to feel concerned that he had been in Salisbury for over a week and had the name of only one person who had participated in the lynch mob. He realized that his investigation was going to take more time than he had expected. Kid Guthrie was on his mind, as was the gang in south Salisbury. From Lankford's Patsy went to Arcade's poolroom and cigar store, after which he reflected further on his progress so far and found solace in the fact that he was slowly gaining the trust of the community that took part in this system of silence. He retired at 11 p.m.[63]

Like the unnamed local who had confessed to Patsy days earlier, Buck Johnson was in the first circle of the conspiracy as a direct participant in the mob, as became clear when he admitted to being one of the men who had kidnapped Williams from the hospital. Unlike Lee Harris, Buck was not concerned about the community's perception; he was the actual muscle behind the lynching, one of the loyal soldiers who stood at the ready to lynch any "nigger" in Salisbury who failed to change his tactics. Perry, on the other hand, in allowing the rope souvenir to remain in his establishment, was endorsing the lynching. This most likely places him in the third circle of the conspiracy.

Patsy spent most of the following day, Tuesday, January 12, talking with locals throughout town, eventually making his way back to Lankford's Sporting Goods store. An important observation he gleaned from this socializing was that the people of the Eastern Shore were loyal to those who were loyal to them. After visiting Campbell and Perry's store, Patsy met up with Sam Preston, the Jewish dress shop owner, to see the 1930 film *Common Clay* at Ulman's Theatre.[64]

Later, the two drove to the town of Delmar to enjoy a little wine at an Italian farm. As they returned to Salisbury, the subject of Williams's lynching came up. Preston continued to express his disgust: "It was the most disgraceful thing you could see or would want to see. I know who was at the head of the party of lynchers and so does everyone else in Salisbury, but they are not talking. The people are just keeping quiet." Preston, like Waller, alluded to a specific leader behind the lynching who had pressured local witnesses to refrain from talking. In spite of his disgust concerning the lynching, Preston still honored the system of silence.

As they made their way out of Delmar, two men hollered for a ride, and before Preston picked them up, he warned Patsy, "Do not talk about the lynching while these two are in the car." Before saying goodnight, Preston assured Patsy that he would tell him more about the lynching shortly. Patsy discontinued his report around 1:00 a.m. As he did so, he reflected that he had not seen Buck in the past few days.[65]

The following day, Patsy traveled around town with Danny Russell, who was set to box the following night. With most of the city keen to see the upcoming event, boxing was the only subject mentioned throughout the town. The *Salisbury Times* set the stage for the upcoming bouts by touting the success of the local boys and their work with the new trainer "Dalarngro" (Patsy): "The local boys have been in intensive training for several days under the tutelage of Pat DeLango [sic], ring instructor."[66] The "local boys" entering the ring included Kid Guthrie, Ben Parsons, and Danny Russell. Patsy soon discovered that one of them had played an active role in Williams's lynching.[67]

At last the big day arrived. Before the bout, Patsy ran into two members of Salisbury's rougher element, Kid Guthrie and his uncle Ellwood Charles Guthrie. The latter, a forty-year-old lifelong resident of Salisbury, owned a grocery store.[68] Naturally, as a fighter, "Kid" Guthrie was a tough guy. Ellwood, on the other hand, was a mean man and unpopular in Salisbury. As the evening drew to a close, Patsy made his way to the Zion Road Arena, about three miles from Delmar, where the boxing matches would be held. Russell, along with Bob Gadsby, another of Patsy's trainees, both won their fights. This helped increase Patsy's popularity in the community. Later that night, Patsy met Mr. Byrd, the local manager of the Western Union telegraph office. When the lynching came up, Byrd, like others, bragged about the job they had done. He also told Patsy that one of the town's prizefighters was among the leaders of the mob. As night came on, Patsy went out to celebrate with his fighters. Byrd's role in the lynching was not clear, but his statement made it obvious that he had played some part. In addition to admitting to his participation, he provided evidence that points to the structure of a private mob by telling Patsy that an unnamed prizefighter, most likely Buck Johnson or Danny Russell, had been among the leaders.[69]

The Best People in Salisbury

The next day, Patsy spent a good bit of time at Lankford's Sporting Goods talking with the local men about the fights. Lee Harris brought up Ben Parsons, a twenty-one-year-old prizefighter whom Patsy had been training for the past week before his successful bout the previous evening. Parsons had been born in Maryland in 1911, but by 1920 his family had moved to nearby Delmar.

Harris mentioned that Parsons had recently gone to court for sticking a pitchfork into a fellow. Howard Campbell asked Harris if this court appearance was for sticking the fork into Williams the night of the lynching.[70] Realizing that he had made a mistake by saying too much, Campbell changed the subject. As the day went on, Patsy decided to invite Harris to dinner. On their way to the diner, they passed the tree where Williams had been lynched the first time, and Harris said, "That's the tree that we hung the dirty nigger on." He then proceeded to lament D.J. Elliott's death, reiterating that Elliott was a good man. The conversation then shifted back to the lynching. "Why," Harris said, "one of our prize fighters went right in the hospital and pushed the nigger out of the window." Patsy wondered which fighter Harris was referring to, but he did not press it. He asked Harris, "Gee, does the law let you people get away with a lynching?" Harris responded, "Hell man, who is going to do any talking? Why, the best people in Salisbury are in on the deal and nobody is going to talk." Harris then claimed that State's Attorney Levin C. Bailey was "in" with the mob and nobody was going to find out anything.

After dinner, Patsy headed over to the Arcade poolroom, then spent time at Lankford's store. Later, preparing to retire for the night, he saw that it was not safe to ask any further questions at Lankford's and planned to get more information on Buck Johnson's role in the lynching. The friendship that Patsy had developed with Harris was beginning to pay off with Harris opening up about Williams's lynching.

Patsy had successfully corroborated Buck Johnson's confession and Mr. Byrd's statement. In his account, Harris not only substantiated previous statements but also solidified his position in the third circle of the conspiracy and provided the first bit of evidence implicating an elected official who had been in charge of the investigation. Harris placed Bailey in the third circle of the conspiracy by suggesting that the state's attorney knew of the plan to lynch Williams and was actually in cahoots with the mob. This spelled trouble for Ritchie's investigation: it was one thing to show favoritism, but another thing altogether to be "in" with the men behind the lynching.[71]

Week Three

Patsy arrived at the Pinkertons' Philadelphia office around 8:30 a.m. on Monday, January 18, for his regular conference. In discussing his pretext for remaining in Salisbury, his superiors decided that Patsy should buy a 50 percent interest in Lee Harris's gymnasium and start giving boxing lessons to locals. When Patsy arrived back in Salisbury that afternoon, he went straight to Lankford's Sporting Goods store. There Lee Harris asked Patsy to go with him to Ocean City to see Captain Powell in preparation for the upcoming fights in Salisbury. Once in Ocean City, Patsy and Harris learned that Powell, along with Ben Parsons, was in Baltimore serving as witnesses for the Euel Lee case. The two returned to Salisbury, passing through Snow Hill, where Harris showed Patsy the house where Euel Lee had allegedly murdered the four white people. He argued that the community near Snow Hill was a disgrace because it had allowed Lee to elude Judge Lynch. Patsy noticed that Harris was beginning to talk a lot more freely with him.[72]

That day's front-page story in the *Salisbury Times* was headed, "Lee Defense Loses Plea for Mixed Jury." The lack of racial equality in jury selection was not a surprise to Harris; in fact, he may have suspected it would happen. Instead, such updates in the local papers concerning the trial of Euel Lee constantly reminded Harris and the racist element of the Eastern Shore that Lee had escaped lynching. It reminded them of what happened when the "Negro" was granted even a modicum of due process, something that whites during this era (and the pre–Civil War era) saw as reserved for those from a particular protected class or with a certain social status. As time went on, it became even more apparent that the lynching of Matthew Williams had been an act of racial terror designed to stoke fear in the hearts of an African American community whose members refused to be broken by the economic and social perils of the Great Depression.[73]

Around 7:00 that evening, Sergeants Walter Martin and Graydon Ware arrived in Salisbury from Baltimore to continue their investigation, hoping to cultivate Black witnesses, some of whom they had already interviewed. Shortly after arriving, they began interviewing an African American man named Howard Purnell; however, they were unable to gain anything of value from him. Shortly thereafter they interviewed Mary Brewington at her home near the intersection of Lake and Isabella streets, but she too was silent.[74]

Commemorating the Spectacle

Two days later, Patsy talked in the evening with Talbot Louis "Toath" Larmore while the two went for a drive. Twenty-eight years old, Larmore had been born in White Haven on Maryland's Eastern Shore. In 1930, he was a high school dropout, single, and working as a clothing salesman. (Ironically, in 1940 he gained the honor of protecting and serving his community by joining the Salisbury Police Department, making $430 a year.) Larmore quickly began to talk about the lynching, telling Patsy that he and Danny Russell had been at the hospital two minutes before the mob took Williams out through the window of the "Negro" ward. Larmore recounted the way the mob had dragged Williams's unconscious body from the hospital.

Earlier that night, the crowd had first gathered in front of the *Salisbury Times* building. From there it headed to the hospital to retrieve Williams. Larmore corroborated previous statements, assuring Patsy that prominent men of the community were behind the lynching. "It was not the rough and drunken element," he said, "but a well picked gang of Elliott's friends that got the 'nigger' out the hospital." Larmore said that after the mob dragged Williams's body all over town from the back of a car, Lorenzo W. Brittingham, the sheriff from Laurel, Delaware, cut the toes off Williams's feet. He then handed out these "nigger toes" as souvenirs to commemorate the spectacle.[75] Larmore's statement was substantiated two months later in the *Baltimore Afro-American* in a similar account of the spectacle.

Patsy then proceeded to ask Larmore what local law enforcement had been doing during the lynching. Larmore told him that Chief Holland and Deputy Sheriff Donald Parks were among the leaders who dragged Williams out of the hospital. He told Patsy that the prominent men in Salisbury had gone earlier to Parks and Holland and told them of their plans. As the conversation continued, Patsy learned that Larmore's father, W. W. Larmore, was the former sheriff of Wicomico County, having served two terms (1907–9).[76]

Talbot Larmore's confession marks a turning point in the investigation, as Larmore placed himself and Danny Russell in the inner circle of the conspiracy. Larmore also shed light on the organized structure of the private mob, alluded to the planning of the lynching by Elliott's friends, and provided evidence that connected another law enforcement officer directly to the lynching. Sheriff Brittingham is the only out-of-state law enforcement officer found to be in the inner circle of the criminal conspiracy. Larmore also placed Chief Holland and Sheriff Parks there.

Thursday was rather slow, and Patsy trained a few of the boys in the gymnasium. After the sessions, he joined Lee Harris and two other men, "Bunk" Perry and Vincent Wheatley Dennis, and they all headed to Deal's Island in nearby Somerset County to attend a party at a place called Webster's. While at the gathering, Patsy became a little worried when Dennis began to press him about why he was in Salisbury. After a while, Harris came to his aid and assured Dennis that Patsy was his partner in the boxing gym. They discussed various topics, but the lynching was not mentioned.[77]

From Pugilist to Private Eye

Maslin Frysinger Pinkett Sr.

After staying the night on the Shore, Martin and Ware continued their work the following day, this time traveling to Snow Hill in Worcester County to investigate a lead that proved unavailing. Leaving Snow Hill, they headed to Princess Anne, where they would finally catch a break after interviewing a local Black leader by the name of Maslin Frysinger Pinkett Sr., who, like Dr. Brown, broke the system of silence, risking his life by providing the names of the men responsible for the lynching. "Fats" Wilson, William Harrington, and Thomas Webster alias "Catfish," he told Martin and Ware, were the men who went into the hospital to get Williams.[78]

Pinkett was the first witness to name Wilson, Harrington, and Webster as individuals who had been at the center of the conspiracy, men responsible for abducting and subsequently lynching Williams. Wilson and Webster's roles in the mob action would later be corroborated by eyewitnesses Patsy would interview.

After talking to Pinkett, Martin and Ware traveled to Fruitland, where they met with the wife of John Creowell, who provided additional evidence revealing the mob's organization and corroborated statements made previously by other witnesses. Mrs. Creowell described the extent to which the lynching had been planned. Her husband's boss, Conrad Long, had given all of his employees the day off when he found out about the impending lynching so that they could join him and participate. In addition, she named Bill Davis, Marion Brown, and a man whose last name was Martin as individuals who had played an active part in the crime.

Meanwhile, for Patsy, Friday turned out to be another slow day, though things picked up after Patsy's training session when he headed to Lankford's Sporting Goods store. Howard Campbell became a little suspicious and asked, "Johnson [Patsy], are you a 'revenue' man or something like that?" Patsy responded, "Howard, be your age. What is the matter?" Campbell joked that for a stranger, Patsy had become awfully friendly and well acquainted with people he had met, and that a few of the local businessmen were remarking that he knew almost everyone in town. Patsy assured him that his popularity had grown so fast as a result of his training Danny Russell, who had won his last fight. This seemed to satisfy Campbell, who

The faculty of Morgan College's Princess Anne Academy,
Princess Anne, MD, 1920s. Professor Maslin Frysinger Pinkett
is at center in the doorway.

promised Patsy that he would tell the businessmen there was nothing to fear.[79] The businessmen Campbell referred to may well have been the ones who had put out the call for silence in response to the investigation.

The next day started successfully for Patsy. There was a good-sized crowd at the gym, and he signed up some new customers for training. Remembering his conversation with Howard Campbell the day before, Patsy decided to slow down a bit in pressing for information concerning the lynching. Later at Lankford's store, Patsy and Harris finished up their business transaction. Patsy paid Harris $40 as a down payment on the gym.

Patsy planned to give Harris the balance of $25 as he earned it from his training sessions. Knowing that news of their transaction would circulate throughout town, Patsy thought that this investment would aid in quelling some of the suspicions. After their deal was completed, Patsy loafed around Campbell and Perry's for the rest of the day and into the evening, retiring around 10 p.m.[80]

January 24 was slow, as usual for a Sunday, and Patsy headed over to a home on Upton Street with Bill Maddox and a man named Sterling. During their conversation, the lynching was mentioned several times. The men assured Patsy that no one would ever find out who was at the head of the lynching, as they all had banded together on the Eastern Shore and made a vow of secrecy. Maddox, a spectator on the night of the lynching, confirmed earlier statements that Chief Holland knew the identity of the men who lynched Williams. Later, Patsy met with William Walter of Delmar, Delaware, who also had been a spectator. He was unable to provide any new information.[81]

Week Four

Monday was surprisingly busy, and a few spectators came to the gym to watch some of the local fighters train. Ben Parsons was among the fighters. Patsy spoke to Parsons in a friendly way and suggested that he come to the gym more often. Patsy hoped Parsons would take him to Berlin, Maryland, where Euel Lee had escaped the mob's clutches a few months prior to the Williams lynching and where Patsy could now ask Parsons what his role had been in the lynching. Later, at Lankford's Sporting Goods store, Governor Ritchie's name was brought up again. Someone in the group there claimed that Ritchie was the one who had ordered the investigation on the Eastern Shore concerning the lynching. Perry's father-in-law offered, "Why, Ritchie has as much chance as a Chinaman on the shore this election, and it is all because Ritchie wanted to know who hung the nigger. Well, a fat chance those Baltimore people have of finding out and if they do, there will be no prosecution nor anyone going to jail." Patsy realized that he needed more time to gather intelligence. He got together with Talbot Larmore later that night while Larmore was collecting furniture bills from the "Negro" section in Salisbury. He was hoping that the lynching would come up, but realized that the proper time had not yet arrived and went back to his hotel around 10.[82]

"The Best Men in Town"

The next day, January 26, Patsy opened the gym as usual and continued to get to know the local men. Questions concerning Patsy's presence had started to fade away, and he was beginning to feel that he was part of the community. Sid Church, who ran a secondhand store at the corner of Camden Avenue and Market Place, lamented that men on the Eastern Shore were thick-headed and ignorant:

> I guess you have heard about the lynching we had here. Well, it was committed by the best men in town, and they got a few fellows worked up to get that nigger and string him up. Well, now those men who strung up the nigger are murderers. It is a shame as these men will not care for anything or what will happen to them. The businessmen about town have pooled some money together to protect any man who is brought up on this carpet.

Patsy responded, "How is it that no one knows who did the lynching and the whole town was there?"

Church shot back, "What in the hell do people want to get mixed up in anything of that sort when our chief of police, police and sheriffs were leading the parade to lynching? Why boy, it was the worst thing I ever saw and it is a shame that it had to happen."

Church thus laid the majority of the blame for the lynching on the police department and the politicians of Salisbury. He then revealed the racial attitudes that had saturated the town and the claim going around that there were a couple more "niggers" in Salisbury who ought to be strung up. He lamented the culture of lawlessness in Salisbury, challenging Patsy to consider the everyday activities in town and the system of silence: "You can see how the citizens are getting paid back. Why there is no law in Salisbury; gambling is wide open, booze all over town and the younger crowd is raising hell speeding with their cars." Church was around fifty-five years old and had spent twenty-one years in New York City in the fishing business. He had moved back to Salisbury just ten years earlier, then lost a fortune speculating in stocks and other securities during the Depression. After speaking with Church, Patsy went to see a film with Lee Harris, had a few drinks, and discontinued his report around 11:30 p.m.

Church corroborated previous statements in identifying the members of the first circle of the conspiracy and pointing to a select group of the towns' "best men" who bought the silence of those directly responsible for lynching Williams by allowing poor whites to conduct crimes such as bootlegging and gambling for their livelihood. At the same time, these elites were exploiting poor whites by having them conduct a lynching, a crime that the elites' status prevented them from joining in.[83] Church also substantiated previous statements that placed the chief of police and sheriffs among the lynching's leaders. Like Buck Johnson, Church suggested that the lynching of Williams would be only the beginning.

A Couple "More Niggers"

Wednesday was a success in both training and investigating. After working with local fighters, he met around noon with Ben Parsons, who lamented that he hated "niggers." Parsons then confessed, telling Patsy that he had been among the crowd and had helped lynch Williams in December. He assured Patsy that Williams was only the first and that there were a couple "more niggers" who were going to "get it" on the Eastern Shore. Patsy was unable to question Parsons any further because of the presence of other people.

Later on, Patsy saw Talbot Larmore, who again told him that those who had committed the lynching were extraordinarily close but committed to silence, and that it would almost be impossible to bring any of them to justice. Larmore said that the chief of police knew everybody who had been at the head of the mob that had lynched the "nigger," and that the chief was well taken care of by the town's prominent men. Intent on changing the subject, Larmore said that Baltimore people should not put their noses into Eastern Shore business. That evening, Patsy reflected on his strategy, realizing that he was going to need still more time to cultivate rapport with the men he had already met. He walked around town to get a little more comfortable with the community before turning in at his usual hour.[84]

The next day, Elwood Waller, a man whose name had come up in previous conversations, walked into the gymnasium. Not long into his conversation with Patsy, the lynching came up. In recounting what had happened to Williams, Waller claimed that the two men pulling the rope to lift Williams up the tree asked people standing nearby for help. According to Waller, fifteen to twenty men ran to the lynching tree and all lent a hand in hoisting Williams's body. He described how the mob then dragged Williams to the local gas station. Waller then admitted the horrifying fact that he had been the one who poured five gallons of gasoline on Williams.

Without providing names, Waller mentioned that the two men who asked for assistance in raising Williams up the tree had fled to Philadelphia the following day but had since returned. Waller told Patsy that he knew who these men were, as well as the other ringleaders of the mob. Waller also explained why people in the community were not talking and reminded him that the locals were always careful when strangers set foot in Salisbury.[85] Waller's confession to having poured gasoline on Williams's corpse places him within the innermost circle of the conspiracy. He also pointed to a still-unnamed ringleader, hinting at the organized structure of the private mob.

"The Night We Lynched the Nigger"

The following morning, January 29, Waller returned to visit Patsy at the gymnasium around 9:00. He was nursing a broken nose and was not working. He picked up where he had left off and mentioned that the Guthrie family was a pretty rough group. Referring specifically to Ellwood Guthrie, he said he never wanted to get into a fight with him, because Ellwood knew how to use a knife. "Guthrie showed how he could use a knife the night we lynched the nigger," Waller said. Patsy, feeling comfortable, boldly asked Waller if Guthrie had stabbed Williams during the lynching. Waller answered, "Hell no. He has no more pull than I, and I am broke and I put the gasoline on the nigger to burn him." Feeling even more comfortable now, Patsy asked, "Well, then what prompted you fellows to do what you did?" Waller responded, "Well, we do not like niggers down here in the first place.

In the second place, a big businessman in town was killed by this nigger and sentiment ran high and that was the way it started. They even announced the lynching at the fights that the main bout would go on directly after the lynching and most everyone at the fights left to come back to town to witness the lynching."[86]

Patsy continued to press Waller, asking him if one of the two men who had charge of the rope the night of the lynching had ever come to the gym. Waller confirmed that this man had visited the gym on several occasions to see the boys train. Realizing that Waller was shaping up to be one of the case's central witnesses, Patsy sought to build upon the information he had obtained from him. Waller was to travel to Philadelphia on February 8 for five days for surgery on his broken nose at the Graduate Hospital of the University of Pennsylvania. It occurred to Patsy that Waller's nose would have made him stand out in the mob. He noted Waller's appearance and dimensions, noting the court plaster that Waller still wore across his nose and estimating he was around twenty-two years of age, six feet tall, and about 170 pounds. Waller had turned out to be a useful informant for Patsy. In recalling that the lynching had been announced at the arena during the fight, he also provided substantial evidence suggesting that it was planned.[87]

In Philadelphia on Saturday, Patsy visited the Pinkerton agency for a conference. Around 2:45 p.m. he boarded the train to return to Salisbury, arriving at 6:50 p.m. Shortly thereafter, he met with Talbot Larmore, who told Patsy he was going to fix him up on a date with a nineteen-year-old girl named Maud Wilson from Princess Anne in Somerset County. Noticing that her last name was Wilson, Patsy hoped she was related to "Fats" Wilson, who was a suspected leader of the mob. Ralph "Fats" William Wilson, a thirty-five-year-old man from Somerset County, was a bouncer along the Eastern Shore and served as the muscle for Captain Powell and Lee Harris during their fights. He also ran a restaurant in Princess Anne and worked the door. As Larmore continued talking, he revealed something promising for the investigation, particularly as to which state police officers may have been involved in the lynching. After Patsy said he was interested in meeting Maud Wilson, Larmore made sure to let Patsy know that he would have to set the date for a time when Maryland State Police sergeant M. D. Brubaker was out of town, since he and Miss Wilson had been dating.[88]

"A Damn Good Job"

Sergeants Martin and Ware sent a summary report on January 30 to Captain Charles H. Burns of the Baltimore City Police stating that one Miss Lillian Serman had deemed the lynching "a damn good job" and had refused to participate.[89] Martin and Ware also reported that a "colored" farmer by the name of John Williams had broken silence in his interview with the two officers in naming Bill Davis as one of the men who threw Williams from the hospital window and in identifying John Martin Sr. and John Martin Jr. as active participants in the lynching.[90] Williams also stated that around 3:30 p.m. on December 4, 1931, a local Salisbury police officer appeared at the tailoring establishment of a "negro" known as "Brown" and told him to close up shop to avoid the trouble coming—additional evidence that the lynching was planned.[91] John Williams was a wealthy truck farmer and realtor who leased land to poor white farmers, and the Martins were his tenants.[92]

Martin and Ware began to develop a theory concerning the lynching, based on the evidence they were compiling, regarding its planning. John Williams's statements suggested that the Martins were in the first circle of the conspiracy and provided further evidence of the lynching having been premeditated.[93]

The Price of Whiteness

Next Martin and Ware caught up with John Creowell of Fruitland, following up on their conversation with his wife a few days earlier. John Creowell confirmed that about 4 p.m. on December 4, 1931, Conrad "Conn" Long of Long Lumber Company gave all his employees the day off and told them to join him to see a lynching.[94] Creowell declined to leave work, however, and the next day when he went to receive his pay, he was fired and told that he was no longer needed. Such were the consequences of refusing to cooperate with the system of silence. The Creowells's cooperation with the Baltimore police investigation stood out. Poor and working-class no doubt, Mr. and Mrs. Creowell, in speaking out, exposed the hypocrisy of the so-called white unity that unraveled before their eyes when they failed to comply with the status quo, a status quo that defined whiteness in terms of

From Pugilist to Private Eye

one's willingness to participate in anti-Black social, economic, and political violence.

As the interview wound up, the Creowells also named Salisbury locals who had participated in the lynching, including Henry Yewell of South Salisbury, whom they said pulled the rope when Williams was hanging from the tree.[95]

The statements of Mr. and Mrs. Creowell placed Conrad Long and Henry Yewell in the first circle of the conspiracy. It also provides additional evidence of planning prior to the lynching. As they concluded their day's work, Martin and Ware interviewed J. R. Waters and Maslin Pinkett in Princess Anne but were unable to get any additional information.[96]

By the end of January 1932, Patsy had gleaned much from his conversations and, slowly but surely, was unmasking the mob. When Sunday arrived, the town was quiet, so Patsy spent most of his time at the home of Ralph Corbin, a twenty-seven-year-old local bootlegger living on Princess Anne Road. Corbin, a native of the Eastern Shore, had previously lived in Dublin and Westover, both in Somerset County. While Patsy was there, Corbin never brought up the lynching. Patsy retired early, around 10 p.m., feeling a growing optimism.[97]

During his first month in Salisbury, Patsy had successfully settled into the Salisbury community on Maryland's Eastern Shore and established his cover identity. He had begun to build relationships with locals. From the outset, he gained access to those behind the lynching and was introduced to individuals who identified other members of the mob or admitted to participating in the lynching themselves. In addition to identifying members of the mob, Patsy was able to befriend witnesses who had given the attorney general very little, if any, information, such as the Jewish store owner Samuel Preston. Patsy also learned that a group of local businessmen and friends of Daniel Elliott had organized the lynching. The detailed information he uncovered about what happened on December 4 and who was involved in the lynching illuminates local power dynamics in Salisbury and how they sustained white supremacy. It was becoming clear that there was a unique structure to the Salisbury lynch mob, consisting of components of both an organized private mob and a hue-and-cry, or mass, mob.

The local businessmen and power brokers who had a hold on the community had demanded silence throughout the city. A number of the local prizefighters and members of Harris and Patsy's gym had been involved in the lynching, and some of them had committed violent crimes against African Americans in the past. The sectionalism and politics of anti-Black racism throughout the state were also evidenced during this first month as Patsy's contacts repeatedly expressed discontent with Governor Ritchie and his demand for an investigation. The near lynching of Euel Lee and his subsequent trial seemed to have inflamed local attitudes toward African Americans and prompted the lynching of Matthew Williams. Finally, Patsy had been able to corroborate existing evidence from the previous investigation, specifically Dr. Brown's testimony. With the grand jury investigation approaching, Patsy needed to continue infiltrating the mob and building the relationships he had established. As the investigation moved forward, it became clearer that a private mob had been behind the lynching of Williams.

Class seems to have been the most salient factor in determining who would break the silence imposed from above. In the case of the Salisbury community, three specific class distinctions shed light on the ways in which white supremacy and class struggle were selected. Oftentimes scholars point to the stark gap between the lower class and the upper class, but in Salisbury it was the middle-class small business owners who also were beholden to the racist and wealthy leaders in the Salisbury community. The census records from the 1930s provide insight into the economic gap between middle class and the upper-class business leaders connected to the lynching. For example, Lee Harris and Frederick Grier were at opposite sides of this socioeconomic gap. Captain Frederick A. Grier Jr. lived at 901 Division Street and his home was valued at $20,000 (the equivalent of $313,196.23 in 2018); his father, Frederick Grier Sr., who lived down the street (at 1001 North Division Street) had a home valued at $19,000 ($297,536.42 in 2018). Lee Harris, on the other hand, lived in a home that he rented for $20 a month in an unappealing part of town.[98]

Harry Waller's statements shed light on how Smead's structure applies to the white supremacist system that killed Williams. As is typical in a traditional mob structure, Waller, a poor laborer, a soda fountain clerk, served as the muscle in direct actions of violence. Waller admitted as much to Patsy early in the investigation when he confessed to being the one who poured gasoline on Williams's corpse after it had been hanged a second time. As Patsy befriended Waller, he began exposing those in power, possibly realizing that, unlike Captain Grier, he had more to lose. Silence in criminal cases is often broken when those at the bottom of socially "homogeneous" brotherhoods, like Waller, become compromised as their social status and station in life remind them how different they are from wealthy racists, such as Captain Grier, whose wealth and status shield them from prosecution. Waller's statements also confirm what Sherrilyn Ifill and other scholars have suspected, that Chief Holland played a direct role in the lynching. Chief Holland was not as wealthy as Captain Grier, but he held a different form of local power, which was legal and direct. In describing such power, Ifill writes, "The first and therefore most important legal actors to respond to real or imagined black criminality were police officers. Their action or inaction set the stage for how a black man suspected of committing a crime against a white person would be treated. Often the police determined whether a black man would face a trial or a lynch mob."[99]

Benjamin Parsons, a widowed lower-class prizefighter, and Talbot Larmore, a middle-class clothing salesman, also quickly opened up to Patsy. Parsons confessed his role in the lynching, and Larmore detailed the positions his coparticipants took and also told Patsy of the covenant of silence concerning the lynching among those in the white community. Clearly, he was breaking the vow of silence in speaking to Patsy, perhaps because he saw Patsy as a fellow white man whom he thought would honor the system of silence. Larmore again broke the covenant of silence when he revealed the role that Danny Russell, Salisbury's most successful prizefighter, played in the lynching.[100] Russell's involvement in the lynching reveals how middle-class white men, too, found themselves beholden to the upper-class elites who were financing the criminal conspiracy.

Lee Harris and Howard Campbell, both middle-class business owners who also were among the first to break the silence, pointed to men in the top social and economic stratum in Salisbury as having issued the mandate for silence throughout the white community. Again, class is essential here, as Harris and Campbell, although business owners, had less status than the elite whites who called on laborers like Waller and subsequently prize-fighters to do the dirty work of lynching Williams. Nonetheless, like Waller, they were among the first people whom Patsy persuaded to inadvertently compromise their oath. By the end of the first week, the inner workings of the local power structure were being revealed, and the foot soldiers were exposing the white leaders at the top of the social hierarchy.[101] In considering the confessions that Patsy documented and the ways those involved in the lynching willingly exposed their involvement, it is important to consider his status as an outsider. In spite of his whiteness, he was still an outsider, and those involved in the lynching broke the silence not in a court of law, but along the lines of white male brotherhood.

As to the role of law enforcement, Patsy's investigation confirms widely held suspicions and corroborates witness statements that law enforcement officers had been complicit in the lynching.[102]

Harry Waller was the first witness to reveal that Chief Grier had supplied the rope used to lynch Williams, thereby offering a glimpse of the mob's inner workings by exposing the corruption and complicity on the part of law enforcement in the lynching of Williams. Waller's statements exposed the first, innermost circle, encompassing those at the core of conspiracy—those who planned and carried out the abduction and murder. This ring also included local law enforcement officers who were implicated. Not only does Waller identify those who were complicit in the lynching, but he also reveals the reason that previous interviews encountered a conspiracy of silence. Waller, along with Lee Harris and Howard Campbell, attributes this call for silence to one specific leader in Salisbury, the man who put the word out for witnesses to remain silent. They provide evidence of a collective group led by one person wielding control over those who participated in the lynching. The possible benefits of remaining silent are evidenced in the interesting financial relationships that developed following the lynching and the investigation, including the relationship between Chief Grier and Ben Parsons.

Regarding motivation, it was clear by the end of January that the lynching was meant to strike fear in the hearts of the Black community. Though not part of a traditional terrorist organization, such as the Ku Klux Klan, this loosely organized mob was formed with the hope of terrorizing African Americans in Salisbury and other communities within Worcester County.

Over the following month and a half, Patsy would continue to unmask those behind the mob, filling in the various layers of the conspiracy.

[5]

Truth, Lies, and
Somewhere in Between

Unmasking the Mob and
Breaking the System of Silence

*The impression was received by the inquirer that the public spirit
of Salisbury is far below what is desirable. Those whom one would expect
to be leaders in a crisis decided to fall in with the ignorant, the prejudiced,
the frightened, the sullenly boastful. Salisbury has given proof of its lack of
civic morality—not only in lynching and burning, but even more pointedly
in the childish defenses offered for the lynching afterward. One feels that
the business organizations stand for nothing better than mere town
boosting, the churches have neglected the application of religion to life.*

Broadus Mitchell, January 25, 1932

Six days before the beginning of February 1932, Johns Hopkins University professor Broadus Mitchell published a report of his investigation into the lynching of Matthew Williams. He had been commissioned two weeks following the crime to investigate it by Frederick Ernest Johnson, executive secretary of the Federal Council of Churches of Christ in America (FCCCA). It is unknown why the FCCCA decided to release this report well over a month and a half after the lynching. Nonetheless, Mitchell's report provides further evidence of the system of silence that permeated the town of Salisbury. To be sure, individual actors carried out the lynching of Williams, but as Mitchell pointed out, it was the "public spirit of Salisbury," or lack of it, that cultivated and covered up the injustice. Mitchell not only faults Salisbury's collective spirit but also illuminates the character of the lynch mob, those who were complicit in the crime, and those who made excuses for it. Ultimately, Mitchell's report sparked a passionate debate between religious and political leaders throughout the state.[1]

The most dramatic response came from the *Salisbury Times*, which made no mention of any concern about the lynching. Instead, this rebuttal focused solely on labeling Broadus Mitchell as a communist: "The report may be worthy of a citation for the distinguished service its author has rendered to the cause of the Soviet government, but what about the humiliation it has brought a Christian, English speaking people here in Salisbury?"[2] The *Times* connected Mitchell to the communist-led International Labor Defense (ILD), which was representing Euel Lee of Snow Hill.

Mitchell's report also prompted politicians to defend the Eastern Shore. Former Democratic US senator from Maryland William Campbell Bruce, for example, echoed the *Salisbury Times* editor in expressing more concern about defending the character of the mob and the Salisbury community than about condemning the lynching. He wrote, "From the recent attack on the character of our Eastern Shore brothers, one might suppose that lynching is peculiar to the Eastern Shore. The fact is that it has occurred over and over again in many states of the Union whenever the incitement to it has been sufficiently intense and widespread to provoke it."[3]

Meanwhile, as Patsy's investigation continued, Governor Albert Ritchie was concluding his presidential campaign tour in the West. His last stop was Kentucky on February 2, where he argued against Prohibition, advocating for home rule and states' rights as the solutions to the Prohibition-related crime wave running throughout the nation. This states' rights approach was succeeding for Governor Ritchie in Maryland, and he hoped his secret investigation into the lynching of Williams would strengthen his case against national anti-lynching legislation.[4]

Week Five

"If It Was Not for Bill Davis"

Patsy Johnson opened the gym around 10:00 a.m. on February 1, 1932, and talked briefly with a few locals. Buck Johnson, who had earlier confided to Patsy that he had killed a "Negro" in Baltimore and had helped lynch Williams, was among the group. Later, when he and Patsy were alone in the gym, Buck bragged that Patsy should have been there on December 4 to witness the lynching party, again admitting that he had helped lynch Williams. Patsy continued to push Buck for information, asking if he had any help. Buck replied, "Sure, the whole town of Salisbury was in on it." As the conversation continued, Buck identified individuals by name, saying that "if it was not for Bill Davis, the lynching would have been a 'flop'" and that "Bill Davis hangs around Campbell and Perry's sporting goods store." He confirmed that Bill Davis was the big fellow previously mentioned who had been seen during the lynching wearing a lumber jacket. Davis, an avid hunter, was a Salisbury local whom Patsy had become friendly with. Davis was a regular at the gym who stopped by every day around noon.[5]

Patsy responded, "Sure, I know Bill," then said, "So he was the leader of the lynching."

"He sure was," Buck replied, "and what a tough guy he is when he gets started." At that point a few men walked into the gym and the conversation abruptly ended. Since this was the second time that Buck had confessed to assisting in lynching Williams, Patsy saw that he was going to be a key witness in the investigation.

During the evening, Patsy headed to Ralph Corbin's place, where he met with Talbot Larmore. Corbin's house was a hangout for the town's rougher element. A few days prior, Larmore had promised Patsy that he would introduce him to the Wilsons of Princess Anne. While at Corbin's place, Larmore confirmed that Bill Davis was a rough character with a lot of pull on the Eastern Shore. At end of the day's report, Patsy noted that Buck Johnson and Elwood Waller should be questioned further, as they had been the first to admit to having played a part in the lynching.[6]

The day's work had produced additional evidence about those at the center of the mob, in the first, or innermost, circle. Bill Davis joined police chief Nicholas Holland in the first circle, though Davis had led both the planning and the implementation of the lynching. Waller's statement that "if it was not for Bill Davis the lynching would have been a 'flop,'" suggests that there was indeed a plan to lynch Williams that was known among a select group of men in the community. Based on his statement, Davis was most likely also behind the taking of Williams from the hospital to the courthouse lawn and from the courthouse lawn to the gas station where his lifeless body was burned.[7]

"We Sure Had a Nice Party"

The following morning, Patsy opened the gym around 9:30. While he was cleaning, Buck Johnson walked in. Right away Patsy tried to get Buck to talk about the lynching, but he was not in the mood. Later on, Patsy headed to Thompson's Grill but had no success at getting any information pertaining to December 4. Shortly after that, Patsy ran into Bill Perry.[8] Bill was the brother of Rufus Perry, co-owner of Lankford's Sporting Goods store. Bill Perry took Patsy to Al's Inn on Princess Anne Road, along with Jack Townsend of Snow Hill. (Later, Perry told Patsy that Jack Townsend and Bill Davis were the leaders of the lynch mob. He warned Patsy to avoid crossing Townsend because he was extremely violent and was known to use a knife.) While Patsy was having a few drinks with Townsend at Al's Inn, he bragged about the night Williams was lynched, asking if Patsy had been in Salisbury at the time. He told Patsy, "You should have been here. We sure had a nice party."[9]

Patsy could now place Herman E. "Jack" Townsend with Bill Davis and Chief Holland within the innermost circle. It is chilling to think that Townsend was only nineteen years old at the time Williams was lynched.[10]

On Wednesday, Patsy opened the gym around 10:00 a.m. and spent most of the morning trying to sign up new members. While he was working, Crawford Keller (Patsy later remembered the name as "Kellar Crawford"), a welterweight boxer and native of Salisbury currently living in Portsmouth, Virginia, walked in. Crawford did not say much about the lynching; however, he mentioned that Ralph "Fats" Wilson of Princess Anne had happened to be in Salisbury the night Williams was lynched. Shortly after talking to Crawford, Patsy lounged around in Lankford's Sporting Goods store, waiting for Bill Davis to show up. Although Davis never came by, store co-owner Howard Campbell confirmed that Davis was a roughneck. Later, Patsy accompanied Campbell and Talbot Larmore to Fats Wilson's restaurant and pool hall, where he finally met Wilson. However, the lynching was not mentioned during their conversation, which focused on boxing.[11]

On the way home, Talbot Larmore told Patsy that Fats Wilson was a regular in Salisbury and that he was well liked by the businessmen around town. Patsy asked Larmore if Wilson had been in on the lynching. Surprisingly, Larmore responded, "Yes, Wilson was in it all right, but I do not see where he did more than the rest of the crowd. The whole town was into the mess and I cannot see how Wilson could be put as one of the leaders."[12] If Larmore was correct, Wilson was not among the leaders behind the lynching but was in the second circle of the conspiracy, working as a coconspirator serving as the muscle for the leaders of the mob.[13]

Patsy began Thursday, February 4, 1932, at the gym around 10:00 a.m. Danny Russell came in and told Patsy that Bill Davis was one of the individuals who hung around Lankford's Sporting Goods store and that on the night of the lynching he had directed the mob as they lynched Williams. Further, he said that Davis was a rough man who, once riled up, was unstoppable. "Don't tell anybody what I told you about Bill Davies [sic]," he said, adding, "There are a few more in Salisbury who got in dutch over the lynching, and it is up to us fellows to keep our mouths shut and not talk about the matter." Evidently expecting that he would be sore from training, Russell asked Patsy if he could give him a rubdown later. Patsy agreed and set up an appointment to see Russell at his home the following day.[14]

Without Davis's Leadership

That evening, Patsy headed to a Mrs. Jones's home on Zion Road in the direction of Delmar with Beulah Smith, who lived in Snow Hill. Smith told Patsy that Sid Church, owner of a secondhand store, was sorry Euel Lee had not met the same fate as Williams. Talbot Larmore and a Miss Todd were present at the gathering, and they commented that the women of the community were doing everything in their power to protect the men who had lynched Williams. Beulah Smith substantiated Waller's previous statement concerning Bill Davis's role in the lynching, declaring that the lynching would have been a "flop" without Davis's leadership.[15]

When the conversation turned to the Baltimore detectives who were in town to investigate the lynching, one in the group referred to them as stool pigeons. As the discussion ended, Larmore told Patsy, "A h[ell] of a chance anyone has to find out who were the leaders of this mob who lynched Williams."

Patsy knew he was continuing to gain the trust of the men involved in the lynching. Russell's and Larmore's statements, like those of previous witnesses, pointed to a group of power brokers, those directly responsible for organizing the lynching, who were now making sure that those actively involved in the lynching remained silent.

Early the following day, Bill Davis stopped by the gym and discussed with Patsy the match scheduled for the coming evening, which would feature Danny Russell. Later, Patsy went to Cinno's cigar store on Division Street to see if he could meet new people. Then he went to Lankford's Sporting Goods, where he met a number of locals. Bill Davis was there when Patsy walked in, but left after a few minutes. As soon as Davis left, Patsy bated the crowd into talking about the lynching. He turned to Howard Campbell and said, "Boy, I bet that Davis is a roughneck when he gets going." Campbell responded, "You would think that Davis was rough if you saw him the night of the lynching. Bill Davis sure did his part in the hanging." No one responded to what Campbell had said. In the evening, Patsy headed to the Del-Mar-Va Fight Arena. Upon arriving, he spotted Davis and asked him to join him and Talbot Larmore for the party after the fights. Davis was not in the mood. After the matches, Russell, Wimbrow, and Patsy, along with a few women, went to Mrs. Jones's home for a while.

Friday ended with Campbell having corroborated other witness statements identifying Davis as one of the leaders of the lynch mob, in its first circle.[16]

Week Six

Just Keep "Catfish" on the Payroll

Sunday turned out to be surprisingly busy for Patsy. Around 1 p.m. he decided to meet up with Talbot Larmore, Bill Perry, and Danny Russell. They all hopped in a car and headed to Crisfield, Maryland, thirty-five miles from Salisbury. They left Crisfield and ended up in Princess Anne about 4:30, where Patsy wanted to visit the store of Fats Wilson's father, a seventy-year-old former police chief of Princess Anne. They all ate ice cream and smoked cigars, and when the visitors were leaving, Mr. Wilson came up to Talbot Larmore. Larmore had dated one of Wilson's relatives, and they apparently knew each other. "Well, Mr. Wilson," Larmore said, "most of the people have forgotten about the matter and no one talks about it at all. I know because I get into every home in Salisbury and surrounding towns collecting [information] and do not hear very much talk about the lynching. Mr. Wilson, just keep 'Catfish' on the payroll for a little while longer and everything will be OK."

"Well, I hope no bad comes from the lynching," Wilson responded. Patsy and the others then headed to Salisbury. During the drive back, Patsy asked Larmore, "Why has Wilson got to take care of this 'Catfish'?" Larmore just laughed and said, "Well, I will tell you. 'Catfish' did a pretty good deed around these parts and he sure must get a little reward." Bill Perry then said, "The hell with the matter, let's not talk about it."[17]

After his conversation with Mr. Wilson and Larmore, Patsy had begun to get the sense that Thomas "Catfish" Webster was one of the men who had led the lynching. Larmore's conversation with Mr. Wilson suggested the latter was one of the men who was paying others to remain silent regarding the lynching. This places Mr. Wilson in the conspiracy's first circle, along with Catfish Webster.

"No Gang in Salisbury"

The following day Patsy worked his usual 10-to-3:30 shift. In the evening, he accompanied Talbot Larmore to Ralph Corbin's place on Princess Anne Road. There they met Fred Ruark, Corbin's brother-in-law. Ruark told Patsy that Catfish Webster and Bill Davis were the leaders of the mob that had lynched Williams. After socializing for a while with Corbin and the others, Patsy was able to extract more information about Ruark's statement.[18] He learned that Corbin's was a place where locals from Salisbury and Snow Hill gathered to fraternize and drink. It appeared that the people of Salisbury had faulted the Snow Hill people for letting Euel Lee get away without being lynched. Suddenly, the men noticed, as if for the first time, Patsy's unfamiliar face and became reluctant to talk. Patsy remained at Corbin's until midnight. Back in his room that night, as he prepared to retire, Patsy wrote that Catfish Webster, Bill Davis, and Fats Wilson had been the leaders of the mob. Fred Ruark's statement placed Catfish and Davis in the first circle of the conspiracy.[19]

On Tuesday, Patsy noted that traffic through the gym had slowed, in part because no fights were scheduled in Salisbury for another two weeks. That afternoon, he met with Howard Campbell and asked him who the rough men were around Salisbury, hoping Campbell would arrange a meeting on his behalf. "You sure must have a few tough men the way you boys lynched the nigger and got away with it," Patsy said. Campbell responded,

> Let me tell you, we do not have any special rough men in town and there is no gang in Salisbury but as far as the lynching goes, that is a different story. Everybody here hates a nigger, but don't repeat this what I am telling you. Bill Davis had more to do with the lynching than anybody else. There were a lot of other people in it that were as much to blame as Davis, but they did not make as much fuss or noise as Davis.

Campbell also told Patsy that, following the lynching, the townspeople had been threatened to keep quiet when questioned by the Baltimore City Police. Campbell's statement corroborated previous statements about who was behind the lynching. He made clear that some businessmen had initiated the lynching, which was then taken up by other residents. He suggested that the police could have stopped the lynching, but they were in it as much as Davis or anyone else.

Patsy attempted to get Campbell to reveal names. "I heard that Buck Johnson and Waller had something to do with the lynching," Patsy said. Campbell replied, "I do not know about them, I would hate like h[ell] to say because I was in the store and only heard of the lynching afterwards." "Well," Patsy quipped, "as long as there is no organizer in Salisbury, I will organize a little gang." They both laughed it off. Besides corroborating other witness statements pointing to Bill Davis, Campbell was the first witness to implicate Holland and the other officers. Campbell also helped to lay out the conspiracy behind the lynching of Williams.[20]

"Hands Off"

The next day, Patsy closed the gym around 2 and joined John Crockett at Fats Wilson's restaurant in Princess Anne to grab a bite to eat.[21] Patsy tempted Wilson to talk about the lynching, mentioning Catfish, but was unsuccessful. However, as Patsy and Crockett headed back to Salisbury, the latter finally opened up about the incident when Patsy tried again.

Patsy said, "Wilson sure is sorry for what he and the 'Catfish' did." Crockett responded, "Well, he was not the only one in the crowd; everybody was in it." Patsy could tell that Crockett did not want to give any names.

Around 5 p.m., Patsy headed back to Salisbury and went to Cinno's cigar store. Cinno (Patsy nowhere gives his full name) was an Italian immigrant who was quite well liked in Salisbury. A native of Genoa, Cinno was known for being a dandy, frequently stepping out on the town at night. The Depression seemed not to have affected his spending habits. Leaving the cigar store, Patsy headed to Lankford's, where he asked Perry whether the piece of rope nailed to the wall was one of many cut as keepsakes? "No," Perry said, "I don't think so. Someone who was really the head of the mob brought the piece of rope in the store." Patsy then asked Perry why the police had not done anything about the lynching. Perry responded, "Why, Holland, the chief, was right in the hospital when they took the nigger out. He did not want to stop the lynching. Why, I was in front of the hospital myself. I could not or did not help because there were already plenty of men on the job. The lynching did not do the community any good, but the niggers were getting too wild and something had to be done."

Perry also corroborated previous statements, telling Patsy that Chief Holland knew the men who took Williams out of the hospital and that he could have stopped the lynching if he had wanted to, but had been given orders by some businessmen to "keep his hands off." Later that night, Patsy's attempts to get information out of Bill Davis and Jack Townsend were less fruitful.

Aside from providing more evidence to corroborate previous statements implicating Chief Holland, John Crockett's statement highlighted the participation of those who happened to be in the area, suggesting a fusion of private and hue-and-cry (mass) mob characteristics.[22]

Wednesday, February 10, was another slow day at the gym. Patsy spent the evening with Howard Campbell delivering a radio. On the drive to the customer's house, Campbell warned Patsy, "Do not say anything, but Bill Davis, who hangs around our store, brought the piece of rope we have nailed to the wall." Campbell repeated, "Do not tell anyone I told you because my business will drop off quicker than hell if people know that I opened my mouth. If you hang around town long enough you will meet up with some of the regular fellows." "Well," Patsy replied, "I am a regular fellow myself and I would like to meet up with them because I might want to do a little bootlegging on the side." Later Patsy headed to Cinno's cigar store, hoping to feel out other locals about the lynching. That night, Patsy had Talbot Larmore drive him to Princess Anne to visit Fats Wilson. However, they left abruptly after Larmore had a confrontation with a local fellow over money. On their way home, they decided to catch a movie, after which, Patsy retired at 10:30.[23]

Campbell's reference to his business potentially dropping off sheds light on the power that the businessmen behind the lynching held over the community. Campbell's statements suggest that there were consequences for breaking the code of silence and speaking out about the lynching. His words provide some of the most compelling evidence Patsy found of the system of silence, as they show the control the lynching organizers had over ordinary citizens who patronized businesses such as Campbell and Perry's.

"Didn't We Do A Good Job on Williams?"

After a couple of slow days at the gym, business was finally beginning to pick up. After work, Patsy walked over to Hastings's Barber Shop, where he ran into Kid Guthrie, who did not bring up the lynching. Shortly after that, Patsy ran into W. Arthur Kennerly, at the Arcade cigar store on Main Street. The fifty-four-year-old Kennerly had served as mayor from 1920 to 1924 and was contemplating running for the office again. He had a close connection to the investigation surrounding the death of Williams, having served as the foreman of the coroner's jury impaneled by Magistrate S. King White on December 5, 1931, to investigate the lynching—the jury that never actually assembled to take testimony.[24] Expressing his approval of the lynching of Williams, and arguing that it represented a model of retribution that should have been used to handle Euel Lee, Kennerly explained to Patsy that, in allowing the lynching of Williams to take place, the state and the county had saved a tremendous amount of money.[25] Kennerly then looked at Lee Harris, who was also present, winked, and said, "Didn't we do a good job on Williams?" Harris agreed. "I say we did." No names were mentioned. Later, Patsy accompanied Talbot Larmore to see the latter's girlfriend in Princess Anne. Afterward, they headed to Fats Wilson's restaurant. Larmore told Patsy and the others that D.J. Elliott and Talbot Larmore's father had been in business together. Eventually the two parted because Elliott was a difficult man to deal with. Around 11:00 p.m., Patsy discontinued his report.[26]

"Jews Were Treated like Williams"

On Friday, Patsy followed up on some leads and finally met with Sam Preston, the Jewish store owner he had been waiting for several weeks to speak with. Preston wasted no time; he talked as if he was clearing his conscience. He began with the frenzy that had ensued on the night of the lynching, describing how everyone had gone crazy, including the women, who later came into his shop and expressed their pleasure at seeing Williams hang over the courthouse lawn. As the spectacle continued, Preston recalled, he fled the scene, unable to bear its barbarism. Preston reminded Patsy that in certain other parts of the country Jews were treated as Williams had been. Undoubtedly, he was referring to the lynching of Leo Frank in Atlanta, Georgia, just seventeen years earlier.

Preston indicated his disgust with Chief Nicholas Holland, who had allowed Bill Davis to coordinate the lynching and direct the men who made up the mob. Preston also corroborated earlier statements that contradicted newspaper accounts, telling Patsy that Williams was hanged not once but twice after the half-drunken men had shown up late for the first hanging. The second time they hanged Williams using a guy wire from a nearby telephone pole.

Inquiring about a possible purse, Patsy asked Preston if the town's prominent businessmen had paid the men anything for the hanging. "This is not Chicago or New York City," Preston answered. "These ignorant shore people have not brains enough to ask for money."[27] Preston had moved to Salisbury nine months earlier from Chicago, where hit jobs were quite common.

Patsy headed to his favored local spots Hastings's Barber Shop and then Lankford's Sporting Goods store, where he was unable to get any more information on the lynching. By 7:30 p.m., he had met up with Talbot Larmore, hoping that Larmore would accompany him to Princess Anne, where Patsy hoped to meet Catfish Webster. Instead, they decided to stay in Salisbury and go to Thompson's Grill. After their meal, in front of the Arcade

Cigar Store, they met Joe Fusco, owner of the George Washington Hotel in Ocean City, and P. I. Rosenberg, a lawyer from Syracuse, New York. As they stood in front of the cigar store, Fusco made Patsy a proposition (addressing him with his brother's boxing name): "Well, 'Bat,' stick around until I open my hotel this summer and I will give you a good job."

Patsy and Larmore went to Ralph Corbin's place, but returned with no leads or information concerning the lynching, so he went back to the hotel. As the night came to a close, he reviewed his list of confessed and suspected members of the mob. Ben Parson was shaping up as someone who had likely played a significant role. Elwood Waller, who was currently laid up in a Philadelphia hospital, had already confessed to pouring the gasoline on Williams. Patsy considered questioning Waller's older brother, the counterman at Thompson's Grill.[28]

Sunday was, as usual, uneventful for Patsy, and after spending a little time at the Arcade and Cinno's cigar store, he left early for his meeting on Monday at the agency in Philadelphia. As he did not return to Salisbury until 7:30 p.m. on Monday, that day, too, produced no new information.[29]

Meanwhile, Martin and Ware had resurfaced in Salisbury the previous Friday morning, from where they called the assistant attorney general and talked from 11 a.m. to 1:40 p.m. Their report highlighted additional evidence corroborating previous statements made by Mr. and Mrs. Creowell. Some of the most valuable of their recent findings were gleaned from the testimony of Howard Purnell, another Black witness who challenged the system of silence and gave an eyewitness account of the lynching.[30]

Purnell told Martin and Ware that he had heard Louis Smith bragging about having gotten gasoline from the garage, pouring it on Williams, and setting his body on fire. A janitor at the Wicomico Hotel, Purnell also saw the lynching from beginning to end. He witnessed the mob form and identified Herman Townsend as one of the men who was holding the rope as the mob took the body away to be burned.

On March 8 Martin and Ware would give what would be their last report to their superior officer, Captain Charles H. Burns. In this brief report, Thompson and Purnell were their key witnesses, and both confirmed that they saw Bill Davis among the mob. Purnell knew a number of the participants and identified Fats Wilson and Lou Smith among the crowd.[31] Martin and Ware also acknowledged in this report the danger that African Americans like Purnell faced if they violated the system of silence, fearing that Purnell would be in danger if he testified. They recommended to Captain Burns that for his and his family's safety, Purnell leave Salisbury.[32]

Years later, Salisbury resident Linda Duyer recalled interviewing Howard Purnell toward the end of his life. After attending a local meeting in Wicomico County, Purnell and a friend were heading out the door when Duyer asked him, "Mr. Purnell, where were you on December 4, 1931." According to Duyer, Purnell "stopped in his tracks," looked at her, and said, "What do you mean, the lynching?" When Duyer replied, "I think that's what I asked you," Purnell responded, "Yes, I was there." "After that," Duyer wrote, "he sat down and gave his account of the lynching of Matthew Williams, his fellow classmate."[33]

According to Duyer, Purnell was working at the Wicomico Hotel, across the street from the courthouse lawn on which Williams was hanged the first time. Purnell, who usually worked nights, had worked that day so he could see a movie in the evening. While he was at the movie, word reached the theater that a lynching was going to take place. Following the film, Purnell witnessed the lynching firsthand because, to get home, he had to walk directly through the mob, past the courthouse and the Wicomico Hotel. As he made a left on Division Street, he heard the mob as they strung up his former classmate several times. He rushed down Church Street to get back home, where he found his father upstairs with his shotgun looking out the window. Through that window, he saw Williams's body being burned after it was dragged from the courthouse to the Black neighborhood of Georgetown.[34]

In their February 12 report, Martin and Ware also revealed that Dr. Stephen R. Collins had told them that W. Arthur Kennerly, the former mayor and the foreman of the coroner's jury, had been a main organizer of the lynching and had recruited men for it. Even more startling, Martin and Ware had managed to get Chief Holland as close as he would ever come to breaking the code of silence. After securing a private meeting with Holland in the home of ex-sheriff Ralph C. Duffy (no one else was present), the sergeants pressed Holland as to why he did nothing on the night of the lynching. He threw up his hands and said, "I had my orders," but refused to say what his orders were or who had issued them. Holland also shared with Martin and Ware something only recently made known—that on the afternoon of December 4, he and Sheriff Murray Phillips had met with Judge Bailey in front of the Wicomico Hotel, just as the judge was heading out of town.[35] What the three discussed is not known.

Week Seven

"We Are Going to Get Williams"

On Tuesday, February 16, Patsy was back to his normal routine, opening the gym around 10 a.m. and conducting boxing lessons. About 3:00 p.m. Patsy headed over to Lankford's Sporting Goods and stayed until the store closed at 6. Patsy had hoped to get Howard Campbell to provide him further details of the lynching, as he believed Campbell to be trustworthy, but he was not successful. After leaving Lankford's, he headed to Cinno's cigar store. Around 8:30 p.m., Patsy met back up with Talbot Larmore, and they went for a drive with two women whose last names were Todd and Mitchell. Patsy brought up the subject of the "colored boy" in Philadelphia who had attacked and allegedly killed the Lutz girl the previous week.[36] Larmore said, "Well, they ought to ship that nigger to Salisbury, we would string him up a tree."

He went on to tell Patsy and their companions what had taken place the night of Williams's lynching. Larmore recalled that he and Danny Russell had been driving down Main Street when they saw a crowd gathering at the *Salisbury Times* newspaper office. Both wondered what was going on. They soon learned that the crowd was preparing to seize Williams from the hospital. Shortly thereafter, they were told that a smaller group was planning to abduct Williams from the hospital and hang him. Soon Russell and Larmore went to Cinno's store. Roger Bailey entered and said, "Come on, boys, we are going to get Williams at the hospital and lynch him."

Larmore and Russell drove out to the hospital and found some four hundred people already there. The two then saw some men hand Williams through a window to other men outside the hospital. They followed the crowd down Division Street. "I saw the two men pulled Williams up the tree to hang him," Larmore said, remembering that they then lowered Williams's body and someone ran up to "the nigger." Just as this man was about to stick a knife into Williams's back, a "colored man" said, "Say, 'Bunky,' don't do that." According to Larmore, Williams was alive when he was lowered from the tree. The men then dragged Williams back behind Thompson's Grill, and someone laid Williams's body over a stump, poured gasoline on it, and set it afire. The crowd then dragged the charred corpse from Main to Lake Street and suspended it from a telephone pole. Finally, after lowering the body, one man stood on it and said, "Now boys, let's all go and see the fights."[37]

Larmore and Russell headed to the arena, where they saw two of the men who had pulled the rope to hang Williams. Larmore said to one man, "I see you helped lynch Williams." "Who, me?" the man replied. "Why, I did not know there was a lynching." Larmore insisted, "Man, I saw you there with my eyes, it was a good job you did." The man answered, "Well, I had Williams by one leg and Murray Phillips had him by the other leg, and if an investigation comes up about this, why I will just say that I let go of the nigger when Murray Phillips did." The man then told Larmore to keep quiet about the lynching.

Larmore also told Patsy that he had witnessed a man cutting off Williams's toes. By this time the women were starting to grow tired of hearing about the lynching, so the conversation ended. However, Patsy came away with a wealth of information that corroborated a number of other statements he had obtained thus far in the investigation. Some of it pointed to Sheriff Murray Phillips as one of the men who had pulled on the rope around Williams's neck, placing him in the conspiracy's first circle. Patsy now knew that Larmore would be his central witness and that he needed to get him away from Salisbury to talk in greater detail.[38]

On Wednesday, after working at the gym, Patsy headed to Lankford's Sporting Goods store around 3:15 p.m. and stayed until 5:20. While he was there, he talked with Lee Harris about a prospective trip to Norfolk, Virginia, where a fight was going to be held. Patsy's main motive, of course, was to get a fuller account of the lynching from Harris. Patsy loafed around the Arcade and Cinno's cigar store without learning anything new. He discontinued his report at 11 p.m.[39]

The following day, Patsy finally met with Bill Davis; however, the two did not get a chance to discuss the lynching. Patsy and Lee Harris continued to plan their trip to Norfolk, hoping to secure some bouts for Salisbury fighters. Campbell asked Patsy if he would like to ride with him to Philadelphia.[40] On Friday, the *Salisbury Times* ran an article on "Battling Johnson" that described how he was training Danny Russell for the upcoming fight. Either Patsy's brother had come into town to assist him in training Danny Russell, or Patsy had assumed the identity of his brother Florine, the original "Battling Johnson," who was now thirty-five years old.[41]

Catfish and Fats Wilson

The gym was closed on Friday because Patsy would be in Portsmouth, Virginia. During the drive there, Lee Harris insisted that on the night of the lynching he was at the fight as he had a couple of men in the ring. Though claiming to have been absent from the lynching, Harris confirmed that fire department chief Frederick A. Grier had furnished the rope. According to Harris, a few of the men had gone to the firehouse to see if Grier had any rope. The chief was said to have responded, "Sure boys, have this rope, and if it is not enough I have a lot more." With a long ride ahead of them, Patsy continued to question Harris. When he asked him whose idea it had been to start the lynching, Harris surmised, "Well, that is a hard thing to say, as Dan Elliott, who was killed, sure had a lot of friends and it would not take much to start what happened."

"I heard that Catfish and Fats Wilson pulled Williams up the tree," Patsy offered. Harris asked Patsy who had told him this, and Patsy said, "Talbot Larmore and Danny Russell were talking about the lynching and they mentioned Catfish and Wilson of Princess Anne."

"Well," Harris said, "I will not say for sure, but I think that Wilson and Catfish did have something to do with the lynching. I do not want to have anyone think that I would accuse any certain person for lynching Williams as that is murder, and if the state could prove anything against Catfish or Wilson, why a first degree murder charge would be preferred against them."[42]

Patsy pushed on, asking Harris if Elliott's son, James, had had anything to do with organizing the lynching. Harris had not heard anything about Elliott's son being involved; rather, he insisted that Williams's lynching was the result of the failure to lynch Euel Lee and George Davis. The "niggers" were getting out of hand, Harris opined, and so it was decided to lynch Williams.

Patsy's ride with Harris to Virginia continued to bear fruit for the investigation as Harris next identified Ben Parsons as one of the mob leaders who had snatched Williams from the hospital; indeed he claimed that Parsons had pulled Williams out of bed and shoved him through the first-floor window. Harris saw Parsons's role in the lynching as connected to his successes in the ring, telling Patsy, "There is a boy for you." As their conversation continued, Harris insisted that Chief Nicholas Holland had known about the lynching an hour before it took place, and that arrangements had been made so that the lynching could go forward—without fear of being stopped. Harris told Patsy that Catfish Webster had left Salisbury for a few days after the lynching, and then returned. According to Harris, everyone in town was nervous about what was going to happen after the lynching. Harris insisted, though, that state authorities would have difficulty gathering evidence against anybody who had taken part in the lynching, as the community was sticking behind the men who had lynched Williams and was remaining silent.

As their conversation continued, Patsy may have become convinced, if he wasn't before, that his presence was necessary. Harris stated, "Boy, didn't we make a fool out of the Baltimore detectives. They were in Salisbury asking questions and going here and there. They could not get anything—and no one else will."[43]

Back in his hotel room a day later, Patsy sifted the concrete facts he had gathered concerning those involved in the lynching. Reviewing the previous entries in his running report, Patsy remembered that Elwood Waller had admitted to having poured gasoline on Williams and that one of the men who had pulled the rope to hang Williams had left town after the lynching and returned a few days later. This matched Harris's account in which he stated that Catfish had left Salisbury for a few days, then returned.

Harris's statement during the Virginia trip placed him in the third circle of the conspiracy. Harris knew about the plan to lynch Williams and approximately when the lynching would occur. As a prominent boxing promoter in Salisbury, Harris was close to the conspirators, some of whom happened to be Salisbury boxers.[44]

Harris and Patsy left Portsmouth around 7:30 a.m. on Saturday morning. On their way back to Salisbury, Harris said that Fats Wilson of Princess Anne was not a rough fellow, that he just liked for people to think that he was rough. According to Harris, on the night of the lynching, Wilson appeared to have been drinking heavily, and took an active part in lynching Williams. Harris even mentioned that Wilson had felt regret afterward, saying he was sorry that he had gotten mixed up in the entire situation. Patsy then said, "Bill Davis, the man who hangs around Lankford's Sporting Goods store, I heard helped a lot." Harris claimed that Davis had directed the entire affair.

At this point, Patsy, sensing that Harris was growing tired of talking about the lynching, dropped the matter. The two arrived back in Salisbury around 3:30 p.m. Patsy hung out at Cinno's cigar store for a while, then took the 11:15 p.m. train to Philadelphia. He arrived at 4:30 a.m. the following morning and remained in Philadelphia until Monday to meet with Pinkerton officials. While other witnesses had alluded to Wilson's involvement in the lynching, Lee Harris was the first witness to state definitively that Wilson had been one of the main leaders in the mob. Based on Harris's account, Wilson belongs with Davis and Holland in the first circle of the conspiracy.[45]

Week Eight

Monday morning, Patsy met with an official of the Pinkerton agency around 8:30. He left Philadelphia on the 10:25 train and arrived in Salisbury at 2. He headed over to Lankford's Sporting Goods store, where Howard Campbell told him that he was going to Philadelphia at 5 the next morning and wanted Patsy to accompany him. At 3:30 Danny Russell entered the store. He told Patsy that he was fighting on March 4 and was going to his father's farm to get himself ready with rigorous training. Patsy asked if he could go with Russell, seeing this practice time with Russell as a way to get him alone to talk. Around 6:30 p.m., Patsy went to Cinno's cigar store and stayed there until around 8. He wrote later that he was trying to get acquainted with Bailey, the man whom Cinno recalled entering his store the night of the lynching and saying, "Come on boys, we are going to the hospital and get Williams." Around 8:15 p.m. Danny Russell and Patsy headed to the Arcade Theatre to catch the latest film, *Two Kinds of Women*. Following the movie Patsy finished his report for the night at 10:30.[46]

On Tuesday, after closing the gym around 3 p.m., Patsy loafed at Lankford's Sporting Goods until 5 p.m. Shortly thereafter, he headed to Thompson's Grill, where he heard no one mention the lynching. While Patsy was at Cinno's cigar store after dinner, Talbot Larmore invited him to a party at Bill Ellers's place. They arrived at Ellers's on Princess Anne Road about 7:30 p.m. Patsy encountered Deputy Sheriff Donald Parks there, and they discussed several topics. Everyone at the party was drunk except for Parks and Patsy. Patsy wanted to keep it that way so that he could cultivate Parks as a witness. Patsy had not yet taken either of the proposed trips with Campbell or Russell. He discontinued his report around 12:30 a.m.[47]

On Wednesday, Danny Russell came to the gym and began training for a fight in Pocomoke, Maryland, on March 4. After leaving the gym that afternoon, Patsy headed over to Lankford's, arriving there around 4 and staying for two hours. He then headed to Hastings's Barber Shop on Division Street and stayed until 7:15, when he moved on to Cinno's cigar store, then the Arcade cigar store. Patsy tried to get people to talk about the lynching, but to no avail. Elwood Waller had returned from Philadelphia, and Patsy wrote, as he finished his report that night, that if he buttered Waller up by taking him to a show one evening soon, he might talk about the lynching, this time laying out the facts.[48]

"Everyone in Town Was in It"

The next day Danny Russell returned to the gym for training. Beginning about 1 p.m., a number of men passed through to see Russell work out. At 3 p.m., after the gym closed, Patsy was invited to a trap shoot (where contestants use shotguns to hit clay targets hurled into the air) on Snow Hill Road. The sheriff of Worcester County was among the many who attended. The conversation ranged over seemingly every topic except the lynching. Around 6 p.m., Sam Preston invited Patsy to his apartment for dinner. Patsy wasted no time during dinner in asking Preston who had been the lynch mob leaders. He said to Preston, "Gee! I would love to know how the lynching started." Preston shared what he knew of the way events had unfolded:

Truth, Lies, and Somewhere in Between

[161]

Everyone in town was in it. I know myself who the leaders were but don't want to say anything about the matter. Why, the *Baltimore News* sent a wire to a Jewish photographer for pictures of the lynching, but the photographer refused. The paper offered as high as a thousand dollars for some kind of picture. These people down here stick together. A minister in town went to the photographer and praised him for not sending pictures to Baltimore. These people here are very clannish and they will not talk. Why, I would not ever testify on the stand as to what I know about the lynching. It is over now so to h[el]l with the matter.

Around 7:30 p.m., after failing to get any valuable new information from Preston, Patsy left. Preston's statement places him in the fifth, outermost circle of the conspiracy, as he had only a passing knowledge of the lynching beforehand, the sequence of ensuing events, and the parties involved.[49]

On Friday, Campbell, Perry, and a few other men Patsy associated with said, "How do you get by here in Salisbury? You are not making any money. Why not go to Ocean City and have a talk with Powell? We think he will give you a job as matchmaker for the fights at the Arena." So Patsy and Harris headed to Ocean City to meet with Captain William Powell. Powell welcomed the two about 10 p.m. and told Patsy he would consider the idea and get back with him in a few days. Patsy then asked Powell if it would be all right to match "colored" fighters. "Oh no," Harris shot back, "to h[el]l with the niggers. We do not want anything to do with them." This was a significant statement, given that some of Lee Harris's white fighters had at least been featured on programs with Black fighters. Five days before the Williams lynching, two Black fighters—Bill Nichols of Salisbury and Ed Bassett of Berlin, Maryland—had opened a boxing card on the same program as local white boxers, including Buck Johnson and Kid Guthrie.[50]

Powell agreed with Harris. "No," he told Patsy, "I do not think it would be advisable to have anything to do with the colored folks." Patsy had hoped mentioning Black fighters would trigger a conversation about the lynching. He began to consider a trip to Philadelphia with Elwood Waller to search for some fighters, during which they could discuss the lynching. As a matchmaker, Patsy hoped that he could strengthen his cover and gain greater access to some of the rough men who had been involved in the lynching, including Catfish Webster. Patsy thought that he might hire Catfish as an usher at the arena and put him in charge of maintaining order. This would give Patsy a reason to hang around Princess Anne for a few days during the week, where he could also meet with Wilson and Brubaker.

Patsy and Harris headed home around 4 p.m., arriving in Salisbury by 5:30. Patsy hung out at the Arcade cigar store and Cinno's cigar store, but heard no mention of the lynching. Later on, he headed to Cambridge, Maryland, with Larmore and Russell and attempted to get them to talk about the lynching, but they seemed afraid to speak. They got back to Salisbury about 12:30 a.m.[51]

On Saturday afternoon, Russell arrived at the gym around 1:30, and Patsy worked with him. Patsy was at Lankford's Sporting Goods store from 3:30 to 5:30, when he headed to Hastings's Barber Shop. He tried to get Hastings's son to talk about the lynching, but the son did not furnish any information. At Cinno's cigar store, Patsy spoke to Bill Green, who ran the gas station. Green wanted Patsy to go out riding and drinking with him. Patsy declined, knowing that he could go out with Green anytime. Around 8:30 p.m. Patsy went to the Arcade cigar store and tried to meet someone to go out with who might talk about the lynching, but he was unsuccessful. He left for Philadelphia around 10:30 p.m., heading to the station and boarding the 11:51 p.m. train. He arrived in Philadelphia around 4:10 a.m. and stayed there until his appointment on Monday.[52]

On Monday, February 29, Patsy arrived at the Pinkerton office around 8:30 a.m. After his meeting, he boarded the train back to Salisbury, arriving a little before 2 p.m. Not long after his return, he met up with Danny Russell for a training session at the gym. By the end of the day, Patsy had stopped by Hastings's Barber Shop and the Arcade cigar store, meeting with Kid Guthrie, Elwood Waller, and Talbot Larmore, all of whom failed to deliver details concerning the lynching. Around midnight Patsy discontinued his report.[53]

[6]

Maryland's Disgrace
The Denial of Justice

We often wonder just what happened to that "sweeping investigation"
of the Salisbury lynching. Perhaps just what most Eastern Shoremen
thought would happen—nothing!

Benjamin Johnson, March 5, 1932

Five days into March 1932, Benjamin Johnson, president, editor, and treasurer of the *Denton Journal*, a regional newspaper headquartered in Denton, Maryland, devoted several lines of his editorial to musing on US foreign policy and the national, local, and state politics of the day.[1] Johnson began by railing against the fiscal incompetence of Hoover, whom he had followed and reported on for eleven years, beginning with his membership in President Warren G. Harding's cabinet. The only thing keeping the economy afloat, in Johnson's view, was the Democratic-controlled House and the nearly equal Democratic-Republican representation in the Senate. Bearing all the markings of a committed Democrat, Johnson wrote, "The solution can safely be left in their [Democratic members of Congress] hands. The country is through with engineering as a governmental science and also with miracle workers." After briefly summarizing the proceedings of the World Disarmament Conference, Johnson praised Maryland's own Senator Millard Tydings as a champion for the Democratic party.

Regarding the sentence that serves as this chapter's epigraph, it is hard to gauge Johnson's thoughts concerning the lynching of Williams. What is clear, however, is his remark speaks to Governor Ritchie's lack of popularity on the Eastern Shore in early 1932. Like most Eastern Shoremen, Johnson saw Ritchie's public call for an investigation of the lynching as nothing more than a political stunt. In his view, Ritchie only alienated himself further from the Eastern Shore, a place whose white society was in many ways a microcosm of white society in the Deep South. It was, however, the public investigation that Johnson referred to, and not the private one that was now entering its third month.

No Remorse

On March 1, 1932—two months since he had arrived in Salisbury—Patsy Johnson had settled in quite well with the locals. He opened the gym a little later than usual for a Tuesday. By 11:30 a.m. he had met up with Lee Harris, and they drove to Ocean City. On the way, they passed the home where Euel Lee had allegedly murdered the white family. Harris argued that Lee would have been lynched if the crime he was accused of committing had occurred in Wicomico County.

Patsy asked Harris if the men who had hanged Williams from the tree would do the same to any other "negro." Harris responded, "Indeed they would," adding that there were some pretty big men in Salisbury who would take care of anyone who had been involved in the Williams lynching. The whole city of Salisbury had been behind the lynching, he told Patsy, and everyone would help anybody who was arrested or sought "justice."

As the two approached Ocean City, Harris showed Patsy the road to Taylorsville, where Ben Parsons lived, a little hamlet about three miles from Berlin. Harris and Patsy met with Captain Powell in Ocean City and discussed their plans to match fighters. Around 1:20 p.m. Harris and Patsy left for Princess Anne, where they met briefly with a fighter. Back in Salisbury, Patsy hung around Lankford's Sporting Goods for a while before going to a speakeasy on Lake Street, in the "colored" section of town, around 7:00 p.m. Later, as he left the speakeasy, he told Fields, the proprietor, that if he saw Elwood Waller the next morning, he should tell Waller that Patsy wanted to see him.[2]

Harris's statement on this occasion, like Russell's and Larmore's, points to a group of power brokers who were responsible for organizing the lynching and were making sure that those who had carried it out and those who had witnessed it firsthand remained quiet. More important, Harris moved beyond the traditional conspiracy and revealed the system of silence, arguing that the whole city of Salisbury was behind the lynching and that all the people would protect one another from prosecution.

On Wednesday, Patsy trained Danny Russell. Around 4:30 p.m., Patsy headed to Thompson's Grill to interrogate Elwood Waller's brother Harry. Patsy wanted Elwood's address in Delmar, Delaware, but it was his day off and he was not at the diner. Patsy had not seen Elwood Waller around for a day or so. He loafed at Cinno's cigar store until 7 p.m. He heard no talk about the lynching. People had dropped the subject, or so it seemed to Patsy. Around 8:30 p.m., Larmore and Patsy went to Ralph Corbin's place on Tony Tank Road but did not learn anything of interest. Patsy ended the day and his report at 11.[3]

On Thursday afternoon, Patsy headed to Hastings's Barber Shop and eventually to Parson's candy store after training several men at the gym. He learned nothing of interest. Around 6 p.m., he accompanied Talbot Larmore to Princess Anne. Shortly thereafter he headed to Wilson's Restaurant to see if Wilson would place some fight cards in his window. Patsy and Larmore remained in Fats Wilson's place talking, but Patsy was unable to gain any additional information about the lynching. During the return trip from Princess Anne, Larmore offered nothing new, either. Around 11:00 p.m., Patsy discontinued his report.[4]

"I Do Not Want a Knife Stuck in My Back"

By Friday, the gym was busier than usual as men were training for fights coming up on March 11. After the training sessions, Patsy headed to Lankford's Sporting Goods and stayed until 5:30. There was no mention of the lynching; instead, everyone was concerned about Danny Russell, who would be fighting in Pocomoke, Maryland, that night. Later Patsy headed to Cinno's cigar store, remaining until 7 p.m. while he waited for Danny Russell to return.

In the cigar store, Patsy struck up a conversation with a fighter named "Kid" Ritchie. Ritchie told Patsy that Kid Guthrie had been fighting the night of December 4 and that Guthrie had not participated in the lynching. Patsy then asked Ritchie who the leaders of the mob were. No one knew the identities of the men, Ritchie said. Continuing to pump Ritchie, Patsy said he'd heard that Catfish Webster was one of the leaders. Ritchie recalled noticing Catfish among the crowd; he had been doing a lot of directing and taking matters concerning the lynching into his own hands. Patsy told Ritchie he needed to know who the leaders had been because he needed a few rough men for security when he held his fight on March 11. Ritchie responded firmly, "I am not going to say anything. I do not want a knife stuck in my back." Directly thereafter, around 7 p.m., Danny Russell came into the store, and he, Bill Wimbrow (Ralph's nephew), Talbot Larmore, and Patsy all left Salisbury and headed for the fights in Pocomoke.

Boxing was the topic of discussion until the men reached Snow Hill, at which point, Euel Lee was brought up. "Well," said Bill Wimbrow, "here is where all the dumb people of Maryland live. If your friend Wilson or Catfish could have gotten their hands on Yuel [sic] Lee we would have had a necktie party all right, the night that Lee was caught." Patsy asked Wimbrow how Catfish or Wilson came to lead the lynching. Wimbrow said, "Who told you they were head men? There were men bigger than Catfish and Wilson at the head of the party and I know the whole d[amn] thing from start to finish and all about the police. I know every one of their faults."

Although Patsy hoped to obtain the full story from Bill Wimbrow, the conversation was interrupted when they stopped to help some fight fans whose car had broken down on their way to Pocomoke. The Salisbury group finally arrived in Pocomoke about 8. Patsy was busy throughout the night, taking care of Russell. Russell's eye was cut during the fight, and he was knocked out in the seventh round. Following the fight, Patsy and Wimbrow took Russell to a Dr. Nack in Pocomoke. After giving Russell two stitches above his eye, the doctor pulled out a pint of good whiskey, and after two or three drinks Wimbrow became talkative. He told Russell he should give up boxing and suggested the three of them go into bootlegging. After leaving the doctor's office, the four headed back to Salisbury. Wimbrow continued talking, this time about opening up a gas station. Russell was silent for the rest of the ride, heartbroken over his defeat and the small percentage he was taking home, $46.00.

Aside from previous speculation concerning the role of Catfish Webster, Patsy still had no eyewitness who would admit to having seen Webster at the head of the lynch mob. Still, Kid Ritchie provided Patsy with the first statement connecting Webster to the first, or innermost, circle—those serving as leaders in the company of Davis.

The group arrived back in Salisbury around 11:30 p.m. Danny Russell went directly home, and so did Larmore. Wimbrow got word of a dance going on at Bradley's Ballroom until 2:30 a.m., featuring a great "nigger orchestra."[5] He wanted to go.

The Great "Nigger Orchestra"

The band known as the Plantation Orchestra was led by Perry Glascoe, a successful reed player and former member of the famous Duke Ellington Orchestra. In spite of the tense racial climate in Salisbury, Glascoe had decided to perform, though he knew without question that he and his orchestra would be playing for an all-white audience. The orchestra's presence in Salisbury reveals much about whiteness on the Eastern Shore. African American musicians were welcomed as long as they stayed in their place. Glascoe's band performed at some of the same venues that hosted boxing matches throughout Maryland sponsored by the Maryland Athletic Commission.[6]

Seizing this opportunity, Patsy accompanied Wimbrow, hoping he could get more information about the gasoline taken from Wimbrow's uncle's garage to douse Williams's corpse. Going with Wimbrow, however, turned out to be less fruitful than Patsy had hoped, and before leaving, he arranged to meet with Wimbrow again and take a look at the gas station. Around 3:00 a.m., Patsy headed home.[7]

Earlier in the day on March 4, with the grand jury hearing approaching, Attorney General Preston Lane wrote Levin C. Bailey in Salisbury, "I think it will be necessary for you to have and go over the information that has been developed in connection to the lynching." Lane was hoping to secure a meeting with Bailey the following Saturday, March 12, to review the evidence that Patsy had compiled concerning the lynching. In addition, he mentioned the prospect of discussing Judge Joseph Bailey's charge to the grand jury.[8] By the time Lane sent this letter to Bailey, he must have known that Patsy had obtained evidence connecting Bailey to the mob. Lane and Governor Ritchie must also have known that Judge Bailey was the uncle of State's Attorney Levin C. Bailey. Certainly, these familial connections could compromise the hearing.

After 10:30 Saturday morning, Patsy headed to Lankford's Sporting Goods store, where all the men present were discussing Russell's defeat the previous night. Leaving Lankford's, Patsy headed to Cinno's and the Arcade cigar stores, and soon began trying to locate Elwood Waller. It had been four or five days since he had seen Waller, and Patsy returned to Waller's usual spot, the Arcade cigar store. Not finding him there, Patsy joined up with Lee Harris, and they walked around town passing out flyers advertising their upcoming fight on March 11. Patsy took this opportunity to see if Harris wanted to go to Princess Anne to try to recruit Wilson and Catfish as doormen. Harris told Patsy he was heading to Dover, Delaware, and would go to Princess Anne later in the week. Patsy did not see Larmore, Russell, or Wimbrow for the remainder of the day. He left Salisbury on the train at 11:51 p.m. and arrived in Philadelphia around 4:10 a.m. He remained in Philadelphia all day Sunday and until his conference at the Pinkerton agency on Monday. When he got back to Salisbury on Tuesday, he continued where he had left off, distributing handbills throughout the community for the upcoming fight. Patsy did not hear anything about the investigation, and at around 10 p.m. Tuesday night he discontinued his report.[9]

"The Smell of Burning Flesh"

On Sunday, March 6, five days before the big fight, Patsy headed to Princess Anne around 10 a.m. to place circulars for the match around town. While there, Patsy headed over to Fats Wilson's restaurant. Wilson told Patsy that he did not think he would attend the fights because he had lost interest since the night Williams was lynched. Patsy asked him if the lynching made him sick. Wilson looked at Patsy and said, "I don't know anything about it. I just did not like the smell of burning flesh." Patsy attempted to get Wilson to say more about the lynching but was unsuccessful. Later he headed to Delmar and put out some flyers. Shortly afterward, he met with Elwood Waller and rode around in John Crockett's car.

Later on, Patsy and Lee Harris headed to Wilmington, Delaware, to see Bob Gadsby, who was boxing there. Patsy declined to attend the fight as he wanted to meet with Buck Wheatelton, Salisbury's leading lawyer, who was going to be at Mrs. Jones's place. Patsy headed to the Jones residence at 8 or 9 p.m. Patsy knew of Wheatelton's reputation as a powerful influence on lawyers, jurists, local judges, and prosecutors, including Levin C. Bailey, the state's attorney. Patsy hoped that Wheatelton would discuss the lynching, but he did not.

Clifford Dreydon, the son of a former sheriff of Wicomico County, was at Mrs. Jones's place while Patsy was there. Patsy later described Dreydon as being rather stuck up and full of himself. Leaning on his father's legacy, Dreydon bragged to Patsy that his father could arrest anyone in Salisbury if he saw fit. Before leaving, unprovoked, Dreydon called Patsy a "vile" name, whereupon Patsy struck him and left to go home.[10]

On Saturday, Patsy spent the day at Perry and Campbell's store. The men around the warehouse were all talking about the fight held the previous night. Later, Patsy headed over to Cinno's cigar store, staying there for the remainder of the day. Patsy then returned to Lankford's Sporting Goods store until it closed. He boarded the 11:51 train to Philadelphia, arriving early Sunday morning.[11]

When Patsy arrived at the Pinkerton offices later that morning for his conference with agency officials, he was instructed to go to Baltimore. He reached Baltimore around 3:30 p.m. and conferred with Superintendent "E.L.P." and Assistant Superintendent "T.J.F.," who would soon be in Salisbury. At 7:55 that evening Patsy took the train back to Philadelphia, arriving around 10:08 p.m.[12] While he was there, the Baltimore Sun ran an article headlined, "75 Are Called in Lynching Case," hinting at the likely topic of his discussion with agency officials and previewing the upcoming grand jury investigation into the lynching of Matthew Williams. The article announced that Levin C. Bailey, with the assistance of Preston Lane, was preparing to call witnesses in the coming week.[13] While Patsy was in Philadelphia, the press descended upon Salisbury. Among the newspapermen was

Paul S. Henderson, the *Baltimore Afro-American* staff photographer who had been to Salisbury before and collected a section of the rope used to hang Williams.

By Monday, the number of witnesses to be called had grown to one hundred; among them were a number of individuals whom Patsy had spoken with. Judge Joseph Bailey selected the grand jury from the sixteen election districts in Wicomico County. From the original list, the court named a foreman and drew twenty-two other names. The resulting grand jury was made up entirely of white men from various stations in life.[14] (See table A.4 in the appendix.)

Following the empaneling of the grand jury, the list of witnesses to be subpoenaed was published in newspapers throughout the state. Of the more than one hundred witnesses summoned on the first day of the investigation, twenty were individuals whom Patsy had identified and spoken with: W. Arthur Kennerly, Lee O. Harris, Howard Campbell, William Perry, Ralph Corbin, Talbot Larmore, Elwood Waller, Benjamin Parsons, Kid Ritchie, Herman Townsend, Leon Skylar, Buck "Petta" Johnson, John Crockett, Steven W. Murray, Rufus Perry, William "Bill" Maddox, Sid Church, Sam Preston, Russell B. Dennis (Danny Russell), and J. Ralph Wimbrow. Patsy was also subpoenaed, which confirms that his daily reports had provided the attorney general and state's attorney with names of people whom they could subpoena for the grand jury investigation.[15]

Under the Lynching Tree

While Patsy was in Philadelphia, *Afro-American* photographer Paul Henderson risked his life yet again by returning to cover the first day of the investigation. Henderson provided the only surviving description of the courtroom where the grand jury proceedings took place:

> A quiet mysterious atmosphere prevails around the old court house where the boy was hanged. The courtroom is one of those old-fashioned places with "built-in" benches, extremely high, clear windows, and bare, dust-worn walls. In the corner is the clerk and, of course the jury box in the other. Twenty-three "gentlemen," all

white, filled the stand as they were selected. Those who were not bald-headed had long, ashy hair extending down their necks. The foreman and another gentleman, however, showed signs of having been freshly barbered. About 200 spectators filled the seats on the "white" side with but two AFRO reporters and four colored men on the "colored" side.[16]

Henderson then described the atmosphere of the Salisbury community and the system of silence that saturated the city:

> As the afternoon session neared, fellow shoremen greeted each other with "Hello, John: what ye doin' here?" "I's a courtin', Jim," was the reply. Across the street another would yell, "How'd yer make out, Joe?" His reply was: "I done all I know, but I don't know much." Presently a group of dusty-faced men and their wives walked up. The females showed as much wear as the males with wrinkled faces and wide-spaced yellow teeth. The men stopped outside to spurt amber while the women entered. One gent assured his spouse, "I'll be thar in a minute; go on in." A bow-legged motorcycle cop kept his eyes set on the "colored boys" [*Afro-American* reporters].[17]

As the officer watched Henderson, a white photographer prepared to take a picture of the grand jury. Henderson followed suit. He grabbed his Graflex press camera and took a few shots of the grand jury. No contemporaneous commentary I found other than Henderson's remarked on it being all white and all male. As Henderson took his photos, the jury members looked at one another, and he took an extra shot just in case. About that time, someone in the crowd said, "What's he going to do with it?" Henderson quickly moved on. Summoning his courage, he walked straight up to Chief Nicholas Holland with his camera. "Beg pardon, Chief," he asked. "How about a picture?" "No pictures," Holland responded before turning away. Henderson considered pressing him, but quickly realized that he was directly under the tree from which Williams had been hanged.[18]

Henderson soon headed into the courtroom one last time, as Judge Bailey had promised the press a copy of his charge to the jury. While Henderson was waiting, one of the jurists handed a piece of paper to the court clerk

Paul Samuel Henderson of the *Baltimore Afro-American*. Henderson was a photojournalist who covered the lynching of Matthew Williams in 1931 and the lynching of George Armwood in 1933. Courtesy of Maryland Center for History and Culture, RS2252 [1991.44.301].

and said, "Give that to the *Afro-American* reporter over there." Every eye in the courtroom turned and stared at Henderson—the "colored boy," as they called him—as he walked up to the bench to thank Judge Bailey, who stood up, took a bow, and left the courtroom.

The charge that Judge Joseph Bailey had delivered to the grand jury and handed to Henderson was endorsed by State's Attorney Levin C. Bailey and Attorney General Preston Lane. The *Salisbury Times* published a copy of the charge that the clerk had given to Henderson and other members of the press. It read:

[T]he four murders in the adjoining County is [sic] not for your investigation—they have already been investigated. . . . Nevertheless, Gentlemen of the Grand Jury, these two murders that occurred in

Maryland's Disgrace

this County on the 4th last December are both for your investigation. The first one is not as far as Matthew Williams is concerned
because he himself is dead. He himself was murdered that night,
but the first of these murders is for your investigation as to whether
or not anyone investigated Matthew Williams to the crime he committed. If so, who? The second one of these murders by the popu-
lace—by the mob—is for your investigation. First, as to who instigated the mob, who instigated the murder and in the second place
as to who were the actual perpetrators of that murder. . . . It is what
a community, it is what an individual, actually is at heart in mind
and soul that makes for worth.[19]

Although the judge's instructions were anything but clear, they seemed to
have suggested to the grand jury that its members tie their determinations
about the lynching of Matthew Williams to whether they thought he had
murdered D.J. Elliott.

I Saw Everything

The following day, the grand jury first dealt with other pending criminal
cases. After lunch, it turned its attention to the lynching investigation. Just
as the first witnesses were called, Attorney General Lane and Assistant Attorney General Anderson returned to Salisbury, carrying boxes of the stenographic records of statements they had taken from witnesses following the
lynching of Williams.[20] With Lane and Anderson in town, seventeen additional witnesses were summoned on the second day of the investigation;
four of them were individuals whom Patsy had identified or connected to
the lynching: Harry Waller, Chief Frederick A. Grier Jr., L. Thomas "Catfish" Webster, and Ralph "Fats" Wilson.[21]

Around 9 that morning, Patsy was summoned by Chief Holland to appear before the grand jury. Patsy, perplexed, told Chief Holland that he
must have made a mistake and confused him for Buck Johnson. Holland
responded, "Well, I was told to tell Johnson, a fighter, so you are a fighter
and you had better be up to the grand jury hearing if you do not want to be
locked up." Along with Patsy, Rufus Perry, Howard Campbell, Sid Church,

Lee Harris, Ben Parsons, Talbot Larmore, Kid Ritchie, and Wicomico County sheriff G. Murray Phillips, in addition to the rest of the identified inner circle, were all summoned to be at the courthouse at 2 p.m.[22]

Upon arriving at the courthouse, Patsy was shocked to see how people were acting. Ex-mayor Kennerly, Bird Sklar, Deputy Sheriff Donald Parks, and some other prominent men were sitting on the main staircase inside, waiting for their names to be called. They were passing the time by holding a mock trial under Kennerly's instruction. About fifty or sixty men were standing around listening as Kennerly instructed the witnesses how to answer questions before the grand jury, which was conducting its investigation in the adjacent room. A number of people became restless as the witnesses were called in one by one, the doctors and nurses first. By 5 p.m., when the interviews stopped, only eight people had been examined, and the rest of the witnesses were told to come back the next morning at 9.[23]

Patsy recorded the unethical, illegal, and unconstitutional practices that he noticed during the first day of the proceedings, describing the scene as a farce. While the grand jury was hearing testimony, State's Attorney Levin Bailey went in and out of the jury room five or six times as Judge Bailey was holding court. Around the third time Bailey left the jury room, he walked up to Kennerly and whispered something in the former mayor's ear. Bailey then headed back into the jury room and Kennerly said to the crowd on the stairway: "Oh, Oh, somebody has bended in that jury room already. I kind of thought someone would spill the beans."[24]

Directly after the proceedings, Patsy headed to Lankford's store. When he stepped foot through the door, all of the men were talking at once. Rufus Perry said, "G[od] d[amn] it, I saw everything and I am not going up and tell them the truth. . . . I know who the big fellow was who was the leader of it all, but I am not going to say who it was. Murray Phillips, the sheriff, knows who he is also. Let Phillips talk, he is sheriff and getting paid for it."[25] Bunk Perry, Rufus's brother, chimed in that he also knew about the lynching, but had been told by the men in the store to keep quiet.

At that moment, Talbot Larmore entered the store but, at first, did not speak about being in the jury room. Moments later, though, he said, "I was with the mob and they did not get anything from me in the jury room this noon." Suddenly, to everyone's surprise, he walked out, and there was a commotion (Patsy did not describe it further). Everyone was shocked and seemed not to know what to do. Kid Ritchie then attempted to speak, but the others quickly silenced him. The crowd broke up after 6 p.m., when Perry closed the store.

Around 7:30, Patsy went into the Arcade cigar store, where Rubin, the clerk, was in the middle of telling twenty-five or thirty men how Larmore had been questioned. Rubin seemed to be very angry about the way things were turning out. His bitterness increased after he observed that the jury was trying to pin the lynching on two men. For anyone to be indicted, he said, would cause an uproar in Salisbury. He thought that the whole town should tear down and burn up the jailhouse.

Now Talbot Larmore entered the store, and Rubin asked Larmore what he had been asked by the jury, so that the witnesses present could prepare for their own questioning the following day. Larmore said he had been asked where he was on the night of the lynching. He had answered, "To the fights." He told the jury that he had heard about the lynching and then went into town. Larmore was then asked, "Did you recognize anybody who was taking an active part in the lynching?" Larmore answered, "No." "Did you notice Murray Phillips?" Larmore responded, "Yes." "Did you notice the man who had a hold of the victim's other leg with Phillips?" Larmore answered, "No." Someone asked Larmore, "But you did later go back to the fights and talk to this man who had a hold of the victim's leg?" Larmore responded, "No." Recounting his testimony to the group at the cigar store, Larmore laughed and said, "They do not think I am crazy and will tell them who or what the names were."[26]

Rubin blurted, "See, what did I say? They are on the right track. Someone has spilled something, and boy, if they lock these two up, hell will break loose." To this, Larmore responded that he had been asked if Ellwood Guthrie was the leader and he had responded, "No." Everyone in the store muttered "Oh." Larmore then recalled he had been asked if he knew a Patsy Johnson. Larmore said, "Yes, but he is a stranger and was not in Salisbury at the time of the lynching." He was also asked, "Do you know Buck Johnson?" Larmore said he had answered, "Yes." "Do you know Ben Parsons?" Larmore answered again, "Yes," and was then excused. Larmore said that he had not been asked if he had known there was going to be a lynching, and that if he had been asked, he would have answered, "Yes, Dr. Dick came in town and said, 'Boys, the nigger is still alive in the hospital, you can go and get him now.'" Larmore told the men, "H[ell], I was with Chief Holland all the time but Lane of Baltimore did not think I was going to tell the truth." At that point, the mood in the store turned angry, and men began making threats, such as "There is going to be more lynching in Salisbury if anyone is indicted."

Patsy left the cigar store and talked to Elwood Waller. Patsy told Waller that he sure was giving Buck Johnson a break: "They are looking for him and I am not saying anything." Waller responded, "You bet that Buck is happy." Patsy said, "Was Buck in the mob?" and Waller replied, "Sure, he was with me, Larmore and the Chief of Police." Waller added that he hoped nothing would come of this, as he had killed a fellow in Pittsburgh two years before and that might be uncovered in the current investigation. Shortly thereafter, Waller and Patsy reentered the Arcade cigar store. As they walked in Rubin said, "D[amn] it all. We all know who the leaders are. I know them all myself but I will not tell the Baltimore police anything about it." The conversation continued into the night as the men expressed their anger and frustration about the situation.[27]

While Patsy and the local witnesses were preparing to appear before the grand jury, the Baltimore president of the International Labor Defense (ILD; the same organization representing the Scottsboro Boys and Euel Lee) wired Judge Bailey, demanding that African Americans be placed on the grand jury and calling him out for furthering the myth that the lynching was the result of outside communist agitators:

> Prominent citizens lynched Matthew Williams December 4th. Judges and the entire shore aristocracy gave repeated encouragement to the mobs. These very same citizens now sit on the grand jury to investigate the lynching. Your remarks to the grand jury about the International Labor Defense justify our belief that the shore mob will be well covered, with you investigating our organization instead. The International Labor Defense regards an investigating body without Negros and poor farmers on it as a lynch party, seeking to protect the murderers of Matthew Williams. We demand that a committee

of Negroes and white workers be permitted to investigate the grand jury to learn whether any of its members were part of the lynch mob leaders.[28]

The white-dominated power structure in the South had used racial imbalance in jury selection to perpetuate racist ideals since the founding of the United States. The ILD understood this perhaps better than any other organization. Its clients Euel Lee and the nine Scottsboro Boys all had to face all-white juries handpicked from the very community that had bred the racial animus. In its telegram, the ILD neglected to mention that Judge Joseph Bailey was also the uncle of State's Attorney Levin Bailey. When Governor Ritchie was later asked about the message, he declined to comment.

The End of Patsy's Investigation

At 8:00 the following morning, Patsy, as earlier arranged, went to the room of S.B., the other undercover Pinkerton agent in Salisbury, and met with Pinkerton assistant superintendent T.J.F. He told Patsy to get out of town as fast as possible. The court would reconvene at 9 a.m., and Patsy had to leave town before he was forced to take the stand. When Patsy said he could not leave until 2:45 that afternoon, his superior told him that the Pinkerton agency would soon reveal the secret investigation, that Patsy's name would be mentioned, and that he should get a taxi and get out of that section of the country quickly.

By the end of the day a total of seventy witnesses had been heard. The grand jury was almost finished with its investigation. Ultimately, the jurors interviewed more than eighty witnesses, including Chief Holland, the key witness of the day, who was questioned for an hour.[29] The record leaves unclear whether Patsy's cover had been blown or if the Pinkerton agency was pulling him out of town because the investigation was drawing to a close. Whatever the case, Patsy packed his gun and took a taxi to Delmar, Delaware. From there, he boarded another taxi to Dover, and from there he hitchhiked home, arriving in Philadelphia around 6:30 p.m.[30]

The grand jury continued its investigation, calling witnesses S. O. Furness of the Salisbury Police Department; Bill Davis of Fruitland, Maryland;

Bill Davis of Salisbury; William Parsons, who was African American; Marlon Hayman of Princess Anne; and Virgil Harmon of Salisbury. March 17 was a big day for Lane in that one of the ringleaders in the first circle of the conspiracy, Bill Davis, was scheduled to testify. Two of the eyewitnesses who could have identified the leaders of the mob—Williams's copatients in the hospital—were, according to the local papers, "unable to be reached." This was, in fact, true. Jacob Conquest could not be reached because he was dead, and Rufus Jernigan had gone missing without a trace.

By the end of the day the grand jury had added more witnesses to the list to be interviewed on the 18th, including Baltimore detectives Graydon L. Ware and Walter Martin and local physicians Arthur Brown and Creston Collins.

After nearly four days of investigation and hearing the testimony of more than 123 witnesses, the grand jury reached its decision on March 18, 1932. Just before the jury was discharged, Judge Bailey released a statement:

> After a thorough and complete investigation of all the evidence, direct and indirect presented to us by Attorney-General William Preston Lane, Jr. and Assistant Attorney-General G. C. A. Anderson in reference to communistic activities, we find that while such organizations do exist in other parts of the State there is no evidence to justify the belief that such an organization exists in Wicomico county. After a thoroughly energetic and complete investigation of all the evidence, direct and indirect, rumors and every lead indicated by the evidence given by more than 100 witnesses produced to us by Attorney-General, the Assistant Attorney-General, the State's Attorney for Wicomico county and members of this grand jury, we find that there is absolutely no evidence that can remotely connect anyone with the instigation or perpetration of the murder of Matthew Williams.[31]

Judge Bailey was playing into the tactic employed by the county's legal authorities since the lynching by addressing the unfounded claim that outside agitators, possibly communists, had caused African Americans, such as Williams, to rebel against the status quo and then had organized the lynching of Matthew Williams. As Bailey's statement suggests, there was no evidence of any such communist organization in Salisbury or anywhere else in Wicomico County. After the statement's release, ILD representatives renewed their attack on the credibility of the investigation by challenging Governor Ritchie to intervene.

The *Baltimore Afro-American* wasted no time in calling out the injustice that had been done in the grand jury investigation and its outcome. The grand jury's critics in the press cited glaring irregularities, in spite of every attempt by local officials to pass off this investigation as legitimate. As Paul Henderson argued, Salisbury was "very anxious to redeem itself in the eyes of the public," and it had used the grand jury to put the embarrassment of the lynching behind it. The *Baltimore Afro-American* pointed out that no one in Williams's family had testified before the grand jury—not either of two aunts, Addie Black and Minnie Handy of Babylon, New York; not an uncle, Matthew Handy, or Williams's only sister, Olivia Simmons of Philadelphia.[32]

In a meeting of the ILD in Baltimore, Louis Berger, a Communist Party lawyer and head of the Baltimore chapter of the ILD, announced two demands that would be presented to Governor Ritchie regarding the investigation. First, the ILD would call on Ritchie to investigate the mysterious death of Jacob Conquest and the disappearance of Rufus Jernigan, the two eyewitnesses who could have identified the mob's leader. Second, it demanded that the governor immediately call for the impaneling of a "new jury of white and Negro workers and poor farmers to investigate county officials" who, Berger argued, had been actively involved in the lynching.[33]

Berger and the *Afro-American* reporters were clearly onto something. However, their calls for Ritchie to intervene went unanswered. Little did they know that Patsy had already provided Ritchie and Lane with enough evidence to put away the leaders and all others involved in the lynching of Matthew Williams.

The second half of Patsy's investigation, from February to mid-March 1932, offers insight into the class-based structure of white supremacy and local power on Maryland's Eastern Shore. Class seemed the most prominent factor in determining at what level of the conspiracy the system of silence was broken. Buck "Petta" Johnson (not to be confused with Patsy) was among the first witnesses called to testify whom Patsy found in the second half of his investigation. The working-class people broke the system of silence in front of Patsy because he had infiltrated their group, posing as one of them, and apparently convincing them that he could be trusted, though it is possible that some became suspicious toward the end of his investigation. His recorded statements suggest how white supremacy and local power in Salisbury align with Smead's conspiracy structure. A local prizefighter, Buck Johnson was, like Elwood Waller, from Salisbury's working class. He served as the muscle and as a foot soldier when it came to the direct actions of violence. He admitted as much to Patsy, while also stating that the whole town were in on the lynching. Like Larmore, Buck Johnson continued to open up to Patsy, revealing others who were in on the crime, declaring that "if it was not for Bill Davis, the lynching would have been a 'flop.'" Unlike Captain Grier and others from the upper class of Salisbury society, Bill Davis was a working-class farmer who was known as a rough man in the community. Again, it was the white laborers who were among the first to break the silence and who were in the innermost circle of the conspiracy.[34]

Bill Perry was the second member of the all-male collective that Patsy infiltrated to break the silence and confess. Perry was a working-class laborer who was employed as a lineman at the local telephone company. Perry, like Larmore, broke the covenant of silence when he informed Patsy that Jack Townsend and Bill Davis had been the leaders of the lynch mob. Townsend, also a member of Salisbury's working class, worked as a moving picture operator.

During the second week of the secret Pinkerton investigation, Larmore recalled that Sheriff G. Murray Phillips had been one of the men who had pulled Williams up the tree in front of the courthouse. Phillips, an officer of the law, had joined Chief Nicholas Holland and Chief Frederick A. Grier Jr. in playing substantial roles in the lynching, namely, making arrangements at the hospital so that others could push Williams out the window and providing the hanging rope, respectively. Howard Campbell, a local business owner, continued to reveal details of the lynching to Patsy, exposing also what was at stake for him if it were to get out that he had failed to remain silent about the lynching.

Those who did keep their pledge of silence, on the other hand, were some of the most respected men in the county, including State's Attorney Levin Bailey and his uncle, Judge Joseph Bailey, who presided over the grand jury investigation (see table A.3).

By March 18, 1932, Patsy's investigation into the conspiracy behind the lynching of Matthew Williams ended. Nearly two weeks before, on March 5, the Philadelphia office of the Pinkerton National Detective Agency completed its final report, which included detailed profiles of those who were involved and or had knowledge of the lynching.[35] Apparently, the agency forwarded this report to the two Baltimore police sergeants who had conducted the original, public investigation, Walter Martin and Graydon Ware. They in turn issued a revised report in which they asserted that they "had subsequently recognized" certain key witnesses and, thanks to the Pinkerton investigation, were now able to identify.[36] After they returned to Salisbury and interviewed some witnesses they had talked to earlier, Martin and Ware obtained revised statements from Maryland State Police officer John J. Thompson, who had, they wrote, "subsequently recognized and identified" Fats Wilson as being in the crowd, and as a leader, as well as Russell Webster. According to Martin and Ware, Thompson recalled talking "to [Fats] Wilson at the time the body was cut down."[37]

Maryland State Police officer M. D. Brubaker also subsequently recognized and identified Ellwood Guthrie as the man whom he had heard bragging about sticking Williams in the back with a knife. Martin and Ware's revised report also provides additional insight into the cooperation of Dr. Arthur D. Brown, who also identified Fats Wilson among the lynch mob and fingered one Martin Clarke as the one who retrieved the rope from the firehouse. Martin and Ware identified other participants in the mob, including Lou Smith, John Martin Jr., John Martin Sr., Henry Yewell, Marion Brown, Conn Long, and former mayor Kennerly.[38] Other than the newspaper accounts, the only surviving evidence as to what went on during the grand jury proceedings consists of brief handwritten notations by Attorney General Lane, most of which are illegible. On March 16 and 17, however, Lane listed three "colored" witnesses—Maslin Frysinger Pinkett Sr., J. R. Waters, and John Williams—and one white witness, John Croswell, all of whom he noted as having identified members of the mob for the grand jury.[39]

In considering the grand jury investigation, it is essential to understand that hearsay was admissible. The purpose of this inquiry for the state's attorney was to obtain an indictment against accused persons, not a conviction. And in such proceedings, the rules against admitting hearsay evidence are less stringent. Patsy's reports were hearsay—evidence based on admissions of guilt that he heard and subsequently documented, rather than actual witnesses' statements as to their firsthand knowledge of the lynching. As grand jury proceedings are secret and no record is made of them, we do not know what Lane and Bailey's strategy was.[40]

Nonetheless, as documented in local and regional newspapers, the state's attorney called witnesses and presented testimony to the grand jury for review. Since this was not a criminal trial, there was no cross-examination of the witnesses. Based on the list of witnesses published in the newspapers, Lane likely used Patsy's reports in determining which witnesses to call and what to ask them. During the weeklong investigation, there were three strategic leaks concerning those subpoenaed. Lane's strategy for calling witnesses seems to have followed Smead's concentric circle theory, but in reverse. Instead of "expanding outward to lesser involvement," Lane was using Patsy's evidence to contract inward to greater involvement.

As of March 14, the day before Patsy's urgent departure, twenty of the forty-seven witnesses whose names had been published in the newspaper were individuals Patsy mentioned in his reports as having played some part in the lynching. The majority of those twenty witnesses could be placed in either the third, fourth, or fifth circles of the conspiracy. The following day, the 15th, with Patsy safely in Philadelphia, the attorney general moved in closer, naming four more witnesses, including Harry Waller, Chief Frederick A. Grier Jr., L. Thomas Webster, and Fats Wilson, all of whom would fit into the first or second circle of the conspiracy. By March 17, Lane had reached the end of Patsy's list. Saving the best for last, he called Bill Davis, the ringleader in the first circle of the conspiracy. (See table A.4 in the appendix.)

In the end, Patsy's investigation and the evidence it turned up were no match for the system of silence that ruled the Eastern Shore. There is no excuse for the failure of the grand jury investigation, given how well informed the prosecution was. Its failure further demonstrates the power of the system of silence in a community where everyone knew who did what, but no one was willing to reveal anything, even under the threat of perjury. Patsy had compiled significant intelligence and evidence, which Lane had used to compile the list of witnesses. Even so, prosecutors were not able to get an indictment.

[Part III]

[7]

A Blot on the Tapestry
of the Free State

The despot's heel is on thy shore,
Maryland!
His torch is at thy temple door,
Maryland!

"Maryland, My Maryland," by James Ryder Randall, 1939

In Maryland memory, lynching is a blot on the tapestry of the Free State, attributed to the "backward" culture of Maryland's Eastern Shore. Indeed, the racial climate of the Eastern Shore has a lot to do with the lynchings. The fact remains that two of our nation's foremost abolitionists, Harriet Tubman and Frederick Douglass, experienced some of the most gruesome dehumanization and violence while they were enslaved on the Eastern Shore. Tragically, this history of violence has been compared to modern-day violence in Maryland's most populated city, Baltimore.

In other words, in the limited analyses of lynchings in Maryland, scholars have devoted the overwhelming majority of their attention to comparing the Eastern Shore to Baltimore. This study focuses less on sectional division and conflict than on the victim, the investigation, and the politics of anti-Black racism. It thereby contributes to a range of work recovering how anti-Black violence has fostered the unification of white communities and has been exploited by officeholders for political capital. Overall, this book shows how Maryland complicates traditional histories of lynching in the American South by taking account of race relations in Salisbury, Maryland, and the extraordinary evidence that brings us closer than ever before to understanding what Black communities have always known.

By examining Black-white relations in Salisbury, we gain insight into what was peculiar to the local community and what reflected more traditional historical experience. Likewise, this research reveals themes that both diverged from and aligned with historians' traditional historical understanding of Black-white relations specifically as they relate to the nature of economic and political power.

When considering racial violence targeting Black communities, the primary historical cases that have been illuminated are the race massacres in Rosewood, Florida, and Tulsa, Oklahoma, during which Black communities were destroyed in order to choke their economic success. Sherrilyn Ifill, based on the sources available to her at the time, has suggested that Black witnesses maintained their silence following the lynching of Matthew Williams. I agree that Williams's lynching was a racial terror lynching; however, based on the evidence uncovered in my investigation, the homogenous characterization of all Black witnesses as refusing to give names is incorrect. Instead, Black leaders and laborers in the community spoke out against the lynching, testified before the grand jury, and cooperated with investigators. Unfortunately, their courage has been hidden in full view. The memories concerning the lynching that have survived in the Black neighborhoods of Salisbury and Maryland give too much credit to the power of white supremacy and racial terror.

As in other episodes of anti-Black violence, in Matthew Williams's case, the stereotype of the "Negro" rapist and murderer was cited to justify the lynching. The elderly man who worked alongside Williams in the mill and who confronted Dr. Arthur D. Brown drew on this tradition. With no evidence at all, he automatically reverted to what Ida B. Wells-Barnett called the "old threadbare lie," telling Brown that "he [Williams] had no business grabbing that white girl." If we stop there, it seems easy to interpret the local responses to alleged Black "criminality" and their justification for the lynching. I could have made the same mistakes that other historians have made and tried to understand the Williams lynching solely through the lens of similar traditions. Indeed, given the secrecy and silence that followed most lynchings, focusing on the public responses within the press makes the most sense, as the sport of lynching Black men had been an acceptable pastime in southern society that was densely covered and sensationalized in southern newspapers. Often what is missing is the local Black voice, such as that of Dr. Brown, who dared to quickly respond to the elderly laborer, "Suppose he did grab a white girl, he didn't have any business to sho[o]t him."[1]

Likewise, Brown was one of the central witnesses to cooperate with the investigation. Aside from a brief mention or a footnote, figures such as Arthur Brown, a radical product of the Great Migration, have mostly been lost. The newly discovered evidence in this study allows the testimony of both Black and white witnesses to be analyzed alongside the sensationalized coverage in the local and national newspapers that has for too long been the only record of lynchings—outside the folklore and legends that are often passed down from generation to generation.

Black Suffering as Political Capital

In looking at the legacy of racial violence in America today, we should consider Governor Albert Ritchie's approach to justice for what it teaches about how Black suffering has been used to build political capital. Ritchie presents another twentieth-century case of an innocent Black body being leveraged to fill ballot boxes. In condemning the lynching while insisting that ending such racial violence should be left to the states, Ritchie was wrestling with the early stages of a transformation that would eventually split the Democratic Party into factions for and against Black civil rights. Ritchie was caught between the identities of the urban liberal and the urban conservative Democrat. As he attempted to appeal to the former by challenging segregation and investigating the lynching of Williams, he ran up against the mores of the Eastern Shore, which had more in common socially and economically with the Deep South than with Baltimore. In the end, choosing to investigate the lynching offended the Democrats' southern wing and cost Ritchie his party's nomination for the presidency. As time would tell, more successful Democrats, such as Franklin D. Roosevelt, found a way to appeal to this racist element while gaining support from African American constituents.

The investigation into Matthew Williams's lynching foreshadowed the response of the Democratic Party's progressive wing to the anti-lynching campaign of the 1930s and '40s, a response that sowed the seeds of the Dixiecrat revolt just fifteen years later. The Great Depression provided a way for Ritchie and other Democratic leaders to hide behind relief programs proposed for all Americans. But states' rights and home rule were of no use when dealing with race lynching. The state was no match for Judge Lynch.

In spite of the outcome of the investigation, there is no excuse for Ritchie's silence following the return of no bill of indictment. Was he embarrassed at having failed to handle the crisis of lynching in the so-called Free State? If he had publicly admitted defeat in his attempt to bring the Williams murderers to justice, Ritchie would have acknowledged that states alone were not strong enough to stop Judge Lynch, and that recognition would have contradicted his criticism of federal anti-lynching legislation. And so it appears as though Ritchie's decision to pursue the investigation was dominated by political calculation. As it happened, however, the failed investigation became political ammunition for his Republican and Democratic opponents, who could have mocked Ritchie by asking how Maryland, considered a champion of states' rights, could have a state's attorney caught in the conspiracy to cover up a lynching.

They could have gone a step further and asked how Ritchie could lead the United States as president if he had failed to prevent a lynching in his own state or bring the perpetrators to justice. After all, as that state's executive, he should have been able to handle the prosecution and subsequent punishment of a small-town mob. Attacking lynching threatened to outrage a portion of Ritchie's constituency, and as a progressive Democratic presidential aspirant, Ritchie feared that exposing those behind the lynching of Williams would show the nation that Maryland was not as progressive as Ritchie and others had claimed; instead, Maryland was just as racist and backward as some of the worst parts of Theodore Bilbo's Mississippi. But failing to expose the perpetrators also implied a failure to uphold justice. The lynching and the investigation left Ritchie twisted in a political knot.

Nonetheless, pondering Ritchie's silence after the investigation is essential to understanding the silence concerning lynching on the part of his progressive Democratic opponent and the country's next president, FDR. Ritchie saw the lynching of Williams as an opportunity to show his strength as an executive leader and appeal to Republicans and racially progressive constituents, for he would need the support of both in the presidential campaign. When there was no indictment, Ritchie went into damage control and, in campaigning across the country, acted as if the lynching had never taken place. He focused his attention instead on the more politically appealing issue of solving the economic problems of the Great Depression.

Pursuing the investigation past the grand jury was not worth the political risk for Ritchie. As it turned out, he did not need justice for Williams in his national campaign. Ritchie became a favorite son in the 1932 presidential campaign, securing strong regional and party support from white voters in the state of Maryland. African American voters, on the other hand, showed their lack of trust in Democrats in the presidential election of 1932. No matter how progressive Roosevelt and Democrats like Ritchie might seem, Hoover carried between 66 and 75 percent of the Black vote in Maryland precincts.[2]

In the early 1930s, most Blacks still supported the Republican Party, not so much because they agreed with its platform or principles as because they could not see themselves aligned with the Democratic Party, whose leaders had historically suppressed their social and political rights throughout the South. Blacks thus distrusted Ritchie for the same reasons they distrusted Roosevelt in the 1932 election—because of his party label and his failure to combat lynching in Maryland, in addition to his inability to meet the needs of Black voters in Baltimore in the 1920s. Former Republican representative John R. Lynch of Mississippi summed up African Americans' distrust of Democrats in the 1930s: "The colored voters cannot help but feel that in voting the Democratic ticket in national elections they will be voting to give their indorsement and their approval to every wrong of which they are victims, every right of which they are deprived, and every injustice of which they suffer."[3]

Racial issues also became politically more significant on the Eastern Shore and in Baltimore in the early 1930s. Paradoxically, Ritchie had succeeded in alienating white Shoremen and Black Baltimoreans alike. Whereas in the 1926 gubernatorial race he received 41.67 percent of the Somerset County vote, in 1930 he received only 31.68 percent. Even his percentage of the vote in Baltimore City dropped slightly, from 64.59 percent to 63.3 percent. These changes may reflect increases in Republican turnout, suggesting opposition to Ritchie was bringing people who had been content to stay home in 1926 out to the polls in 1930. (See tables A.5 and A.6 in the appendix.)

What else could Ritchie have done to pursue justice after two investigations failed to produce indictments against Williams's murderers? For the most part, Ritchie was in dangerous territory. There he was, a Democrat, attempting to seek justice for an alleged "Negro" murderer who had been strung up by a lynch mob. To explore this question, it is useful to compare Ritchie with his Democratic counterpart in Florida, then look at Ritchie's handling of a similar case on the Eastern Shore that confronted him just two years later: the lynching of George Armwood.

Perhaps the most that Ritchie could have done would was to have followed the playbook of Florida governor Doyle E. Carlton, the only progressive Democrat whose response to lynching seemed to go a step further than Ritchie's. Carlton showed more public involvement and more vigorously pursued evidence and potential culprits in the double lynching of Charles and Richard Smoke in Blountstown in August 1931. Nonetheless, after the investigation, Carlton, like Ritchie, ran up against corrupt local officials and an unsurprising return of no bill of indictment against men known to have been responsible for the murders. Carlton was no match for Judge Lynch and the system of silence that permeated the South. Indeed, the Florida governor represented the less subtle progressive stance that equated Black lives with white lives—but only to the extent that when the Smokes had been lynched, he argued, so had all of Florida. Ritchie's responses, by contrast, were all centered on vague, politically motivated appeals for justice and an investigation.

The Case of George Armwood

In understanding Ritchie's investigation into the lynching of Williams, it is helpful to compare how Ritchie responded to the lynching of George Armwood two years later, on October 18, 1933. Whereas the governor made no remark following the failed prosecution of Williams's murderers, he was outspoken in his dismay regarding the lynching of George Armwood and the subsequent failure to obtain an indictment, even though state police officers made eyewitness statements identifying the culprits.

Armwood was lynched in Princess Anne after being accused of the attempted assault of seventy-one-year-old Mary Denston on October 16, 1933. Remembering how the Williams investigation had gone, Ritchie did not trust the local authorities, including Judge Robert F. Duer and the state's attorney, and ordered Attorney General Preston Lane to conduct a secret investigation into Armwood's lynching. Just as in the case of Williams, the investigation revealed the identity of mob members. In contrast to his reaction to Williams's lynching, Ritchie was extremely vocal concerning the performance of the local authorities, who had failed to keep Armwood safe. In the end, Judge Lynch still prevailed as the system of silence proved too strong; the grand jury chose not to indict anyone, claiming that witnesses could not identify anyone in the mob.

This is where Ritchie departed from his 1932 precedent. This time, he disregarded the grand jury, displaced State's Attorney John Robins, and took over the investigation. Ritchie ordered the National Guard to arrest the four men whom the investigation had identified as leaders of the lynch mob. The next day in Somerset County, four men accused of Armwood's lynching appeared in court for a habeas corpus hearing. Ultimately, Judge Lynch would again prevail. One thousand white supporters cheered as the jury returned a verdict of not guilty and the judge ordered the release of the accused and dismissed the case permanently.[4]

How the Unknown Becomes Known: The Nuance of Silence

With access to newly discovered evidence, this study complicates the existing narrative and provides nuance to the overall story. Nonetheless, as

Patsy Johnson's investigation and Dr. Arthur D. Brown's statements revealed, the system of silence in Maryland could be broken. This took place when white and Black citizens broke their nonverbal contract by exposing the criminal conspiracy and the identities of the leaders of Salisbury's white establishment who had supported the lynching and enforced it through economic and social control.

Indeed, all of those revealed to have known about or participated in the lynching were complicit. The most shameful of these were officers of the law, such as Chief Holland, Sheriff Parks, and Captain Grier—either because they agreed with the underlying premise of lynching in general or because they did not do what was needed to stop the lynching. The complicity of law enforcement not only affected Black people but also squelched white dissent. Whites in Salisbury came to understand that they would pay a price for supporting any Black person who tried to gain equality with white people.

The ultimate truth is that more than one thousand white citizens watched as this young Black man was kidnapped and pushed through a hospital window, dragged to the courthouse lawn, lynched—not once but twice—and then set ablaze. In 1931, Salisbury's total population consisted of some 10,000 citizens, 6,000 of whom were white and 4,000 of whom were Black. That means that a sixth of the white citizens of Salisbury witnessed the lynching of Williams. These figures leave out others who were in town for the Wicomico County High School football game and those attending the fights at the Zion Road Arena, so possibly even more whites observed or heard firsthand accounts of the lynching.[5]

Taking these numbers into consideration, the notion that historians Morton Sosna and David Chappell put forth, that whites were victimized by radical violence as much as Blacks, is hard to credit. Nonetheless this particular school of thought provides a window into understanding that there is a nuance of silence.[6] When it comes to the attitudes of white southern communities following an episode of racial lynching, the silence that saturated these communities was not absolute or monolithic. Indeed, all whites may have been racist, but not necessarily to the same degree. In the case of Matthew Williams, there were the racists who were willing to hang and burn this man to death, the racists who were willing to be present and did not muster the courage to stop it, and the racists who were not even concerned enough to be aware of what was happening.

In considering the confessions that Patsy Johnson documented and the willing confessions he recorded of those involved in the lynching, it is important to remember Johnson's status as an outsider. In spite of his whiteness, he was still a stranger in town, yet those involved in the lynching broke their silence—not in a court of law, but to Johnson, whose whiteness, class, and virtual friendship persuaded them to break the virtual contract of white brotherhood—maintaining the silence.

[8]

Confronting the Legacy
of Anti-Black Violence
in the Age of Fracture

*"The past both sets the stage for the present [and] it exists
in the present in new form."*

Dread Scott (2020)

On Monday, April 27, 2015, I was, like many in Baltimore, glued to the TV for hours, watching the violence that erupted following the home-going service for Freddie Gray, then the latest fatality at the hands of police. What happened to Gray puts one in mind of something that Maryland has not witnessed since the lynchings of Matthew Williams. On April 12, 2015, eighty-eight years after Williams's lynching, Freddie Gray was arrested and thrown into the back of a police van. Seven days later, he was pronounced dead after his spine had been 80 percent severed. Those who undertook this violent act were not nameless vigilantes, but rather public servants sworn to protect and serve—Baltimore City Police officers.[1]

While writing this book, I continually reminded myself that Matthew Williams represented one of the several thousand victims of racial terror lynchings in US history. In light of the murder of unarmed Black men and women by law enforcement, it is essential to ask what the story of Matthew

Williams's lynching tells us about what some have described as "modern-day lynchings," given the fact that police in their official capacity shot unarmed Black people in the nineteenth and twentieth centuries, as well. While there are many differences in geography and nature between traditional and "modern-day" lynchings, there are also several similarities, specifically related to the social, economic, and political vulnerabilities of African American communities, such as that in Salisbury, Maryland. I find three salient features that have remained consistent between historical and modern-day lynchings:

1. Both leverage the state's power through the participation of law enforcement in the actual lynching and then the inaction or complicity of prosecutors, judges, and jurors.
2. Both use spectacle as a way to satisfy white voyeurs and terrify Black citizens.
3. Both historical and modern-day lynchings are motivated by a desire to exert social control and maintain white supremacy.

In 2019, I took a Greyhound bus to Salisbury to pay my respects to Williams and his family. The long ride gave me a chance to prepare for the heaviness of the trip. Before arriving, I had arranged to meet with local historian and author Linda Duyer, who would become a dear friend until her passing. A geographer by training, Duyer gave me a historical driving tour through what remained of the Black community of Salisbury. She showed me the locations of the scenes I describe in the foregoing pages. The most sacred moment was at Potters Field Cemetery, where Williams's remains are buried with those of his ancestors and the former enslaved residents of Poplar Hill plantation. As I stood on this hallowed ground, images of Williams's burned and mutilated flesh as described in the report of his autopsy filled my mind. After paying my respects, I went to the courthouse lawn, the scene of the spectacle's climax, when Williams's lifeless body hung suspended in the air. I imagined the size of the crowd that filled the streets and how local police officers directed traffic, thinking that routine action "the most humane thing to do."[2] The widespread cooperation of law enforcement, members of the grand jury, and state officials in ensuring the impunity of Williams's murderers is consistent with the prevailing legacies of lynching that have been so visible in what one historian has called the "age of fracture."[3]

This complicity is hauntingly relevant to the recent murders of Ahmaud Arbery (2020), George Floyd (2020), Breonna Taylor (2020), and Rayshard Brooks (2020), all of whom were unarmed when they were killed by police, as a result of our nation's failure to address systemic anti-Black racism. Indeed, such killings are normal in the sense of "not unheard of," just as lynching was normal in the South in the 1930s; and these four souls are casualties of our democracy, represented as it is by local, state, and national officials whose silence has allowed and made room for the ongoing state-sanctioned legal and extralegal murder of Black men and women.

In confronting the legacy of lynching, we must consider the historical utility of lynching. Indeed, as Williams's case shows, lynching was an act of terror, employed by white people to stoke fear, maintain social control, and police Black bodies. Lynching is rooted in dehumanization. Like slavery, it was a tool designed to maintain the racial hierarchy. In examining lynching and its ramifications, it is essential to consider its normalization, which is one of the threads that connects the Salisbury lynching tree to the back of a Baltimore paddy wagon. Certainly by the time of Williams's lynching, coverage of spectacle lynching in the media was nothing new.

Blow-by-blow accounts of spectacle lynchings have filled millions of newspaper pages in the United States. Today, with the advent of social media, you don't have to wait for the Sunday paper; you can watch footage of modern-day lynchings; some even play out live for the world to see. Just ask the families of Eric Garner and Philando Castile.

These senseless, seemingly relentless killings and the failure of the American justice system to hold the murderers accountable for their acts of violence signify to the world how little the United States values the Black body. From the acquittal of George Zimmerman for the killing of Trayvon Martin to the insignificant punishment handed out to officer Amber Guyger, who was sentenced to only ten years for the murder of Botham Jean, these unrelenting acts of systemic racial violence have traumatically shaped the identity of Black citizens and communities in the United States.

My goal for this book from the outset was to salvage the humanity of the victims that has often been lost in traditional studies of lynching. I was not necessarily concerned with reconciliation; instead, I was focused on justice. This book puts the evidence out in the open for the city of Salisbury, the Eastern Shore, and the state of Maryland to wrestle with. The evidence reveals what people of color have known all along: local, state, and government officials "colluded in the commission of these crimes and conspired to conceal the identities of the parties involved."[4] As with lynchings in many other states, no one was ever tried, convicted, or otherwise brought to justice in Maryland for participating in these racially motivated mob actions, and no victim's family or community ever received a formal apology or compensation for their loss.

Thanks to the work of Nicholas M. Creary, Will Schwarz, and state assembly delegate Joseline Peña-Melnyk, Maryland cities may be a little closer to confronting the legacy of lynching. House Bill 307 was signed by Governor Larry Hogan on Thursday, March 18, 2019, thereby establishing the Maryland Lynching Truth and Reconciliation Commission (MLTRC). MLTRC is the nation's first statewide truth-and-reconciliation-style commission dedicated to investigating racial terror lynchings and addressing their continuing legacy.

The act's preamble states that at least forty African Americans were lynched in Maryland between 1854 and 1933, "by white mobs acting with impunity."[5] While the law is a groundbreaking first step in confronting the legacy of racial terror lynching in the Free State, in only acknowledging these crimes against humanity, the state runs the risk of suggesting that catharsis is akin to retributive justice.

Systemic Anti-Blackness and Historical Trauma: The Case of Salisbury

As we reflect on lynching's legacy and look to confronting persistent anti-Black violence, we have to examine the systemic anti-Blackness that can be traced back to the lynching of Matthew Williams, a message crime targeted not only at an individual but at the Black community of Salisbury as well.

In laying out the history of Georgetown in chapter 2, I sought to give life to the community in which Williams was born; however, we have to also understand how the lynching impacted Black businesses and economic welfare, Black wealth, and the Black community in Salisbury and the Eastern Shore. The best way to examine such systemic issues is through the lens of historical trauma; failing to account for this trauma, I argue, renders social transformation a futile hope.

To briefly trace the generational impact of anti-Black violence in Salisbury and on Maryland's Eastern Shore from the 1930s to the twenty-first century, I employ Michelle Sotero's "conceptual model of historical trauma" and concept of "mass trauma experience." In doing so, we have to understand the tactics of domination and control—subjugation. For any minority not considered white, specifically African Americans, subjugation is the overarching tactic.[6] The tools or subtactics of subjugation include "military force, bio-warfare, national policies of genocide, ethnic cleansing, incarceration, enslavement, [and] laws that prohibit freedom of movement, economic development, and cultural expression."[7] The ultimate outcome of subjugation is deep-rooted trauma to the subjugated population's psyche, physiology, and culture. Because of subjugation and its subtactics, past traumas reverberate and compound in multiple generations of individuals, families, communities, and society. To seek solutions for healing, several theories have emerged to understand, for example, trauma experienced by descendants of slaves in the United States. These theories include post-traumatic stress disorder (PTSD), post-traumatic slave syndrome, race-based trauma, root shock, epigenetics, and historical trauma.[8]

Sotero lays out a unique set of requirements for subjugation to succeed through "mass trauma experience," including: "(1) overwhelming physical and psychological violence, (2) segregation and/or displacement, (3) economic deprivation, and (4) cultural dispossession."[9] Historical trauma occurs when an experience passes to subsequent generations that follow the primary generation without connection to the original trauma. The legitimacy of the subjugation may be rescinded over time, but the universal experience of domination persists in the form of significant physical and psychological trauma for the affected population. The legacy of the trauma remains in the forms of anti-Black racism, discrimination, and social and economic disadvantage.

In the following pages, I explore the manifestations of three forms of subjugation on Maryland's Salisbury and on the Eastern Shore.

The Eastern Shore's Overwhelming Physical and Psychological Violence

After reading the previous chapters, the reader should find Sotero's first requirement, overwhelming physical and psychological violence, clearly evident in Salisbury and Wicomico County, from the 1898 lynching of Garfield King to the lynching of Williams in 1931 and George Armwood in 1933. Anti-Black violence in Maryland was not confined to the Eastern Shore, nor did it cease after the Armwood lynching, even though historians have declared 1933 as marking the end of lynching in Maryland. In fact, Northeastern University's Civil Rights and Restorative Justice Project has identified an additional 37 named, 36 potential, and 12 unknown victims of racially motivated homicides in Maryland between 1930 and 1956.[10]

Physical and psychological violence have persisted on the Eastern Shore to the present day. In 1932, just four weeks following the lynching of Matthew Williams, an "anti-negro mob" descended on the small town of Ridgely, Maryland, fifty miles from Salisbury. A curfew was established for the town's Black people after members of the mob attempted to drive "colored people out of stores and off the streets."[11] In September 1934, almost one year following the lynching of George Armwood, future civil rights activist and chief lobbyist of the NAACP, Clarence M. Mitchell Jr. covered a story in the *Baltimore Afro-American* highlighting the continued assault on Black citizens of Princess Anne after reports circulated of a mob of white hoodlums attempting to drive "the entire black population" from town. Upon following up on several leads, Mitchell ran into a wall of silence as local Black leaders insisted that all was well in the community. The fear evident in this claim suggests the extent of "psychological violence." It was later revealed by eyewitnesses that the mob had, in fact, descended on the Black community and bludgeoned one Roy Shields in the presence of the local sheriff, Luther Daughtry, who would eventually rescue Shields from the hands of the mob. Alongside Sheriff Daughtry was Judge Robert Duer, the same individual who had given a speech a year earlier to a white mob before they murdered and mutilated George Armwood.[12]

During the latter half of the 1930s, mob violence continued to occur throughout the state of Maryland, but the next known instance of white domestic terror took place in 1940 in Snow Hill in Worcester County, where members of the Black community had been attacked by a white mob just nine years before. This time a mob of forty men descended on the Worcester County jail preparing to lynch two African American women. They dragged thirty-one-year-old Martha Blake and her fourteen-year-old daughter, Lillian, out of the jail, where they were being held for questioning in regard to the recent murder of a local white farmer, Harvey Pilchard, in Stockton, Maryland.[13] As the mob of white hoodlums stormed the jail with nooses in hand, Blake was crying while her daughter was praying in the corner of the cell. On gaining entry to the cell, the attackers inside the jail pushed the women through a broken window, delivering them to the white mob of over one thousand men, who were said to have been dancing around them, "dangling a rope in their faces and shouting, 'How would you like to have this around your neck?' "[14]

Meanwhile local law enforcement stood watching as the two women were quickly shoved into a car by leaders of the mob. With a caravan of more than two hundred cars following them, the leaders headed to Stockton with their two captives in search of Martha's husband, who had allegedly murdered Pilchard. After getting word of the incident, the governor ordered state officers, including those on the scene, to "protect the women at all costs."[15] Fearing that an outbreak of racial violence would spread throughout the Eastern Shore, the governor summoned a team of twenty-five state officers to Cambridge, Easton, and Salisbury and ordered them to uphold the law. Shortly thereafter, a team of four state officers opened fire on the mob, rescued the two women from its hands, and drove them out of town to Baltimore.[16]

Meanwhile, on the other side of the Shore, African Americans in Baltimore led protests against police brutality in that city—against law enforcement tactics that had been overshadowed by the sectional divisions between the Eastern Shore and Baltimore and the white politics of paternalism and anti-Black racism practiced in Annapolis and Baltimore. This was a politics seen in other cities that sought to distance themselves from the "backward" Democratic apparatus of the Deep South where the uncivilized practices of racial terror lynching continued to be the norm.

By the 1950s, as the Ku Klux Klan emerged in its third wave, Maryland was not spared from the resurgence of the "Invisible Empire." Klan activity was revealed in the Free State in January 1950 when "Klan rosters and other secrets" were discovered by the "Non-Sectarian Anti-Nazi League" and turned over to the Internal Revenue Service, which would soon uncover widespread tax evasion.[17] Meanwhile, Maryland did not ratify the Fourteenth Amendment to the US Constitution, guaranteeing due process of law and equal protection of the laws to all Americans, until 1959.[18]

In the 1960s, as Peter Levy and C. Fraser Smith show, the Eastern Shore once more drew national attention for racial violence when riots occurred in Cambridge in 1963 and again in 1967.[19] As Rhonda Y. Williams notes, in 1963 the "Black Power" movement arrived on the Eastern Shore in effect, if not in name, as Black women "mobilized outside" yet in the "context of" Black Power radicals to bring most of the changes those radicals sought to Maryland.[20] In the spirit of Harriet Tubman, Gloria Richardson, leader of the Cambridge Nonviolent Action Committee (CNAC), confronted the anti-Black violence of the Eastern Shore head on, denouncing the "inheritors of lynch mob terror" represented in both local police and white citizens of the Eastern Shore.

On June 11, 1963, following a sit-in demonstration at a local restaurant led by Richardson's CNAC, a group of white patrons descended on the students and assaulted them. A riot ensued. On June 12, the *Salisbury Times* ran the story on its front page above the fold with the headline "Two Wounded in Cambridge Race Riot, Fires Flare." The article was positioned just beneath Kennedy's call for the "END OF RACIAL CRISIS" and above the heart-wrenching news of the slaying of thirty-seven-year-old civil rights leader Medgar Evers in Mississippi. The Magnolia State represented everything that progressive white politicians in Maryland sought to distance themselves from. The aging members of the white mob who had murdered and mutilated Matthew Williams, and who had gone on to become business owners and lead law enforcement agencies, now enjoyed the spoils of the progressive politics that masked the specter of racial terror lynching in their own state while claiming that race-motivated murder had been virtually monopolized by the Magnolia State.[21]

Segregation and Displacement

Regarding segregation, Salisbury was no different than any other city below the Mason-Dixon Line. Segregation was well established by the 1930s and continues today. Following the Civil War, whites in Wicomico County looked to segregation to provide spatial and social separation from the Black community and to reinforce the racial hierarchy. This involved setting aside four neighborhoods for Black residents, including Cuba (1909), Georgetown, Jersey, and California, all of which were built on "undesirable" land near the Wicomico River and its affluents.[22]

Indeed, Wicomico County was in line with existing national trends. However, a pattern emerged in Cuba and Georgetown following the Great Depression that accelerated in direct correlation with episodes of racial violence, including the near lynching of Richard Ford and the lynching of Matthew Williams. Williams had substantial connections to both of these communities, which together formed the center of the Black community's economic power in Salisbury.

For example, before State Route 13 was constructed in the 1930s, there were two Black neighborhoods designated with the names Cuba and Georgetown. According to the records of many local historians, police considered Cuba and Georgetown crime-ridden, and whites found them unattractive to the eye; one might infer from these descriptions that these were the ghettos of that era. What little remains of these neighborhoods is now considered part of the Church Street area.

The Case of Cuba and Georgetown: Displacement and Economic Deprivation

Under the guise of a response to "white socioeconomic advancement and population increase," there was a direct assault and destruction on the

Black communities of Cuba and Georgetown. In the 1930s, Salisbury acquired a reputation for harboring white mobs that ran through Black neighborhoods, wreaking destruction. Like the African American communities of Tulsa, Oklahoma, and Rosewood, Florida, the Black communities of Cuba and Georgetown were also attacked, in their cases in the form of multiple incidents of targeted, systemic anti-Black violence, which served the same purpose of stoking fear and regaining control of Black bodies.

It was at this time, in 1930, that the first upgrades to Route 13 were made in the Salisbury-Fruitland area and the area north of downtown Salisbury along Division Street, was traversed by a bypass near the New York, Philadelphia, and Norfolk Railroad.[23] Local historian Richard Waller Cooper has documented this assault on Salisbury's Black neighborhood. In describing the realignment of Route 13 in the 1930s, Cooper writes of the two communities: "There was a section of the town that could be generally described as being between old East Church Street and the former Lake Humphreys and adjacent to the railroad that had the local name Georgetown—and sometimes Cuba. It had the distinction of being in today's language a 'depressed area'; back in the 1930's it was a poverty-stricken, dirty eyesore—a slum."[24] Cooper wishes the reader to believe that Georgetown and Cuba just happened to be in the way of advancement in the 1930s. In describing the displacement with his problematic characterization of the Black neighborhoods, though, Cooper practically admits that the need for a new highway was nothing more than an excuse to "clear out the residue of this problem area," the Black communities of Cuba and Georgetown, areas he describes as being well known to the local police department as crime infested. This was the same police department shown to have been complicit in the lynching of Matthew Williams in 1931.

By 1939, the first phase of the Route 13 realignment was complete.[25] As the bypass took the portion of the community between Main Street and College Avenue, Bob Toulson's Tailor Shop was destroyed, along with the St. Paul AME Zion Church on Church Street and several homes owned or rented by Black residents on Commerce, Cathell, and Water streets. The second phase of Georgetown and Cuba's slow but sure destruction occurred in the 1950s when Route 50 was completed through Salisbury. Cooper describes the intentions behind laying out the path this highway would take through town:

Helpful as the effort was, it still did not do a too-thorough job; there were still the remnants of 'Cuba' and 'Georgetown,' as these little enclaves were known—especially by the police department who were often called there to help keep peace. The nearness of the new highway had established a high value on nearby property. . . . It just so happened that the through-town route, considered for U.S. Route 50, would just about clear out the residue of this problem area; again another plan for a national highway would serve a dual purpose, and Salisbury would once again come out "smelling like a rose."[26]

By the end of the 1950s, the damage had been done, and nearly all the residents were forced out of the community that they and their ancestors had helped build. Some joined the Great Migration that left the Free State and headed northward, but most had to relocate to the West Side and Jersey Heights. White citizens of the Salisbury Housing Association did not waste time in starting to plan for an additional bypass, this one targeting Jersey Heights. That project would commence in the 1970s.[27]

Having to start anew, the resilient former citizens of the Cuba and Georgetown community and their relatives and descendants made a way out of no way and, by the late 1990s, had formed two communities in Jersey Heights, a growing middle-class neighborhood, and the low-income neighborhood of the West Side. Yet again, the African American community would be targeted.

This time, the West Side was used as a tool to promote resegregation by establishing low-income public housing (Booth Street Projects) solely in the Black community, housing that would not be managed or maintained properly, causing health risks as piles of trash contributed to crumbling sewer lines, automobile runoff, and fast-food waste. The Booth Street Projects would remain until they were finally demolished in 2016.

When the city proposed widening Route 50 to alleviate the traffic congestion anticipated from the development of Ocean City Resort, the American Civil Liberties Union was among the first to sound the alarm. The ACLU admonished the federal government not to fund the planned bypass, arguing that it "targeted a Wicomico County area (Jersey Heights) with a Black population exceeding 90 percent."[28] This time the Black community of Salisbury did not take the assault quietly. Under the leadership of acclaimed civil rights attorney Sherrilyn Ifill, then with the Public Justice Center, and Deborah A. Jeon of the ACLU, the Jersey Heights Neighborhood Association (JHNA) brought seven suits against the state and federal highway officials challenging the construction of the bypass next to their residential area.[29] After the JHNA secured legal representation by the ACLU and the Public Justice Center, its campaign to save the neighborhood received national attention. The memory of the Eastern Shore's racist past was present in the minds of local leaders. Charles Whittington alluded to it following an early dismissal of the association's federal lawsuit: "Throughout Maryland's history, government officials have gotten away with shutting up the Shore's black community."[30] A few years earlier Jersey Heights resident Ann Church revealed the historical trauma caused by having to relive the nightmare of displacement again after her family had been uprooted by the previous bypass construction: "Just as I was displaced by Route 13 as a 9-year old, my 9-year old daughter will see her all-black neighborhood singled out as a highway construction site."[31]

The twofold destruction of Georgetown was not so much about physical displacement as about dismantling Black wealth and social and economic power. Unlike Cuba, which was seen as a slum, Georgetown included a Black business district and a developed community. As highlighted in chapter 2, Georgetown boasted historic Black churches, Black businesses, and Black-owned homes. This community represented the most prominent Black business concentration in Wicomico County, if not throughout the lower Eastern Shore. Yet, like Greenwood in Tulsa, Oklahoma, Georgetown was all but erased after a highway was built through it.[32] When members of the Black community of Salisbury pass the intersection of Lake and West Main streets, they are haunted by the memory of the bodies in the Black cemetery there, exhumed to make room for urban development. Indeed, there is no vestige of this community—only parking lots and the offices of Perdue Farms. Today, only one of the estimated nineteen original structures, including residences, business, and churches, remains from the original neighborhoods of Cuba and Georgetown: the Chipman Cultural Center, which was John Wesley Methodist Episcopal Church, Matthew Williams's home church.

Today, Salisbury grassroots activists such as Amber Green of Fenix Youth Project, Inc., and James Yamakawa of the Wicomico Truth and Reconciliation Initiative bear witness to the prevailing subjugation that is the legacy of anti-Black violence and psychological violence, displacement, and economic deprivation, tangible impacts of the lynching of Williams in 1931. For the past four years, Green and Yamakawa have dedicated a large portion of their lives to anti-racist activism in Salisbury. Their journey began in the fall of 2016 when they held their first joint Black Lives Matter protest following the murder of Philando Castile. They first learned of Williams and his story after walking past a sign honoring Confederate general John Henry Winder.[33]

A Sign of the Times

The racial demographics provide background for understanding race relations in Salisbury and across Maryland. According to the most recent American Community Survey, African Americans make up 29 percent of the state's population, and whites make up 56 percent, whereas in Salisbury, Blacks make up 39 percent of the population, and whites 56 percent.[34]

In describing the current racial climate in Salisbury, Yamakawa pointed to the recent protest against a petition calling for the removal of the marker commemorating southern war hero Winder, located within fifty feet of where Williams was lynched.[35] Winder was a Confederate general who was only indirectly affiliated with Salisbury. He was born in Nanticoke, Maryland, which during the early nineteenth century was in Somerset County. President Jefferson Davis appointed Winder as assistant inspector general of the camps of instruction (prisoner of war camps), and as such was responsible for overseeing the death, starvation, and torture of thousands of Union soldiers in the infamous Andersonville prison. This was the prison described by historian Robert Scott Davis as "the world's first modern-day concentration camp." More than 30 percent of the Black Union soldiers imprisoned there would die before being released.[36]

Carrying Confederate flags that waved in the wind, the protesters marched back and forth on the sidewalk next to the marker, trampling the ground where Williams's body was dragged nearly ninety years earlier.

David Lee, a Salisbury resident who claimed descent from Robert E. Lee, argued:

> The Mayor, of course, has put a big effort into removing the only monument that I know that we have down here. If they had any other monument, they could leave it up, why don't they put another one up, why don't they put another one up, why does everything have to be down, whether it's down south up north, they want to tear everything down. I have to tell you my name is Lee, and I am a first cousin of Robert E. Lee his self. You know, I don't think my ancestor was such a racist or anything like that, there is people that ought to learn and read about Robert E. Lee, he was the first one after the civil war that went in there to a church when they were trying to say to Black people couldn't pray and went in there and prayed with them in the church.[37]

Lee's comments were echoed by citizens and government officials alike in the Salisbury community; during a public hearing on the sign's proposed removal, one concerned citizen said: "Again, I honestly could care less about the sign, I am not here as some kind of Nazi White supremacist, I am just here on the side of reality. Where do we draw the line, if everything is offensive, everything has to come down? Maryland was a Confederate state, do we hit the reset button and start over." After being told that he was incorrect and that Maryland was not a Confederate state, he laughed, saying, "Yeah, it was, read a little bit."[38]

On September 5, 2017, John Canon, the Wicomico County Council president, remarked:

> I have mixed emotions about the marker; I feel, as was suggested earlier, that there is some sense of hysteria across the county about this. I don't think we are in a racist society, as you are hearing in the news. Removing the marker can, I think, create racial divisiveness. I understand; he was a bad general; ironically, he probably killed more white soldiers than Black soldiers. The one thing I would like to see this group do. They suggest that they were going to put markers up or plaques up for the lynching that occurred. I would much

rather encourage this group to put up a marker for Frederick Douglass.[39]

In listening to the words of the above individuals, it's no wonder that Black citizens in the still-segregated city of Salisbury, to this day, are reluctant to go downtown, haunted as it is by the legacy of lynching, a haunting renewed by citizens who make statements such as those quoted above. These views represent some of the many ways the legacy of lynching is visible and audible within the Salisbury community. In June 2020, following the lynching in May of George Floyd, a Black man, at the hands of Minneapolis police, and four years after Green, Yamakawa, and a number of their close friends started the grassroots movement to have the sign removed, it was taken down.[40]

The legacy of lynching is also visible within institutions of higher learning in the lower Eastern Shore. In October 2019, Salisbury University students reacted to racist messages written on a building wall. "I'm not completely surprised, but it is really sad to hear about these things continuing to happen. I know I went through my fair share of racist discrimination type of things that go on here. My first year, I had someone call me the n-word," remarked Salisbury University senior Julia Kwedi.[41]

Presenting further evidence of lynching's legacy in Salisbury today is Mayor Jake Day, who argued, "If you grow up in certain parts of our city or potentially if you are of a certain race, or a certain economic class, you are going to be limited in your potential because people are going to maybe, judge you, see you a certain way, or you just don't have access to the same resources within striking distance as you do if you are born somewhere else . . . that's wrong."[42] This rhetoric, these haunting feelings, and the continued economic, educational, and legal injustice represent the lingering impact of Judge Lynch not only in Salisbury but throughout the United States.

On Saturday, September 15, 2018, three years after the death of Freddie Gray, and two years after the acquittal of the officers involved in his case, Anton Black, a nineteen-year-old African American man—just three years younger than Matthew Williams when he died—became the latest victim of anti-Black violence in the Free State, at the hands of police. His death in the small Eastern Shore town of Greensboro was overshadowed by the media attention that saturated Baltimore following the riots that ensued after the Freddie Gray verdict was rendered, reawakening sectional divisions within the state.[43] The African American members of this community were familiar with the spirit of anti-Black violence in Caroline County, a little over fifty miles from Salisbury and less than six miles from Ridgely, Maryland, where eighty-six years before, a white mob descended on the African American community.

A white couple called 911 to report what seemed to be a fight between two young Black men, one of whom was five-foot-nine, 159-pound Anton Black. According to one of the officers who arrived on the scene, Black was "roughhousing" with the other, younger boy. Later, Black's mother revealed that the young boy was Black's friend, who was in no danger.

The other police officer was Thomas Webster IV. His arrival on the scene underscores the irony of Dread Scott's suggestion. Officer Webster had recently been hired onto the force after having been suspended from the police department in neighboring Dover, Delaware, following a 2016 legal settlement involving an African American man, Lateef Dickerson, who had been in his custody.[44] Following his acquittal for felony assault by an all-white Delaware jury, Webster received a $230,000 settlement from the city of Dover. The jury that found Webster not guilty had seen dashcam footage showing him kicking the unarmed Dickerson in the head, knocking him unconscious, and dislocating his jaw. Beaten, bruised, and traumatized, Dickerson nevertheless escaped the incident with his life. Black, on the other hand, would not make it out of his interaction with Webster alive.

After arriving on the scene, Webster told the nineteen-year-old Black to place his hands behind his back. Black soon took off running, and Webster began chasing him and could be heard over the radio acknowledging that Black had suffered from mental health issues. The chase soon led to Black's home, where the young man would take his last breath as his mother watched in confusion as Webster and a group of other white officers descended upon the high schooler. To these four men seeking to restrain him, Black must have somehow evoked the stereotypical anti-Black caricature of the violent superhuman Black "brute." Trevor Hewick, the private investigator hired to work on the case, likened the night of Black's death to the scene of a "lynch mob."[45] After seeing the thirty-eight-minute body camera footage, Antone Black Sr., the young man's father, declared "They lynched him," notwithstanding that the officers and one civilian "didn't use a rope and a tree, they used a gun and a badge."[46]

Scott's words are fitting as we consider how to go about dismantling the legacy of social, legal, educational, and economic anti-Black violence. Indeed, in the age of Blue and Black Lives Matter, the provocative statement that the police are the "inheritors of lynch mob terror" is undeniable and poignant, and points to the need for both social transformation and racial healing. We must recognize that the police are an integral part of this nation and that the ongoing racial conflict now claiming so much media attention has beset this nation since its creation, a founding based on "constitutional commitments" to freedom, justice, and equality, at a time when no such equality and social harmony existed, certainly not between races. In fact, the nation and its founding principles were conceived in racism and anti-Blackness. If the police reflect that founding, they are the inheritors of anti-Black violence, including lynch mob terror, just as all of our institutions are the inheritors of anti-Black violence.

If the police are the inheritors of anti-Black violence, then states like Maryland, and cities like Salisbury, that create and equip police forces are the inheritors of anti-Black violence. Now that the unknown has been made known, at least in Matthew Williams's case, the once faceless lynch mob has been revealed. What is the next move for Salisbury, the state of Maryland, and for the United States? The answer is simple: our nation, our communities, and our institutions must relinquish this inheritance of anti-Black violence, which will require reimagining our America as a country that honors narratives of the oppressed and promotes a collective commitment to social, legal, educational, and economic reform—a nation rooted not in a "belief in a racial hierarchy" but in acknowledging and protecting the humanity in all people.[47]

Afterword

A Message from a Living Relative

The early days of the coronavirus pandemic, in 2020, had already turned out to be quite a roller coaster ride. Then I got a call from my cousin on my father's side, who had received a call from Dr. Charles Chavis, a history professor at George Mason University, who believed that I might be related to a young man who was lynched in Salisbury, Maryland, in 1931.

Knowing that relatives sometimes get things crossed up, I wanted to follow up with Dr. Chavis myself to see what he had to say. I was forwarded his phone number, and I requested that he send me the genealogical information that he had compiled. Upon reviewing the family tree, it became clear that Matthew Williams Handy was my relative, initially thought to be on my father's side. However, a closer look revealed that this twenty-three-year-old young man was a distant cousin on my mother's side. His aunt, the woman who helped raise him, Mrs. Addie Black, was my great-grandmother.

Working for years as a professional in broadcast radio and TV, I have reported and heard about many kinds of heinous incidents in the United States, but I had never expected to find family history among them. To this day, I remember my mother, Carolyn, and my grandmother Rachel discussing memories and some secret details about the history of the Eastern Shore of Maryland. It seemed like centuries ago, but only ninety years had gone by. Reading the interview of Addie Black, or "Grandma Addie," as we called her, left my emotions raw. I've read about other lynchings that seemed to dominate the Deep South—but this happened in Maryland, the so-called Free State. I live in Los Angeles, where I am a journalist, media personality, producer, and director, but nothing in my professional experience prepared me for the content of this book. The system of silence ran even deeper than I could have imagined.

After reading a newspaper article where my great-grandmother Addie described young Matthew's character, I can see clearly he could well have been considered a decent citizen. He dropped out of school as a young teen to work to help support his family; he was thrifty and avoided the wrong crowds. If this could happen to him, it could happen to anyone. When I think about my loved one whose life was cut down, I cannot help but be reminded how this type of activity continues today and similarly goes unpunished. Matthew Williams did not receive the justice he deserved. The legal system failed him as it has also failed so many today who have lost their lives at the hands of police, who should have protected them, according to their professional vows.

The detailed day-by-day and point-by-point account of the horrific lynching of Matthew Williams is rare, but as the revealed truth, it is necessary—no matter how painful it is to me or the descendants of other individuals involved. Dr. Chavis has done us all a great service, but what is of particular importance is how this case is handled from this point forward and how it will set a precedent for the way other similar cases—the more than 6,000 recorded lynchings in the United States—are researched, investigated, and addressed by the justice system. Along with the election of President Joe Biden and Vice President Kamala Harris, this book will usher in a new day in seeking equality in the justice system and rooting out systemic racism in this nation. I'm not proud of this history, nor am I proud that this happened to my relative, but I am proud of the profound effect it will undoubtedly have on the American consciousness, or as President Biden says, on the restoration of "the soul of America."

Tracey "Jeannie" Jones
Los Angeles, California
January 2021

Acknowledgments

This book would not have been possible without the guidance and support provided by so many. It is the product of the prayers of my ancestors, relatives, and friends. To my grandmothers, the late Cora Lee Hammonds and Alice Marie Howard, thank you for raising two of the strongest people I know, Charles L. Chavis Sr., whose namesake I am, and Karen D. Chavis. Charles and Karen, Mom and Dad, thank you for nurturing my passion and for fighting for me throughout my life's journey. To my sister, Brittney White, my first friend, thank you for your listening ear during the good times and the bad times, and thank you for holding me accountable and keeping me grounded. To my wife, Erica L. Chavis, the love of my life, thank you for always believing in me and for helping me maintain balance throughout this journey. To my son, Charles "Noah," your life challenged me to understand the importance of this work in shaping the future of America, an America which I pray will learn from the mistakes of its past.

This book was supported by a number of intellectual relationships that continue to guide and sustain me along this journey. The influences of Omar H. Ali, Victor Anderson, Houston A. Baker, Tara T. Green, Forrest E. Harris Sr., David A. Michelson, Bruce Morrill, Amy E. Steele, and Naurice Frank Woods Jr. helped carry me through some of the most challenging times of the project.

I am extremely grateful for the guidance, advice, and honesty of Brett Berliner, Jeremiah Dibua, Peter Levey, Lawrence Peskin, and David Taft Terry during the formative and most trying stages of this project. Simone Barrett, Chris Haley, Ida Jones, Pace J. McConkie, Earl S. Richardson, and Matthew Washington all gave informal and formal feedback that kept me on track.

To Susan Allen, Kevin A. Brown II, Eola Dance, Benita Dix, Busola Enola, Marc Gopin, Dean Herrin, Douglas Irvin-Erickson, Yasemin Irvin-Erickson, Karina V. Korostelina, Noel Lopez, Tehama Lopez Bunyasi, Solon Simmons, and Naomi Nontumni Tutu, thank you for the dialogue, for the critical engagement, and for being there not only to see this project through but also as I navigated through a scholarly and personal journey.

I am grateful to Kevin Avruch and Alpaslan Özerdem and to the Jimmy and Rosalynn Carter School for Peace and Conflict Resolution at George Mason University, which supported the final stages of this project. I am especially grateful to my dedicated team in the John Mitchell, Jr. Program for History, Justice, and Race, including Gbenga Dayslyva, Chinyere Erondu, Christie Jones, Ajanet Rountree, Tanja Thompson, and our most loyal supporters, Bruce Aft, Joshua Levin, Janet Rountree-Hudson, Andy Shallal, Kimberly Wilson, Judge Owen Wilson, and Audrey Williams. I also thank Kate Epstein, Jane Jones, and Steven Baker for their editorial support as well as Damita Green, master genealogist, for assisting me in verifying and tracking down the living relatives of Matthew Williams and Black witnesses, including Maslin Pinkett. Special thanks to the scholars, historians, activists, leaders, and change agents whose work has inspired me in more ways than I can express, including Gail Christopher, Nicholas M. Creary, David Fakunle, Amber Green, Kirkland Hall, Corey J. Henderson, Sherrilyn Ifill, Michaela Moses, Clara Small, James Yamakawa, and the late great Linda Duyer. Thank you to Chris Haley and Maya Davis at the Maryland State Archives, and the staff at the following institutions and repositories: the amazing Ian Post of the Edward H. Nabb Research Center at Salisbury University, the Lillie Carroll Jackson Civil Rights Museum, the Robert M. Bell Center for Civil Rights in Education, the Jacob Rader Marcus Center of the American Jewish Archives, Maryland Historical Society, Moorland-Spingarn Research Center at Howard University, Wilson Special Collections Library at the University of North Carolina at Chapel Hill, and the Benjamin A. Quarles Humanities and Social Science Institute at Morgan State University.

To my dear friend Iris Barnes, thank you for giving your wisdom, guidance, and most important, your friendship during this process. Deep thanks to Johns Hopkins University Press for welcoming me onboard. Thank you, Laura Davulis, Kathryn Marguy, and Esther Rodriguez for your continued advocacy and support. Last and most important, I would like to express my deepest gratitude to Ms. Tracey "Jeannie" Jones, for entrusting me with the story of her loved one and her family.

[Appendix]

Table A.1.
Population of Baltimore and Eastern Shore Cities, 1920–1930

	Population	% increase since 1920
Baltimore	804,874	9.70
Salisbury	10,997	45.60
Princess Anne	975	9.93

Source: Fifteenth Census of the United States (Washington, DC: Government Printing Office, 1930), 1:486, 493.

Table A.2.
Racial Composition of Somerset and Wicomico Counties, 1930

	State of Maryland*	Somerset	Wicomico
Native White	1,259,077	15,169	24,268
Percentage	77.17	64.90	77.70
Black	276,379	8,111	6,750
Percentage	16.94	36.80	21.60
Total	1,631,526	23,382	31,229

Source: Fifteenth Census of the United States (Washington, DC: Government Printing Office, 1930), 3:1043, 1056.
*Percentages for the state are derived.

Table A.3.
Concentric Circles of Conspiracy: The Case of Matthew Williams

a. First, innermost circle

The group of conspirators who actually planned and carried out the abduction and murder; occupied the very core of the conspiracy to commit abduction and murder[1]

- Bill Davis—Directed the lynching[2]
- Jack Townsend—Directed the lynching[3]
- Sheriff Murry Phillips—Abducted Williams[4]
- Sheriff Donald A. Parks—Among the mob (led the parade) and participated in the criminal conspiracy[5]
- Chief Nicholas H. Holland—Among the mob (led the parade) and participated in the criminal conspiracy[6]
- Ellwood Guthrie—Stabbed Williams with knife[7]
- Thomas "Catfish" Webster—Leader of the mob[8]
- Benjamin Parsons—Confessed to having lynched Williams
- Lorenzo W. Brittingham—Participated in the lynching[9]
- Elwood Waller—Confessed to helping hang Williams, pouring the gasoline on Williams, and participating in the larger criminal conspiracy
- Ralph "Fats" Wilson—Participated in the lynching[10]
- Buck Johnson—Confessed to having helped abduct and lynch Williams

[1] A criminal conspiracy exists when two or more people agree to commit almost any unlawful act, then take some action toward its completion. The action taken need not itself be a crime, but it must indicate that those involved in the conspiracy knew of the plan and intended to break the law. A person may be convicted of conspiracy even if the actual crime was never committed.

[2] Identified as the leader of the lynch mob by Buck Johnson, Bill Perry, Danny Russell, Beulah Smith, Fred Ruark, Howard Campbell, and Samuel Preston.

[3] Identified as one of the leaders (along with Bill Davis) by Bill Perry.

[4] Identified by Talbot Larmore as one of the men who carried Williams to the lynching.

[5] Identified by Larmore as being among the men, along with Chief Holland, who abducted Williams from the hospital. Larmore also stated that Parks and Holland were informed by "prominent men" regarding what the plan was for the lynching.

[6] Identified by Larmore, Sid Church, and Rufus Perry as being among the mob.

[7] Identified by Ellwood Guthrie as having stabbed Williams with a knife.

[8] Identified by Talbot Larmore as being involved in the lynching and by Fred Ruark as being a leader of the mob, along with Bill Davis.

[9] Identified by Talbot Larmore as having cut off Williams's toes. This is also corroborated in the *Baltimore Afro-American* newspaper.

[10] Identified by Kellar Crawford and Lee Harris as having taken an active part in the lynching.

b. Second circle

The men who helped plan the lynching and served as lookouts (including law enforcement); coconspirators (conspiracy to commit murder)

- Roger Bailey[1]
- Chief Frederick A. Grier—Provided the rope used to lynch Williams[2]
- Talbot Larmore—Identified as being at the hospital
- Danny Russell—Identified as being at the hospital when Williams was abducted[3]

[1] Identified by Larmore as having entered Cinno's cigar store and announced the plan to get Williams

[2] Identified by Harry Waller (Red Star counterman) and Lee Harris as having provided the rope

[3] Identified by Talbot Larmore as being at the hospital a few minutes before Williams's abduction

c. Third circle

People who knew of the conspiracy and the approximate time when the crime would occur but had no direct role in the lynching

- Sid Church—Confessed to having witnessed the lynching and having been aware of the conspiracy
- Thompson (proprietor of restaurant)—Phoned a New York–based newspaper to give a play-by-play of lynching
- Harry Waller—Was aware of the conspiracy
- Bill Perry—Identified Jack Townsend as one of the leaders of the mob
- Lee Harris—Knew about the conspiracy and those involved
- Howard Campbell—Knew about the conspiracy and those involved
- William Walter—Witnessed the entire lynching

d. Fourth circle

People with direct, though ex post facto, knowledge of the lynching, including who had witnessed at least part of the abduction but claimed not to have recognized any of the men

- Bill Maddox
- Rufus Perry
- Byrd
- Samuel Preston
- Hospital staff

e. Fifth circle

People who had only passing knowledge of the conspiracy, of the parties involved, and of the probability that something was going to happen. Many of the residents of Salisbury and Wicomico County belong in this circle.

- Rufus Perry—Was given a piece of the rope
- Beulah Smith—Had only passing knowledge of the conspiracy
- Kellar Crawford—Had only passing knowledge of the conspiracy
- Fred Ruark—Had only passing knowledge of the conspiracy

Table A.4.
Members of the Grand Jury Impaneled in the Case of Matthew Williams

	Race	Sex	Occupation
Leonard M. Morris	White	Male	Farmer (truck farm)
C. Herbert Chatham	White	Male	General farmer
Wm. C. Brewington	White	Male	Salesman (furniture store)
Wm. T. Vincent	White	Male	Farmer (truck farm)
Roger Malone	White	Male	Farmer
Edmund Humphreys	White	Male	Farmer (truck farm)
Thomas R. Phillips	White	Male	Railroad brakeman
Lloyd Jones	White	Male	Laborer (truck farm)
Lee C. Messick	White	Male	Farmer (truck farm)
Benjamin W. Turner	White	Male	Assistant foreman (railroad)
Leslie Truitt	White	Male	Laborer (basket factory)
Lemuel J. Harrington	White	Male	Farmer (truck farm)
William C. Gray	White	Male	Retired naval officer
Josiah Johnson	White	Male	Carpenter
Harvey W. Mariner	White	Male	Farmer (truck farm)
J. Herman Downes	White	Male	Farmer (truck farm)

Source: "100 to Be Called in Lynching Case," Baltimore Sun, March 14, 1932.

Table A.5.
Gubernatorial Election Results, Lower Eastern Shore Counties and Baltimore City, November 2, 1926

	Albert C. Ritchie (Democrat)	Addison E. Mullikin (Republican)
Somerset County	2,377	3,328
Wicomico County	4,179	3,397
Worcester County	3,134	2,087
Baltimore City	103,304	56,646
Statewide Total	207,345	148,145

Source: "General Election for Maryland, November 2, 1926: For Governor of Maryland," Maryland Manual 137 (1926): 251, http://msa.maryland.gov/megafile/msa/speccol/sc2900/sc2908/000001/000137/pdf/am137--251.pdf.

Appendix

Table A.6.
Gubernatorial Election Results, Lower Eastern Shore Counties
and Baltimore City, November 4, 1930

	Albert C. Ritchie (Democrat)	William F. Broening (Republican)
Somerset County	2,411	5,200
Wicomico County	4,965	4,930
Worcester County	3,003	3,181
Baltimore City	156,728	90,867
Statewide Total	283,639	216,864

Source: "General Election Results, November 4, 1930: Candidates for Governor," *Maryland Manual* 147 (1930): 251, http://msa.maryland.gov/megafile/msa/speccol/sc2900/sc2908/000001/000147/pdf /am147--240.pdf.

Table A.7.
Lynchings in Maryland, by County

County		City	Name	Date
Allegany (1)				
	1	Cumberland	William Burns	10-6-1907
Anne Arundel (5)				
	2	Annapolis	John Sims	6-7-1875
	3	Jacobsville	George Briscoe	11-26-1884
	4	Annapolis	Wright Smith	10-5-1898
	5	Annapolis	Henry Davis	12-21-1906
	6	Brooklyn	King Johnson	12-23-1911
Baltimore Co. (2)				
	7	Towson	Howard Cooper	7-13-1885
	8	Rosedale	William Ramsay	3-8-1909
Calvert (1)				
	9	Prince Frederick	Charles Whitley	6-6-1886
Caroline (2)				
	10	Denton	David Thomas	10-10-1854
	11	Oakland	Jim Wilson	11-4-1862
Carroll (1)				
	12	Westminster	Towsend Cook	6-2-1885
Cecil (2)				
	13	Cecilton	Frederick [?]	9-26-1861
	14	Elkton	John Jones	7-27-1872

(continued)

Appendix

Frederick (3)				
	15	Point of Rocks	James Carroll	4-17-1879
	16	Frederick	John Bigus	11-23-1887
	17	Frederick	James Bowens	11-16-1895
Harford (3)				
	18	Belair	Isaac Moore	7-22-1868
	19	White Hall	Jim Quinn	10-2-1869
	20	Belair	Lewis Harris	3-27-1900
Howard (1)				
	21	Ellicott City	Jacob Henson	3-28-1895
Kent (1)				
	22	Chestertown	James Taylor	5-17-1892
Montgomery (3)				
	23	Poolesville	George Peck	1-10-1880
	24	Darnestown	John Diggs	7-27-1880
	25	Rockville	Sydney Randolph	7-3-1896
Prince George's (4)				
	26	Piscataway	Thomas Juricks	10-12-1869
	27	Notley Hall	John Henry Scott	3-23-1875
	28	Upper Marlboro	Mike Green	9-1-1878
	29	Upper Marlboro	Stephen Williams	10-20-1894
Queen Anne's (2)				
	30	unknown	John Fields	early 1860s
	31	Centreville	Asbury Green	5-13-1891
St. Mary's (1)				
	32	Leonardtown	Benjamin Hance	6-17-1887
Somerset (4)				
	33	Princess Anne	Isaac Kemp	6-8-1894
	34	Princess Anne	William Andrews	6-9-1897
	35	Crisfield	James Reed	7-28-1907
	36	Princess Anne	George Armwood	10-18-1933
Wicomico (3)				
	37	Salisbury	Garfield King	5-25-1898
	38	Salisbury	Matthew Williams	12-4-1931
	39	Salisbury	unknown	12-4-1931
Worcester (1)				
	40	Pocomoke	Edd Watson	6-14-1906

Source: Maryland Lynching Memorial Project.

Appendix

[Notes]

Abbreviations

ED Enumeration District
FHL Family History Library
LOC Library of Congress, Washington, DC
MdHR Maryland Hall of Records
MSA Maryland State Archives
NRC Edward H. Nabb Research Center for Delmarva History and Culture at Salisbury University
PSP Polly Stewart Papers, Edward H. Nabb Center for Delmarva History and Culture, Salisbury University, Salisbury, MD
RG Record Group

Preface

1. As is common across cases of mass violence historically, the acts of killing members of marginalized groups are not ignored or denied across the wider society. Instead, they are "hidden in plain sight," either because they have become normalized or because such violence is viewed as legitimate, justified, or good. See Douglas Irvin-Erickson, Thomas La Pointe, and Alexander Hinton, "Introduction: Hidden Genocides," in Irvin-Erickson, La Pointe, and Hinton, *Hidden Genocides*, 13–14.

2. Ishmael, "Reclaiming History"; Gibbs, "The Heart of the Matter."

3. By a joint resolution, the Maryland General Assembly created the Maryland Interracial Commission in 1924, but it would not begin operating until 1927. Earl Bragg's "The Interracial Commission: To the Editor of the Evening Sun," *Baltimore Evening Sun*, April 3, 1924; "Commission on Civil Rights: Origin and Functions," *Maryland Manual On-Line*, accessed January 9, 2021, https://msa.maryland.gov/msa/mdmanual/25ind/html/44humanf.html.

Introduction

1. Emmett Till Unsolved Civil Rights Crimes Reauthorization Act of 2016, Pub. L. No. 114-325, 130 Stat. 1965 (2016), https://www.congress.gov/bill/114th-congress/senate-bill/2854/text.

2. Work, "Lynching, Whites & Negroes, 1882–1968"; "2015 Police Violence Report"; Charles L. Chavis Jr., "The Promised Land and the Myth of a Post Racial America: Strange Fruit in the Age of Obama," in Woods, *Rooted in the Soul*; Charles L. Chavis Jr., "'Strange Fruit' Is Still Hanging from the Trees," *Baltimore Afro-American*, October 5, 2017.

3. Ore, *Lynching*, 6.

4. Dread Scott, "Morning Remarks," in "Lynching: Reparations as Restorative Justice," virtual conference, 33:08, Civil Rights and Restorative Justice, November 17, 2020, https://crrj.org/efforts/lynching-reparations-as-restorative-justice-conference/.

5. Frederick Douglass, "Why Is the Negro Lynched?" address in Metropolitan A.M.E. Church Lesson of the Hour, Washington, DC, January 9, 1894, available at Internet Archive, https://archive.org/details/whyisnegrolynched00doug/mode/2up.

6. "Eye Witness to Lynching Tells How Mob Acted," *Baltimore Afro-American*, December 12, 1931.

7. See part II for more evidence on the connection to racial violence and labor violence; and Battat, *Ain't Got No Home*, 15–16.

8. "Ritchie Orders Mob Members' Arrested: Lee Trial Deferred; Demands," *Baltimore Sun*, December 6, 1931.

9. "Rabbi Israel Urges Action on Lynching: Clergyman Here Calls on Eastern Shore Ministers to Remove Disgrace," Newspaper Clippings and Correspondence Relating to the Lynching of Matthew Williams, Courthouse lawn, Salisbury, MD, December 4, 1931, Governor Albert Ritchie Collection, Maryland State Archives, Annapolis, MD. For more on Rabbi Israel, see Chavis, "Rabbi Edward L. Israel."

10. "Rabbi Israel Urges Action on Lynching"; Chavis, "Rabbi Edward L. Israel."

11. "Rabbi Israel Urges Action on Lynching"; Chavis, "Rabbi Edward L. Israel"; "Ritchie Orders Mob Members' Arrested."

12. Ida B. Wells-Barnett, "Lynch Law in America," *Arena* 23, no. 1 (1900). Williams's case was not devoid of such characteristics: at least one white witness's testimony presented a case of sexual subtext. See chapter 2.

13. Curtin, *The Atlantic Slave Trade*, 3; Inikori and Engerman, *The Atlantic Slave Trade*; Darity, "The Numbers Game and the Profitability of the British Trade in Slaves"; Eltis and Richardson, "The 'Numbers Game' and Routes to Slavery"; Eltis and Richardson, *Atlas of the Transatlantic Slave Trade*.

14. Hill, *Beyond the Rope*; Wood, *Lynching and Spectacle*; Carrigan and Waldrep,

Swift to Wrath; Waldrep, African Americans Confront Lynching; Rice, Witnessing Lynching; Dray, At the Hands of Persons Unknown; Brundage, Under Sentence of Death; Brundage, Lynching in the New South.

15. This scholarly perception concerning Maryland's number of documented cases of lynching can be traced back to the 1920s when criminal psychologist Robert H. Gault admonished his readers to "look at the figures and see how dear old Maryland shines— no lynchings there—she is not over organized; she has only 24 good counties; therefore, she has good government." See Gault, "Lynching, an Evil of County Government."

16. McGovern, Anatomy of a Lynching; Smead, Blood Justice. See also Mathews, At the Altar of Lynching; Armstrong, Mary Turner and the Memory of Lynching; Tyson, The Blood of Emmett Till; Bernstein, The First Waco Horror; and Capeci, The Lynching of Cleo Wright.

17. Frazier, Lynchings in Missouri; Capeci, The Lynching of Cleo Wright; Konhaus, "'I Thought Things Would Be Different There'"; Roberts, A Lynching in Little Dixie; Rolph, "To Shoot, Burn, and Hang"; Trotter and Trotter, Coal, Class, and Color; Williams, "Permission to Hate"; Wright, Racial Violence in Kentucky; McCulley, "Rape, Lynching, and Mythmaking in Missouri, 1804–1933."

18. Clegg, Troubled Ground.

19. Arnold-Lourie, "'A Madman's Deed, a Maniac's Hand,'" 1032; Polly Stewart, "Regional Consciousness as a Shaper of Local History: Examples from the Eastern Shore," in Barbara and Thomas, Sense of Place, 74–87; Ifill, On the Courthouse Lawn.

20. To date, the only book that has addressed the history of race lynching in Maryland is Ifill, On the Courthouse Lawn, which offers two brief case studies of which Matthew Williams is one. The present book is thus the first on a single lynching in Maryland.

21. Dray, At the Hands of Persons Unknown.

22. Ifill, On the Courthouse Lawn, 57.

23. Václav Havel, "The Power of the Powerless," International Journal of Politics 15, no. 3/4 (1985), 5–6. For more on post-Reconstruction white conformity with anti-Black ideas in the United States, see Cash, The Mind of the South; and Tindall, The Emergence of the New South.

24. Havel, "The Power of the Powerless," 6.

25. Havel, "The Power of the Powerless," 9.

26. Havel, "The Power of the Powerless," 9.

27. When using the term forensic reconstruction, I refer to what forensic scientists Tom Bevel and Ross Gardner have described as "event analysis." As they explain, "Reconstruction is the end purpose of analysis; it requires not only the consideration of the events identified but whenever possible the sequence of events." Bevel and Gardner lay out event analysis as follows: collect data; establish specific event segments (time snapshots); establish which event segments are related to one another and the sequence of these event segments, establishing a flow for the event; consider all possible arrangements, auditing the evidence when necessary to resolve contradictions; and, based on the event segment sequence, establish the final order of the segments; and flowchart the entire incident and validate the sequence. Bevel and Gardner, Bloodstain Pattern Analysis, 20. See also Chisum and Turvey, Crime Reconstruction, 186.

28. Ross, "At the Bar of Judge Lynch."

29. Brundage, Lynching in the New South, 15–19.

30. This observation complicates conventional notions of a "private mob," which becomes problematic when considering the role and involvement of public officials and law enforcement officers involved in its activities. However, law enforcement officers throughout the South during the 1930s were often members of white supremacist organizations such as the Ku Klux Klan. This may have been the case on Maryland's Eastern Shore, which saw a rise of Klan activities beginning in 1923. Castle, " 'Cops and the Klan' "; Brown, *Setting a Course*, 186; Harcourt, "Kleagles, Kash and the Klan," 10; John W. Owens, "Forces of Ku Klux in Counties Now Rated Far below Claims: Opinion Expressed among Impartial Observers in Recent Election That Membership of Klan Has Been Greatly Overstated" (part 2), *Baltimore Sun*, November 21, 1923; Cohen, " 'The Ku Klux Government.' "

31. Howard Smead, telephone call with author, April 6, 2020.

32. Smead, *Blood Justice*, 152, 8.

33. Adam Weishaupt was a German philosopher and founder of the Order of the Illuminati, a secret society whose members were organized in a set of concentric circles. According to Weishaupt, all organization members were given the impression that they were on the inside. However, members of the inner circle regarded those in the outer ring as a means to an end, who were useful because they could be made to believe anything. For more information on concentric circles and conspiracy theories, see Byford, *Conspiracy Theories*.

Chapter 1

1. "Lynchers in Salisbury Had Right-of-Way," *Baltimore Afro-American*, December 12, 1931.

2. Levi H. Jolley, "Aunt Sobs, Declares 'Buddie' Mob Lynched Was a Good Boy," *Baltimore Afro-American*, December 12, 1931; Matthew Handy in the household of Mary Handy, Salisbury, Wicomico County, Maryland, US Census, 1920, database with images, *FamilySearch*, accessed February 4, 2017, https://familysearch.org/ark:/61903/1:1:M 677-8V7, citing ED 136, sheet 2A, line 13, family 29, NARA microfilm publication T625, roll 678, FHL microfilm 1,820,678.

3. Matthew Handy in the household of Mary Handy, Salisbury, Wicomico County, Maryland, US Census, 1920.

4. Minnie Handy in the household of Mary Handy, Salisbury, Wicomico County, Maryland, US Census, 1920, database with images, *FamilySearch*, accessed February 4, 2017, https://familysearch.org/ark:/61903/1:1:M677-8VQ, citing ED 136, sheet 2A, line 12, family 29, NARA microfilm publication T625, roll 678m FHL microfilm 1,820,678.

5. "Fellow Worker of Lynched Man Says He Was Quiet, Industrious," *Baltimore Afro-American*, December 12, 1931.

6. "Fellow Worker of Lynched Man Says He Was Quiet, Industrious."

7. Jolley, "Aunt Sobs."

8. "Lynched Man's Sister Doesn't Believe Brother a Killer," *Baltimore Afro-American*, December 12, 1931.

9. "Lynched Man's Sister Doesn't Believe Brother a Killer"; Jolley, "Aunt Sobs."

10. In attempting to salvage Williams's humanity, it is essential that I identified sources that would provide a blueprint of everyday life in Salisbury, Maryland, in 1931.

Sanborn maps are a unique source that provide detailed land-use and property records. They also indicate the racial boundaries and racial segregation in the city. When combined with other primary sources such as census records, genealogical data, and city directories, Sanborn maps not only provide an extra layer of corroboration but offer a clearer picture of what life was like for Williams and the citizens of Salisbury, Maryland. Oswald, *Fire Insurance Maps*, 24–29; Nehls, "Sanborn Fire Insurance Maps at the University of Virginia," 9.

11. Fields, *Slavery and Freedom on the Middle Ground*, xii.

12. Wilson, *The Book of the States*, 46.

13. "Maryland at a Glance: Land," *Maryland Manual On-Line*, accessed February 14, 2021, http://www.mdarchives.state.md.us/mdmanual/01glance/html/area.html#area.

14. "Maryland at a Glance: Land."

15. Omo-Osagie, *Commercial Poultry Production on Maryland's Lower Eastern Shore*, 2.

16. DiLisio, *Maryland Geography*, 15.

17. Truitt, *Historic Salisbury, Maryland*, 78.

18. Levin Handy Family Bible, 1816, Nabb Research Center for Delmarva History and Culture, Salisbury University, Salisbury, MD; Earle and Skirven, *Maryland's Colonial Eastern Shore*, 188; Armstead, *Freedom's Gardener*, 152–55; Jacob, *Salisbury in Vintage Postcards* (1998), 39.

19. The church building now houses the Charles H. Chipman Cultural Center. Paul B. Touart, *John Wesley Methodist Episcopal Church*, 2.

20. Touart, *John Wesley Methodist Episcopal Church*, 2.

21. *Eastern Shore of Delaware, Maryland, and Virginia Directory, 1908–1909*.

22. "Humphreys Dam Breaks—Emptying Lake Humphreys; Many Persons View the Unusual Spectacle," *Salisbury Advertiser*, May 29, 1909.

23. Duyer, *'Round the Pond*, 50.

24. For more on Grant's proclamation, see "Proclamation of the Fifteenth Amendment—New Registration Law," *Baltimore Sun*, March 31, 1870.

25. Levine, "Standing Political Decisions and Critical Realignment."

26. "Wright Smith Lynched," *Annapolis Advertiser*, October 6, 1898.

27. "Governor Lowndes' Callers," *Baltimore Sun*, May 28, 1898.

28. Donald, "The Southern Rite of Human Sacrifice," 27; "A Murder and Lynching," *Salisbury Advertiser*, May 28, 1898.

29. "A Murder and Lynching."

30. "Hanged at Salisbury: Garfield King, Colored, Taken from Jail and Lynched; Strung to a Tree and Shot; Summary Vengeance of a Mob in Wicomico County; the Victim was a Colored Youth of Eighteen Years Who Shot Herman Kenney, a White Boy at Twigg's Store on Saturday Last," *Baltimore Sun*, May 26, 1898.

31. "Shooting in Wicomico: A White Youth Fatally Wounded by a Young Negro with a Handy Pistol," *Baltimore Sun*, May 23, 1898.

32. "A Murder and Lynching: Garfield King, Colored, Shot Herman Kenny, White, and a Mob Lynched the Negro; Details of the Lynching Which Took Place at the County Jail," *Salisbury Advertiser*, May 28, 1898; "Hanged at Salisbury," *Baltimore Weekly Sun*, May 28, 1898.

33. Huston was a notable Black leader in Salisbury who owned and operated a bank and was a close friend to Frederick Douglass, whom he hosted when Douglass came to speak in the Salisbury courthouse for a fund-raiser in 1880. "Dead Salisbury Negro

Made Fortune in 'Tips,'" *York (PA) Gazette Daily*, January 17, 1916; "Frederick Douglass," *Baltimore Sun*, February 24, 1880; "A Lecture to be Given," *Salisbury Advertiser*, February 21, 1880.

34. Lloyd Lowndes Jr. was the first Republican governor of Maryland following the Civil War and maintained a close relationship with Black Republicans throughout the state and nation. He served in the US House of Representatives during Reconstruction between 1873 and 1875. White, *Governors of Maryland, 1777–1970*, 221–24.

35. William Ashbie Hawkins, one of Baltimore's first Black lawyers, was quite familiar with lynching cases, having represented Jacob Henson, who had been lynched in Ellicott City, Maryland, just two years prior. "Henson Convicted," *Baltimore Sun*, March 29, 1895; "Condemnation Resolution," *Salisbury Advertiser*, June 4, 1898; "Ashbie Hawkins, Attorney for 50 Years, Dies at 78," *Baltimore Afro-American*, April 12, 1941. Graham was a Republican politician who lived in Salisbury around the time of the lynching and practiced law locally. Following his service as state tax commissioner (1898–1902), he was appointed secretary of state by Governor Phillips Lee Goldsborough in 1912. "Robert Patterson Graham," in Hall, *Baltimore*, 726–27.

36. "Senate, Wicomico County (1868–1966)," in Papenfuse et al., *Archives of Maryland, Historical List*.

37. "Wicomico Aroused: People in One of the Districts Excited over the Recent Lynching," *Baltimore Sun*, May 28, 1898. Reports of white lynch mob leaders in blackface appear as early as the 1870s and are documented in the accounts of the lynching of Charlotte Harris, the only recorded lynching of an African American woman in the state of Virginia. "Local Matters: The Lynching of Charlotte Harris in Rockingham County," *Richmond Dispatch*, March 18, 1878. Seven years later, Nicholas Snowden, an African American man, was lynched in Howard County, Maryland, allegedly by Black community members. However, the only eyewitness to the kidnapping was the white warden, John T. Ray. Ray described a group of twelve men who took Snowden from the jail: "They were dressed as ordinary citizens but had veils and other disguises over their faces, and I could recognize none of them. I thought beyond doubt they were colored. Their veils did not fully cover their faces, and I could see they were colored." "Lynching in Howard: A Mob of Colored Men Take a Colored Prisoner from Jail and Hang Him," *Baltimore Sun*, September 19, 1885.

38. The witnesses were most likely referring to the lynching of William Andrews in nearby Princess Anne the previous year. "Andrews Lynched!," *Cambridge (MD) Democrat and News*, June 12, 1897. As it relates to the lynching referenced in Caroline County, there is no documented victim of color on record; however, they might have been referring to Marshall E. Price, a white victim lynched on July 2, 1895. "Wicomico Lynching: The Mysterious Tall Leader at Salisbury Jail," *Cecil (MD) Whig*, June 4, 1898; "Price Lynched," *Baltimore Sun*, July 3, 1895.

39. "Wicomico Lynching: The Mysterious Tall Leader."

40. *Report of the Adjutant General of Maryland, 1906–1907* (Baltimore: Geo. W. King Printing Co., 1908), 299; "Secretary of State," *Maryland Manual* (Baltimore, MD: King Bros., 1898), 1.

41. "Governor Lowndes' Callers: Colored Men Urged That a Reward Be Offered for the Apprehension of Lynchers," *Baltimore Sun*, July 18, 1898; Mather, *Who's Who of the Colored Race*, 181; Wright, *Centennial Encyclopedia of the African Methodist Episcopal Church*, 280; Waring, *Work of the Colored Law and Order League*, 4; "Colored Masons

Meet: Councilman Hiram Watty Is Chosen Imperial Potentate," *Baltimore Sun*, October 22, 1902.

42. "Governor Lowndes' Callers."

43. "Governor Lowndes' Callers."

44. "Stewart, Negro Leader, Is Dead," *Delmarva Daily Times*, December 3, 1949.

45. "Stewart, Negro Leader, Is Dead."

46. "Colored People of Salisbury Protest Interference of Ades," *Delmarva Daily Times*, December 6, 1933.

47. On November 7, 1931, Bernard Ades and a female companion were attacked and beaten as they attempted to have lunch at a restaurant in Snow Hill across the street from the courthouse. "Pledge Snow Hill Killer Fair Trial in Dorchester County," *Snow Hill News Journal*, November 7, 1931; "Murder Trial Will Be Held in Cambridge: Snow Hill Quiet after Several Days of Unrest; Defense League Lawyer Attacked," *Hagerstown (MD) Morning Herald*, November 7, 1931.

48. During the Progressive era, labor unions throughout the United States began circulating a short article entitled "About the Outside Agitator," which satirized the nomenclature associated with the various attacks that corporations leveled at the movement as a whole to discredit it. The article begins by arguing that "certain employers who are trying very hard to keep their industrial policy back in the middle ages are fond of pointing to the outside agitator." Further, the unions argue, "it is a modern industry that made trade unionism indispensable to the welfare and safety of the race." See *Commercial Telegraphers' Journal* (Milwaukee: Commercial Telegraphers' Union of America, 1918), 572.

49. Pedersen, *The Communist Party in Maryland*, 53; Allen and Schlereth, *Sense of Place*, 81.

50. Gilmore, *Defying Dixie*, 5. For more information about the NAACP's and the ILD's efforts, see Berg, "Black Civil Rights and Liberal Anti-Communism"; Pedersen, *The Communist Party in Maryland*, 53.

51. "Colored People of Salisbury Protest Interference of Ades."

52. "Colored People of Salisbury Protest Interference of Ades."

53. "Colored People of Salisbury Protest Interference of Ades."

54. Thurston, *Industrial Salisbury*, 1934.

Chapter 2

1. "Negroes Out of Work," *Nation* 122 (April 22, 1931): 441–42.

2. Louis J. O. Donnell, "Guard against New Racial Outbreak at Scene of Lynching," *Baltimore Sun*, December 6, 1931. Dallas M. Ellis, Wicomico County, Maryland, US Census, 1920, ED 130, sheet 16B, line 53, family 217, NARA microfilm publication T625, roll 678, FHL microfilm 1,820,678; John C. K. Trader in household of Sall Trader, Wicomico County, Maryland, US Census, 1920, ED 122, sheet 4B, line 81, family 97, NARA microfilm publication T625, roll 678, FHL microfilm 1,820,678.

3. "Angry Residents Seeking Negro in Delmar Murder: Fear Mob Violence," *Wilmington (DE) Morning News*, September 16, 1929.

4. "Angry Residents Seeking Negro in Delmar Murder."

5. This membership number was a distant second to neighboring Somerset County, with between 600 and 700 members. John W. Owens, "Forces of Ku Klux in Counties

Now Rated," *Baltimore Sun*, November 21, 1923. Louis J. O'Donnell, "Guard against New Racial Outbreak at Scene of Lynching," *Baltimore Sun*, December 6, 1931.

6. Truitt, *Historic Salisbury Updated*, 147.

7. Mattie L. Leonard in household of John Leonard, Worcester County, Maryland, US Census, 1920, ED 147, sheet 7A, line 50, family 177, NARA microfilm publication T625, roll 677, FHL microfilm 1,820,677k; "Berlin Mayor Denies Riots Stories," *Baltimore Afro-American*, October 24, 1931.

8. "Four Negros Injured in Disorders in Berlin," *Baltimore Sun*, October 19, 1931.

9. "Negro Wanted for Attack on Woman in M.D. Jailed Here," *Wilmington (DE) News Journal*, November 23, 1931.

10. "Mob on Eastern Shore Seeking Negro is Foiled: George Davis," *Frederick (MD) News*, November 24, 1931; "Jailers Foil Lynch Threat," *Cumberland Evening Times*, November 24, 1931.

11. "Husband Is Flogged for Beating Wife," *Salisbury Daily Times*, September 18, 1931. Joseph Bailey was born on December 12, 1862, in Quantico, Maryland, to Levin Collier and Mrs. Elizabeth Russell Bailey of Quantico. In 1885, after completing his education, Joseph moved to Salisbury. There he served one term as deputy registrar of wills for Wicomico County. In 1932, after Bailey completed his first term as associate judge of Maryland's First Judicial Circuit, Governor Albert C. Ritchie appointed him to remain on the bench until the general election of 1934. At the time of his death in 1939, Bailey was recognized as one of the leading attorneys and jurists in Wicomico County. For more on Judge Bailey, see "Former Judge Joseph Bailey Succumbs Here," *Salisbury Daily Times*, May 15, 1939.

12. "Judge Duer Says He Made Error in Judgement Regarding Trouble," *Baltimore Sun*, October 19, 1933.

13. Earle, *Curious Punishments of Bygone Days*, 84; Pleck, *Domestic Tyranny*, 120.

14. "Husband Is Flogged for Beating Wife."

15. "Husband Is Flogged for Beating Wife."

16. "Husband Is Flogged for Beating Wife."

17. The scholarship exploring correlation between economic strife and lynching is not new and has been consistently engaged within lynching historiography. See, for example, White, *Rope and Faggot*; Raper, *The Tragedy of Lynching*; Hovland and Sears, "Minor Studies of Aggression"; Johnson, "The Economics of Lynching"; Jaynes, *Branches without Roots*; Williamson, *The Crucible of Race*; Shapiro, *White Violence and Black Response*. Stewart Tolnay and Elwood Beck argue that economics was in fact the most influential factor: "Economic motives played an important role in mob violence against southern blacks. . . . [W]hen economic fortunes of marginal whites soured (e.g., because of shifts in farm tenure or a swing in the price of cotton), violence against blacks increased." Tolnay and Beck, *A Festival of Violence*, 221.

18. Whyte, *Hoover*, 478.

19. Herbert Hoover to Mr. Eugene Kinckle Jones, April 1, 1929, reprinted in *Opportunity: A Journal of Negro Life* (National Urban League) (May 1929), 139.

20. US Census Bureau, *Occupation Statistics*, 1910, 1920, and 1930.

21. See S. Lebergott, "Labor Force, Employment, and Unemployment, 1929–1939: Estimating Methods," *Monthly Labor Review* 66 (July 1948): tables 1–2, pp. 50–53; S. Lebergott, "Annual Estimates of Unemployment in the United States, 1900–1954," in Universities—National Bureau Committee for Economic Research, Measurement and Be-

havior of Unemployment, NBER Special Conference Series 8, Princeton University, 1957; Bureau of Labor Statistics, *Historical Statistics of the United States, Colonial Times to 1970, Part I* (Washington, DC: Government Printing Office, 1975), series D, 85–86, Unemployment: 1890–1970, 135; *Fifteenth Census of the United States, 1930: Unemployment* (Washington, DC: Government Printing Office, 1931); M. R. Darby, "Three-and-a-Half Million U.S. Employees Have Been Mislaid: Or, an Explanation of Unemployment, 1934–1941," *Journal of Political Economy* 84, no. 1 (1976): 1–16.

22. For more information, see Cezar Tampoya Jackson, "A Comparative Study of Perceptions of the Media Relating to Lynchings on the Eastern Shore of Maryland, 1931–1933," master of arts thesis, Salisbury State University, Salisbury, MD, 1996.

23. "All over America," *Salisbury Times*, February 7, 1931.

24. Charles S. Johnson, "Present Trends in the Employment of Negro Labor," *Opportunity: A Journal of Negro Life* (May 1929), 146; T. Arnold Hill, "The Present Status of Negro Labor," *Opportunity: A Journal of Negro Life* (May 1929), 143; Broadus Mitchell, "The Negro in the Industrial South," *Opportunity: A Journal of Negro Life* (May 1929), 149.

25. Sitkoff, *A New Deal for Blacks*, 26.

26. Reid, "The Forgotten Tenth," 22–23, 26.

27. "Negroes Out of Work."

28. Unemployment Committee to Register Idle," *Salisbury Times*, October 6, 1931.

29. Reid, "The Forgotten Tenth," 14.

30. Hale, *Making Whiteness*, 48.

31. Daniel Jefferson Elliott was born near Mardella, Wicomico County, Maryland, on October 22, 1862, to James and Julia Elliott, two farmer-merchants. Elliott was educated in the Green Hill School, Maryland, and went on to attend a business college in Baltimore. Before opening his factory in Salisbury, Elliott was the proprietor of a general store in White Haven, Maryland. Shortly after that, Elliott made his way to Virginia, where he took up an interest in milling. Around 1884, Elliot married Charlotte Elizabeth "Lottie" Vickers, and in 1900, they were living in Tyaskin, Wicomico County, Maryland, along with their three children Laura (age fourteen), James (seven), and Alice (one). For more information, see Daniel J. Elliott, ED 3, Tyaskin, Precinct 2, Wicomico, Maryland, United States, US Census, 1900, citing ED 113, sheet 17A, family 332, NARA microfilm publication T623, FHL microfilm 1,240,629; Daniel J. Elliott, Salisbury, Wicomico, Maryland, United States, US Census, 1930, citing ED 9, sheet 26A, line 5, family 604, NARA microfilm publication T626, roll 882, FHL microfilm 2,340,617.

32. Statement of Dr. Arthur D. Brown, December 11, 1931, 2, Attorney General (Transcripts), MSA: S T2282-5, MdHR: 87W9; "Doctor Deserts Home after Seeing Mob," *Baltimore Afro-American*, December 12, 1931; F. W. Besley, "Maryland's Lumber and Timber Cut and the Timber Supply," in Hu Maxwell, *The Wood-Using Industries of Maryland* (Baltimore: United States Forest Service, 1910), 47, 49.

33. For more on each of these historic massacres, see Zucchino, *Wilmington's Lie*; Godshalk, *Veiled Visions*; Krehbiel, *Tulsa, 1921*; González-Tennant, *The Rosewood Massacre*.

34. "Doctor Deserts Home after Seeing Mob."

35. "Arthur D. Browne, M.D.," in *Biography–Business* (Salisbury, MD, 1935), 56; James S. Brawley, *The Rowan Story* (Salisbury, MD: Rowan Print Co., 1953), 207, 264–66; Arthur D. Browne World War I Draft Registration Card, 1917, US Selective Service System, *World War I Selective Service System Draft Registration Cards, 1917–1918*, NARA, M1509, 4,582

rolls (image from Family History Library microfilm); Kiwanis display ad, *Salisbury Times*, September 13, 1954; *Thirty-Second Annual Catalog of the Officers and Students of the Leonard Medical School: The Medical Department of Shaw University* (Raleigh, NC: Edwards & Broughton Printing Company, 1912), 31.

36. Hale, *Making Whiteness*, 200.

37. Bailey and Tolnay, *Lynched*, 92–93.

38. Franklin and Franklin, *My Life and an Era*, 192.

39. "Lynched Man's Sister Doesn't Believe Brother a Killer."

40. *Wicomico Telephone Directory* (Salisbury, MD: Chesapeake and Potomac Telephone Company of Baltimore City, 1930), 59. The directory lists "Elliott DJ crate" as located on Lake Street and the residence at 617 Park Avenue.

41. Born in March 1893, James Martindale Elliott was the only son of Daniel Jefferson Elliott and Lottie Elliott. Little is known about his early life, though he was more than likely born in Virginia. James was a graduate of Randolph Macon Academy, an all-boys college-prep school in Front Royal, Virginia. After graduation, he joined his father in the company business, which would eventually be named "D.J. Elliott and Son." Later in life, James moved to Florida and worked with the Gulf Oil Company. During the last few years of his life, he returned to Salisbury, where he lived to be seventy. For more information, see James M. Elliott in household of Daniel J. Elliott, ED 3, Tyaskin, Precinct 2, Wicomico, Maryland, US Census, 1900, *FamilySearch*, accessed March 27, 2020, https://familysearch.org/ark:/61903/1:1:M32J-17Q, citing ED 113, sheet 17A, family 332, NARA microfilm publication T623, FHL microfilm 1,240,629; "James M. Elliott Sr.," *Salisbury Daily Times*, February 25, 1964; obituary of Daniel Jefferson Elliott, Personal Collection of Elliott Neal White (Salisbury, MD), 1931.

42. Statement of Dr. Arthur D. Brown, 2.

43. Statement of Dr. Arthur D. Brown, 2.

44. Statement of Dr. Arthur D. Brown, 2.

45. Statement of Dr. Arthur D. Brown, 2. The older white man with whom Brown spoke was one of at least two whites in the community who suggested a sexual subtext for the lynching. This myth of the Negro rapist would resurface in interviews of white citizens who recalled the events of the lynching in the 1970s. See White Painter (Age 74), "Informant Interview—Salisbury Lynching," Delmar, Delaware/Maryland, November 24, 1970, Box 7, Folder 5: Lynching Interviews, 1970–1973, PSP.

46. The conversation that Brown describes is an example of what Ida B. Wells-Barnett named the "old threadbare lie." Ida B. Wells-Barnett, "Lynch Law in America," *The Arena* 23, no. 1 (1900): 15–23.

47. See Freedman, *Redefining Rape*; Gunning, *Race, Rape, and Lynching*; Sommerville, *Rape and Race in the Nineteenth-Century South*; Nowatzki, "Race, Rape, Lynching, and Manhood Suffrage."

48. White, *Rope and Faggot*, x.

49. Statement of Dr. Arthur D. Brown, 2.

50. Statement of Dr. Arthur D. Brown, 2.

51. Statement of Officer J. C. Peroutka, December 17, 1931, 2, Attorney General (Transcripts), MSA: S T2282-5, MdHR: 87W9.

52. Charles H. Burns, Captain (Summary of Statements); Attorney General (Transcripts), MSA: S T2282-5, MdHR: 87W9, Levin C. Bailey (1927–35); The phone directory lists "Long Curtis W.," as a lawyer with offices in the Salisbury Advertising Building,

and "White William W." as located at 1415 E. Church Street. The directory also lists "Baily Levin Claude, lawyer," with offices located on East Main Street and his personal residence on Camden Avenue. *Wicomico Telephone Directory*, 64, 72, 55; "Bailey, Levin Claude," in *America's Young Men: The Official Who's Who among the Young Men of the Nation* (Los Angeles: Richard Bank Publishing Company, 1934), 26.

53. Statement of Dr. Arthur D. Brown, 4; *Wicomico Telephone Directory*, 69. The directory lists "Smith Marion K.," with his residence at 213 Washington Street. "Pope & Hitchens General Auto Repairs: For Real Service, Lake Street, near Willow," in Thurston, *Industrial Salisbury*, 1934, 5.

54. Statement of Dr. Arthur D. Brown, 3.

55. Statement of Dr. Arthur D. Brown, 22–23; "One Alleged Member of Rowan County Mob Has Been Arrested," *Winston-Salem (NC) Twin-City Daily Sentinel*, August 7, 1906; "Photograph of the Bodies of Nease Gillespie, John Gillespie and Jack Dillingham" (1906) from Kluttz's Studio, E. Council St., near Court House, Salisbury, N.C., National Museum of African American History and Culture, accessed March 21, 2021, https://nmaahc.si.edu/.

56. Statement of Dr. Arthur D. Brown, 3.

57. B.J. Reports, January 8, 1932, 1, Attorney General (Transcripts); *Wicomico Telephone Directory*, 69. The directory lists "Smith Marion K." with residence at 213 Washington Street.

58. B.J. Reports, January 8, 1932, 1.

59. As time went on, white community members recalled a similar story that directly connected the lynching of Williams to the failed lynching attempts of Euel Lee and George Davis. See White Housewife (Age 71), "Lynching in Salisbury," September 23, 1972, Salisbury, Maryland; and White Proprietor of Store, both in "The Salisbury Lynching," Salisbury, Maryland, June 21, 1973, Box 7, Folder 5: Lynching Interviews, 1970–1973, PSP.

60. Report of Sergeants Martin and Ware, February 12, 1932, 2, Attorney General (Transcripts), MSA: S T2282-5, MdHR: 87W9.

61. Sergeants Martin and Ware to Captain Charles H. Burns, Police Department: City of Baltimore, January 16, 1932, Attorney General (Transcripts), MSA: S T2282-5, MdHR: 87W9.

62. Report of Sergeants Martin and Ware, February 12, 1932, 2, Attorney General (Transcripts), MSA: S T2282-5, MdHR: 87W9.

63. W.H.M. (Pinkerton detective code name), Wednesday, February 17, 1932, New York; W.H.M., Thursday, February 18, 1932, New York; W.H.M., Tuesday, February 23, 1932, New York, all in Attorney General (Transcripts).

64. Krech, *Praise the Bridge That Carries You Over*, 124.

65. Krech, *Praise the Bridge That Carries You Over*, 124.

66. Smith, *More than a Whisper*, 125.

67. Additional accounts that point to James as the one who killed his father can be found at the Edward H. Nabb Research Center for Delmarva History in the interviews with Black and white citizens who recalled oral traditions and reflected on their memories of the incident, in "The Lynching of the Innocent," 1972, FK69.027, Folder 1, Folklife Collection—African American Oral Traditions and Stories, Edward H. Nabb Center for Delmarva History and Culture, Salisbury, University, Salisbury, Maryland; White Attorney (Age 72), "Salisbury Lynching," Salisbury, Maryland, June 15, 1973; Black Amer-

ican (Age 31), "Lynching in Salisbury," 1970s; White Housewife (Age 71), "Lynching in Salisbury," September 23, 1972; White Female Eyewitness—Anonymous (Age 70), "Lynching in Salisbury," June 18, 1973; Black Male Eyewitness (Age 67), "Historical Legend," Cambridge, Maryland, June 25, 1973; White Informant (Age 51), "Lynching," Salisbury, Maryland, November 23, 1970; White Informant, Retired (Age 62), "The Last Lynching," July 15, 1973, Salisbury, Maryland all in Box 7, Folder 5: Lynching Interviews, 1970–1973, PSP.

68. Elliott Neal White, interview by author, May 10, 2020, transcript in author's collection, Fairfax, VA.

69. "Salisbury Paper Omits Story of Lynching," *Baltimore Post*, December 5, 1931; "Maryland's Disgrace—The Shame of the Eastern Shore," *Baltimore Post*, December 5, 1931; "Comment of Eastern Shore Newspapers on Lynching," *Baltimore Sun*, December 6, 1931; "Sees Father Killed, Shoots Attacker," *Evening Sun*, December 4, 1931; "Lee to Be Tried on Shore Tuesday," *Baltimore Sun*, December 4, 1931; Moore, *Murder on Maryland's Eastern Shore*, 69–70.

70. "Motive for Slaying Is Not Known," *Salisbury Times*, December 4, 1931.

71. Obituary of Daniel Jefferson Elliott.

72. "Farmers and Merchants Bank of Salisbury," *Salisbury Daily Times*, September 12, 1929.

73. Daniel J. Elliott, 08 Dec 1931, in "Maryland Probate Estate and Guardianship Files, 1796–1940," database with images, *FamilySearch*, accessed March 12, 2018, https://familysearch.org/ark:/61903/1:1:F9XH-QZQ, citing Wicomico County courts, Maryland.

74. Daniel J. Elliott, 08 Dec 1931, in "Maryland Probate Estate and Guardianship Files, 1796–1940."

75. Daniel J. Elliott, 08 Dec 1931, in "Maryland Probate Estate and Guardianship Files, 1796–1940." Modern-day amounts calculated using the Consumer Price Index (CPI) Inflation Calculator, United States Bureau of Labor Statistics, accessed March 26, 2020, https://www.bls.gov/data/inflation_calculator.htm.

76. Thurston, *Industrial Salisbury*, 1934, 14; *P. G. H. Memories*, 1904–54, 26.

77. Statement of Sheriff G. Murray Phillips of Salisbury, December 18, 1931, 1, Attorney General (Transcripts), MSA: S T2282-5, MdHR: 87W9.

78. Statement of Sheriff G. Murray Phillips of Salisbury, 1.

79. Statement of Sheriff G. Murray Phillips of Salisbury, 1.

80. Statement of Sheriff G. Murray Phillips of Salisbury, 1.

81. Hossfeld, *Narrative, Political Unconscious, and Racial Violence in Wilmington, North Carolina*, 20.

82. *Primum non nocere*. The Latin precept is not actually from Hippocrates but is a phrase in the *Epidemics*. Ifill, *On the Courthouse Lawn*, 57. Hippocrates's words are as follows: "Whatsoever houses I enter, I will enter to help the sick, and I will abstain from all intentional wrong-doing and harm, especially from abusing the bodies of man or woman, bond or free. And whatsoever I shall see or hear in the course of my profession, as well as outside my profession in my intercourse with men, if it be what should not be published abroad, I will never divulge, holding such things to be holy secrets. Hippocrates of Cos, "The Oath," *Loeb Classical Library*, 147:298–99, accessed October 6, 2015, doi:10.4159/DLCL.hippocrates_cos-oath.

83. "Report of Harry Greenstein on Visit to Salisbury, Wicomico County," Tuesday, September 13, 1932, Ritchie Executive Papers, Hornbake Library, University of Maryland.

84. Statement of Sheriff G. Murray Phillips of Salisbury, December 18, 1931, 2, Attorney General (Transcripts), MSA: S T2282-5, MdHR: 87W9.

85. Onofrio, *Maryland Biographical Dictionary*, 19. Ward, a Democrat, had served as a member of the Maryland House of Delegates from 1915 to 1917 and as chair of the Democratic State Central Committee of Wicomico County from 1918 to 1926. In 1931, he was serving as a member of the Maryland State Senate, a post that he would hold until 1939. In 1939 Ward left the state legislature to serve as the US representative for Maryland's first congressional district after T. Alan Goldsborough resigned. Ward was part of the Democratic coalition that Roosevelt depended on for his reelection. Ward was a man of the South and the Free State, working as a farmer, lumberjack, and merchant.

86. Statement of Sheriff G. Murray Phillips of Salisbury, 2.

87. Statement of Sheriff G. Murray Phillips of Salisbury, 2.

88. Statement of Sheriff G. Murray Phillips of Salisbury, 2.

89. Statement of Sheriff G. Murray Phillips of Salisbury, 2.

90. Statement of Sheriff G. Murray Phillips of Salisbury, 2.

91. Statement of Mary Massey, Salisbury, Maryland, December 19, 1931, in *Stenographic Transcript in the Case of Statements in Re Lynching of Matthew Williams*, 44–45.

92. Statement of Helen E. Fisher, Salisbury, Maryland, December 19, 1931, in *Stenographic Transcript in the Case of Statements in Re Lynching of Matthew Williams*, 61.

93. Statement of Helen V. Wise, Salisbury, Maryland, December 18, 1931, *Stenographic Transcript in the Case of Statements in Re Lynching of Matthew Williams*, 79.

94. Statement of Helen V. Wise, 81.

95. Statement of Helen E. Fisher, 66; P. G. H. *Memories, 1904–54*, 16.

96. Statement of Mrs. Florence S. Smith of Salisbury, 1.

97. Statement of Mrs. Florence S. Smith of Salisbury, 1.

98. Statement of Mrs. Florence S. Smith of Salisbury, 1.

99. Statement of Mrs. Florence S. Smith of Salisbury, 1.

100. Jennie V. Easton, in household of Joshua Cropper, Salisbury, Wicomico, Maryland, United States, US Census, 1930, database with images, *FamilySearch*, accessed January 15, 2017, https://familysearch.org/ark:/61903/1:1:X3H3-TCT, citing ED 9, sheet 16A, line 27, family 332, NARA microfilm publication T626, roll 882, FHL microfilm 2,340,617; 405 W. Isabella St., *trulia*, accessed February 24, 2021. https://www.trulia.com/homes/Maryland/Salisbury/sold/1446376-405-W-Isabella-St-Salisbury-MD-21801.

101. John Easton (Colored), Salisbury, Maryland, December 18, 1931, in *Stenographic Transcript in the Case of Statements in Re Lynching of Matthew Williams*, 97.

102. William Handy (Colored), Orderly, Salisbury, Maryland, December 18, 1931, in *Summary of Stenographic Transcript in the Case Statements in Re Lynching of Matthew Williams*, 3; Report of Sergeants Martin and Ware, 2.

103. Statement of Mrs. Florence S. Smith of Salisbury, December 18, 1931, 1, Attorney General (Transcripts), MSA: S T2282-5, MdHR: 87W9.

104. Statement of Rufus Jernigan (Colored), Salisbury, Maryland, December 19, 1931, *Stenographic Transcript in the Case of Statements in Re Lynching of Matthew Williams*, 2–3.

105. Statement of Rufus Jernigan (Colored), 3.

106. Statement of Rufus Jernigan (Colored), 4.

107. Statement of Jacob Thomas Conquest (Colored), Salisbury, Maryland, December 18, 1931, in *Stenographic Transcript in the Case of Statements in Re Lynching of Mat-*

thew Williams, 205; Tom Conquest, Salisbury, Wicomico County, Maryland, United States, in "United States Census, 1930," *FamilySearch*, accessed April 15, 2017, https://familysearch.org/ark:/61903/1:1:X3H3-W5W, citing ED 8, sheet 7A, line 44, family 160, NARA microfilm publication T626, roll 882, FHL microfilm 2,340, 61.

108. Statement of Jacob Thomas Conquest (Colored), Salisbury, Maryland, December 18, 1931, in *Stenographic Transcript in the Case of Statements in Re Lynching of Matthew Williams*, 202.

109. Statement of Jacob Thomas Conquest (Colored), 203.

110. Statement of Jacob Thomas Conquest (Colored), 203.

111. Marie Johnson Waller, videotaped interview by Susan Holt, November 2009, Waller (Marie) Salisbury Lynching Oral History Collection, Edward H. Nabb Center for Delmarva History and Culture, Salisbury University, Salisbury, Maryland.

112. Johnson Waller, interview with Susan Holt.

113. Johnson Waller, interview with Susan Holt.

114. Statement of Alfred T. Truitt, editor of *Salisbury Times*, December 18, 1931, 25, Attorney General (Transcripts), MSA: S T2282-5, MdHR: 87W9.

115. Statement of Alfred T. Truitt, 25.

116. *Wicomico Telephone Directory*, 69. The directory lists the "Arcade Theatre" as located on West Main Street.

117. Statement of Carl William Wilson, December 19, 1931, 168, Attorney General (Transcripts), MSA: S T2282-5, MdHR: 87W9.

118. Statement of Carl William Wilson, 168.

119. Statement of Carl William Wilson, 171.

120. Statement of Nicholas H. Holland, Salisbury Chief of Police, December 19, 1931, 27, Attorney General (Transcripts), MSA: S T2282-5, MdHR: 87W9.

121. Samuel C. Broughton, Salisbury, Maryland, December 19, 1931, *Stenographic Transcript in the Case of Statements in Re Lynching of Matthew Williams*, 220.

122. Samuel C. Broughton, 214.

123. Samuel C. Broughton, 215.

124. Walter Dashields (Colored), Salisbury, Maryland, December 19, 1931, *Stenographic Transcript in the Case of Statements in Re Lynching of Matthew Williams*, 184.

125. Walter Dashields (Colored), 187.

126. Randolph Ralph (Colored), Salisbury, Maryland, December 19, 1931, *Stenographic Transcript in the Case of Statements in Re Lynching of Matthew Williams*, 200.

127. Statement of Nicholas H. Holland, Salisbury Chief of Police, December 19, 1931, 14.

128. Statement of Nicholas H. Holland, Salisbury Chief of Police, December 19, 1931, 17.

129. Statement of Nicholas H. Holland, Salisbury Chief of Police, December 19, 1931, 15.

130. Statement of Nicholas H. Holland, Salisbury Chief of Police, December 19, 1931, 19.

131. "Student Masses and Cheering Section Will Provide Color for Charity Game," *Salisbury Daily Times*, December 3, 1931.

132. "Mob Described by Brockman," *News & Salisbury Times*, December 5, 1931.

133. White Female Secretary (Age 59), "Hanging, 1933," Fruitland, Maryland, August 8, 1971, Salisbury, Maryland, Box 7, Folder 5: Lynching Interviews, 1970–1973, PSP.

134. The eyewitness who recalled attending the lynching with his mother saw Williams being hanged a second time, from a guy wire, after his body had been burned. White Male Informant—Eyewitness (Age 59), "Salisbury Lynching." See also White Female Secretary (Age 59), "Hanging, 1933."

135. Statement of Nicholas H. Holland, Salisbury Chief of Police, December 19, 1931, 17.

136. Statement of Nicholas H. Holland, Salisbury Chief of Police, December 19, 1931, 17.

137. Markovitz, *Legacies of Lynching*, xxviii; Evans, *Cultures of Violence*, 4.

138. Statement of Officer J. C. Peroutka, December 17, 1931, 2, Attorney General (Transcripts), MSA: S T2282-5, MdHR: 87W9.

139. Statement of Officer J. C. Peroutka, December 17, 1931, 2.

140. Statement of Will White, December 17, 1931, 2, Attorney General (Transcripts), MSA: S T2282-5, MdHR: 87W9.

141. In the 1970s, a number of informants pushed back against the myth that outsiders were responsible for the lynching of Williams. White Teacher (Age 48), "Informant Interview—Salisbury Lynching," Ocean City, Maryland, June 15, 1972, Box 7, Folder 5: Lynching Interviews, 1970–1973, PSP.

142. Tulani Salahu-Din, "The Evidence of Things Unsaid," National Museum of African American History and Culture, July 6, 2017, https://nmaahc.si.edu/explore/stories/collection/evidence-things-unsaid.

143. Handwritten note and rope used to lynch Matthew Williams, December 1931, Gift of The Estate of Paul S. Henderson, National Museum of African American History and Culture, Washington, DC.

144. Apel, *Imagery of Lynching*, 22, 15; Harris, *Exorcising Blackness*, 22; Apel and Smith, *Lynching Photographs*, 47; Lightweis-Goff, *Blood at the Root*, 10–11. W. E. B. Du Bois remembered seeing such trophies on display in storefront windows in the South. In route to the *Atlanta Constitution*, Du Bois walked by a meat market that "exhibited the fingers of Sam Hose" in its display cabinet. Du Bois, "The Reminiscences of W.E.B. Du Bois" (transcript of interview with W. T. Ingersoll, 1960), Columbia University Oral History Research Office, New York.

145. Havel, "The Power of the Powerless," 5–6.

146. Jones, Nfa, and Stephenson, *Performing the Body/Performing the Text*, 83; Apel, *Imagery of Lynching*, 22.

147. Statement of Sheriff G. Murray Phillips of Salisbury, 2.

148. Statement of Sheriff G. Murray Phillips of Salisbury, 3.

149. Statement of Sheriff G. Murray Phillips of Salisbury, 3.

150. Statement of Sheriff G. Murray Phillips of Salisbury, 5.

151. Statement of John J. Thompson of Landsdowne, Maryland, December 16, 1931, 1, Attorney General (Transcripts), MSA: S T2282-5, MdHR: 87W9.

152. Statement of John J. Thompson, 1.

153. Statement of John J. Thompson, 1.

154. Statement of John J. Thompson, 1.

155. Statement of John J. Thompson, 1.

156. Statement of Wallace H. White, Advertising Manager of the *Salisbury Advertiser*, Salisbury, Maryland, December 18, 1931, 1, Attorney General (Transcripts), MSA: S T2282-5, MdHR: 87W9.

157. Statement of Wallace H. White, 1.

158. Statement of Alex Pollitt, Salisbury, Maryland, December 19, 1931, 1, Attorney General (Transcripts), MSA: S T2282-5, MdHR: 87W9.

159. Statement of Alex Pollitt, 1.

160. Statement of Alex Pollitt, 1.

161. Statement of Dr. Arthur D. Brown, 6.

162. Statement of Dr. Arthur D. Brown, 7.

163. Statement of Dr. Arthur D. Brown, 7.

164. "Indict Sho' Doctor on Narcotic Charge," *Baltimore Afro-American*, January 26, 1929; "Sho' Doctor Gets Year on Dope Charge," *Baltimore Afro-American*, February 9, 1929.

165. Statement of Dr. Arthur D. Brown, 10.

166. Statement of Dr. Arthur D. Brown, 10.

167. Equal Justice Initiative, *Lynching in America*, 5. Years later, one eyewitness who attended the lynching with his mother recalled interpreting the incident as a message crime targeted at the entire Black community. He recalled that the mob dragged Williams's lifeless body "down to Lake and Main and strung him up again so all the colored people can see him." White Male Informant—Eyewitness (Age 59), "Salisbury Lynching," June 28, 1972, Box 7, Folder 5: Lynching Interviews, 1970–1973, PSP. Others recalled being told of the events by their parents who described Williams's lynched body as a "symbol." See, for example, White Male (53), "My Father Described the Hanging," Maryland, 1970s, Box 7, Folder 5: Lynching Interviews, 1970–1973, PSP.

168. Ifill, *On the Courthouse Lawn*, 57.

Chapter 3

Epigraph: Ritchie quoted in "Shore Mob Lynches Negro: Salisbury Killer Is Hanged from Tree at Courthouse," *Baltimore Sun*, December 5, 1931.

1. "Governors Confer amid Pleasant Surroundings," *Indianapolis Star*, June 2, 1931.

2. Ritchie's appeal to states' rights was not new. Most southern Democrats were champions of states' rights as justification for avoiding federal enforcement of civil rights measures. Indeed, this stance can be tracked from the antebellum period to the early civil rights era, when Democrats fought against Reconstruction-era civil rights laws, to the twentieth century, which saw anti-lynching legislation and eventually the Civil Rights Acts of 1964 and 1965. See Chepaitis, "Albert C. Ritchie in Power," 399; Frederickson, *The Dixiecrat Revolt and the End of the Solid South*, 238.

3. Brown, "The Election of 1934," 416, 420. For more information on Ritchie and the Democratic Convention of 1932, see Levin, "Governor Albert C. Ritchie and the Democratic Convention of 1932."

4. "Sho' Lynching May Decide the Next President," *Baltimore Afro-American*, January 2, 1932.

5. Frymer, *Uneasy Alliances*, 93.

6. Farrar, *The Baltimore Afro-American*, 66.

7. Feldman, *Before Brown*, 276, 279.

8. White, *Governors of Maryland*, 258–59.

9. White, *Governors of Maryland*, 258–59.

10. Mark S. Watson, "Albert Cabell Ritchie," in *Dictionary of American Biography*, 20:560; William M. Bowen Jr., "The Period of Ritchie—and After," in Radoff, *The Old Line State*, 129–30.

11. "Gorman Makes Bluff," *Washington (DC) Evening Star*, September 29, 1905; P. Henry, "That 'Poe' Amendment," *Baltimore Afro-American*, July 1, 1905; "Republican Leaders Will Work Hard to Defeat Amendment," *Baltimore Afro-American*, July 22, 1911; Calcott, *The Negro in Maryland Politics*, 114–15; Valelly, *The Two Reconstructions*, 123–24;

Perman, *Struggle for Mastery*, 231–34; "Voters Are Aroused: Preparing to Make a Most Vigorous Fight against the Poe Amendment," *Baltimore Afro-American*, October 21, 1905; Smith, *Here Lies Jim Crow*, 66. The Legal Information Institute defines grandfather clause as "a provision of several Southern states' constitutions in the late 1800s designed to keep blacks from voting; now unconstitutional, these grandfather clauses denied the vote to people who were illiterate or did not own property, unless their descendants had voted before 1867." "Grandfather Clause" (definition 2), Legal Information Institute, Cornell Law School, accessed April 5, 2021, https://www.law.cornell.edu /wex/grandfather_clause. An "understanding clause" required a person registering to vote to explain a provision of the state constitution well enough to satisfy the (white) registrar.

12. Fields, *Slavery and Freedom on the Middle Ground*, 10.

13. Ritchie Citizenship League, *What Governor Ritchie Has Done for the Colored Race*; "Beall Heads Maryland Klan," *Wilmington (DE) Evening Journal*, October 23, 1923.

14. "Ritchie for Governor," *Baltimore Afro-American*, October 19, 1923; State Klan Plans for Political Debut . . . Particularly on Eastern Shore," *Baltimore Sun*, July 9, 1923; John W. Owens, "Ku Klux Rated as Poor Third in Anti-Ritchie Country Fight," *Baltimore Sun*, November 20, 1923; "Beall Heads Maryland Klan."

15. "Why the 'Afro' Is for Ritchie," *Baltimore Sun*, November 2, 1923; "Ritchie Wins by over 40,000 Plurality: 15,000," *Baltimore Afro-American*, November 9, 1923.

16. "Ritchie Names Commission," *Baltimore Afro-American*, September 5, 1924.

17. See "Resentment Rises against Ritchie," *Baltimore Afro-American*, January 10, 1925; "Gov. Ritchie Replies to Afro Questions," *Baltimore Afro-American*, May 16, 1925; "Maryland: Governor Stands for Equal Schools," *Baltimore Afro-American*, June 13, 1925.

18. *US House Journal* 65, no. 2 (1918): 297.

19. "Ritchie, in Virginia, Urges Protection of States Rights, Calls Dyer Bill, 'Label' to Capture Negro Vote," *Washington Post*, March 6, 1926.

20. "Ritchie, in Virginia, Urges Protection of States Rights."

21. "Ritchie, in Virginia, Urges Protection of States Rights."

22. Press Service of the NAACP, Press Release: "Senator France, Representative Dyer to Urge Federal Anti-Lynching [Law]," November 29, 1920, NAACP Papers, Part 7: The Anti-Lynching Campaign, 1912–1955, LOC, Microfilm Reel 26, Frames 407–8.

23. "Mass Meeting Asks Congress to Pass Anti-Lynching Law," *Brooklyn Daily Eagle*, December 10, 1920.

24. Joseph France, "Senator France against Lynching," *Baltimore Afro-American*, February 18, 1921. "On May 6, 1921, [Representative George H.] Tinkham interrupted consideration of an Army appropriations bill by introducing a resolution instructing the House Committee on the Census to investigate disenfranchisement efforts by the states and to report back to the full House with information on how to reapportion and expand the chamber's membership. As usual, he did not mince words, describing southern disenfranchisement schemes as 'the most colossal electoral fraud the world has ever known.' He added, 'On this question moral cowardice and political expediency dominate the Republican leadership of the House.'" "The Negroes' Temporary Farewell: Jim Crow and the Exclusion of African Americans from Congress, 1887–1929," United States House of Representatives: History, Art & Archives, https://history .house.gov/Exhibitions-and-Publications/BAIC/Historical-Essays/Temporary-Fare

well/Reduction/ and the primary citation. See also *Congressional Record*, House, 67th Cong., 1st sess. (May 6, 1921): 1124–26; the entire debate is on 1124–31. For a brief account, see Sherman, *The Republican Party and Black America*, 170–71.

25. Senator Joseph France, Anti-Lynching Bill S. 2791, December 6, 1921, 67th Cong., 2nd sess., Cong. Rec. S35 (1921).

26. Alice Gram and Velma Hitchcock, "Public Conduct Legislation: History of Anti-Lynching Legislation in Congress," in *Congressional Digest* (Washington, DC: Congressional Digest Corporation, 1922), 1:10.

27. Gram and Hitchcock, "Public Conduct Legislation."

28. "The Colored Peoples' Strong Defender . . . Senator France's Record," in *The First Colored Professional, Clerical, and Business Directory of Baltimore City*, 10th ed. (1922–23) (Baltimore: R. W. Coleman, 1922), 2.

29. "Negro Vote May Swing Election: Figures Show Kentucky and Maryland Have Largest Colored Vote," *Baltimore Afro-American*, September 24, 1920.

30. "City's 1920–30 Population Shows 34,000 Increase, History's Largest: Baltimore Tops D.C.," *Baltimore Afro-American*, February 21, 1931. To place these statistics in historical perspective: the Maryland population in 1920 was 1,449,661, and in 1930 Baltimore's population was 804,874. Maryland State Data Center, "Maryland Historical Census," accessed December 29, 2020, https://planning.maryland.gov/MSDC/Pages/census/censusHistorical.aspx.

31. "Interracial Commission Discusses Finance Plans."

32. "Ritchie Won't Back Program of Commission," *Baltimore Afro-American*, March 5, 1927.

33. "Carroll Gibson to Be Hanged Here February 13: Governor Ritchie Signs Death Warrant," *Baltimore Afro-American*, January 17, 1925; "Gibson Guilty, Says Governor: Chief Executive Declares Report," *Baltimore Afro-American*, February 7, 1925; "Ritchie Won't Stay Hanging: Walter White Makes Appeal to Governor," *Baltimore Afro-American*, February 14, 1925; Walter White, Memorandum of visit, February 7, 1925, NAACP Papers, Part 12, Series A, Reel 16, Frame 16, LOC.

34. Wallace Shugg, "Capital Punishment History: A Historical Perspective," Maryland Department of Public Safety and Correctional Services, accessed February 28, 2021, https://dpscs.maryland.gov/publicinfo/capitalpunishment/historical.shtml; "Index by State: Maryland, 1876–1961," *DeathPenaltyUSA*, accessed February 28, 2021, https://deathpenaltyusa.org/usa1/state/maryland2.htm; "Capital Punishment History: Persons Executed in Maryland since 1923," Maryland Department of Public Safety and Correctional Services, accessed February 28, 2021, https://www.dpscs.state.md.us/publicinfo/capitalpunishment/demographics_persons1923.shtml. For more on the Kent County Nine, see G. Kevin Hemstock, *Injustice on the Eastern Shore: Race and the Hill Murder Trial* (Charleston, SC: Arcadia, 2015).

35. Frank R. Kent, "Ritchie of Maryland," *Scribner's Magazine* (October, 1927), 410.

36. "Young Men's League Offers to Campaign for Ritchie: Organization," *Baltimore Sun*, June 27, 1924.

37. W. Preston Lane Jr. to Albert C. Ritchie, December 6, 1931, Attorney General (Transcripts), Correspondence, MSA: S T 2282-5, MdHR: 87W9.

38. Townsend and Boeschenstein, *Illinois Democracy*.

39. "Chicago Board of Trade Hails Governor Ritchie," *Cumberland (MD) Evening Times*, December 7, 1931.

40. "Chicago Board of Trade Hails Governor Ritchie." Cermak, the thirty-fourth mayor of Chicago, had accepted the post on April 7 of that year. His tenure as mayor was cut short when he was assassinated by Giuseppe Zangara in Bayfront Park, Miami, Florida, in 1933 while shaking hands with then president-elect Franklin D. Roosevelt; it was the same year that George Armwood was lynched in Princess Anne, Somerset County, Maryland. "Freedom of Information Act: Franklin D. Roosevelt (assassination attempt)," Washington, DC: Federal Bureau of Investigation; Smith, FDR, 297–98.

41. Ritchie for President to W. Preston Lane Jr., December 7, 1931, Attorney General (Transcripts), Correspondence, MSA: S T 2282-5, MdHR: 87W9.

42. Ritchie for President to W. Preston Lane Jr.

43. Ritchie for President to W. Preston Lane Jr.

44. Theodore Holmes, "Gov. Ritchie, Possible Presidency Candidate, Shies from Mob Issue," *Negro Associated Press*, December 11, 1931.

45. Holmes, "Gov. Ritchie, Possible Presidency Candidate, Shies from Mob Issue."

46. *Maryland Population, 1930–1960: By Election Districts, Cities, and Towns* (Baltimore: Maryland State Planning Department, 1961), at *Internet Archive*, http://archive .org/details/marylandpopulati113mary.

47. Clegg, *Troubled Ground*, 85.

48. "Coroner's Jury to Investigate Slayer's Death," *Salisbury Times*, December 5, 1931. Bailey, a Salisbury native and Democrat, graduated from the University of Maryland Law School in 1913 and started his career shortly thereafter, becoming a partner at Miles, Bailey, and Williams. By 1920 he had begun to pursue politics, serving as city solicitor from 1920 to 1924 and as state's attorney for Wicomico County from 1926 to 1934. Howes, "Bailey, Levin Claude," in *America's Young Men*, 26.

49. Albert C. Ritchie to Levin C. Bailey, telegram, December 5, 1931, Attorney General (Transcripts), Correspondence, MSA: S T 2282-5, MdHR: 87W9.

50. Levin C. Bailey to William Preston Lane, Contemporaneous Notes of Phone Call, December 7, 1931, Attorney General (Transcripts), Correspondence, MSA): S T 2282-5.

51. Levin C. Bailey to William Preston Lane.

52. Levin C. Bailey to William Preston Lane.

53. "Mystery Death Believed to Be Second Mob Victim," *Baltimore Afro-American*, December 12, 1931.

54. "Mystery Death Believed to Be Second Mob Victim."

55. Albert C. Ritchie, n.d., quoted in Kneier, *Illustrative Materials in Municipal Government and Administration*, 519–20.

56. General Assembly (Laws), Chapter 367, 1867, MdHR 820942, 2/2/6/19.

57. Catledge, *My Life and the Times*, 53.

58. "Lane Confers at Salisbury on Lynching," *Cumberland Evening Times*, December 14, 1931.

59. Assistant to Mr. Lane, Contemporaneous Notes of Phone Conversation, December 11, 1931, Attorney General (Transcripts), Correspondence, MSA: S T 2282-5, MdHR: 87W9.

60. "Lane Confers at Salisbury on Lynching," *Cumberland* (MD) *Evening Times*, December 14, 1931; "Lane Arrives Here, Confers with Bailey," *Salisbury Times*, December 14, 1931.

61. "William Preston Lane, Jr., Attorney General, will come to Salisbury Wednesday to assist the State's Attorney. They also will be assisted by Deputy Attorney General

Anderson, who, with detectives from Baltimore, have conducted an investigation for several weeks, during which they made stenographic reports of statements made by scores of persons questioned." "Somerset Folk to Appear at Trial," *Princess Anne Marylander and Herald*, March 18, 1932.

62. For additional background information on the Pinkerton National Detective Agency, see Morn, "*The Eye That Never Sleeps*"; Ward Churchill, "The Pinkerton Detective Agency: Prefiguring the FBI," in Stokes, *Race and Human Rights*, 53–118; and O'Hara, *Inventing the Pinkertons*.

63. Frymer, *Uneasy Alliances*, 93; Farrar, *The Baltimore Afro-American*, 66.

Chapter 4

Epigraph: "Sho' Lynching May Decide the Next President," *Baltimore Afro-American*, January 2, 1932.

1. Wilbur J. Cash dated the birth of the savage ideal to Reconstruction and argued that it extended throughout the United States. In his seminal work, Cash wrote that the savage ideal "had not been established in any Western people since the decay of medieval feudalism. . . . Tolerance, in sum, was pretty well extinguished all along the line, and conformity made a nearly universal law." Indeed, this conformity translated to both ideals and behavioral norms. Cash, *The Mind of the South*, 134–35. For more on the savage ideal see, Tindall, *The Emergence of the New South*, 184.

2. Indeed, as noted, the Williams lynching was similar to the spectacle lynchings of the 1890s; however, it should be pointed out that a year earlier, a similar spectacle lynching had taken place in Marion, Indiana. On August 7, 1930, three young Black men, Thomas Shipp, Abram Smith, and James Cameron, were abducted by a mob of ten to fifteen thousand whites from the Marion jail. Sixteen years old, James Cameron slipped out of the hands of the mob after being beaten. Shipp and Smith did not escape, and the mob lynched them. The climax of the spectacle lynching is captured in an iconic photograph by Lawrence Beitler. Madison, *A Lynching in the Heartland*; Cameron, *A Time of Terror*. For more on public brutality and exhibitionism and the structure of lynch mobs, see Tolnay and Beck, *A Festival of Violence*; Stovel, "Local Sequential Patterns"; and Wood, *Lynching and Spectacle*.

3. Through the detailed background of Johnson's life that follows, we gain insight into the lived experience of poor whites in Baltimore. These life experiences allowed Johnson to blend in with Salisbury's non-elite white community. The social structure of this community would serve as a vital piece of the lynching apparatus.

4. J. Loos, "Syracuse Foreign Born Population, Some Statistics," *Syracuse Sunday Herald*, March 19, 1897, 28.

5. New York State Census, 1915, United States Census, 1917–1918, U.S. World War I Draft Registration Cards, all in "New York State Census, 1915," database, *FamilySearch*, accessed November 8, 2014, https://familysearch.org/ark:/61903/1:1:K9LP-LVD; Patrick Petta, Syracuse Ward 04, Onondaga, New York, United States, "New York State Census, 1915," citing p. 10, line 23, state population census schedules, 1915, New York State Archives, Albany.

6. "Karpe's Comment on Sports Topics," *Buffalo Evening News*, December 15, 1916.

7. Gems, Borish, and Pfister, *Sports in American History*, 189; Gems, *Boxing*, 158.

8. Roediger, *Working toward Whiteness*, 135; Gems, *Sport and the Shaping of Italian-American Identity*; 116; Algren, *Never Come Morning*, 261.

9. "New York's Legalized Prize-Fights," *Literary Digest*, September 16, 1911. New York continued to prohibit boxing until the 1920 Walker Law created the New York State Athletic Commission.

10. "Jersey Legalizes Eight-Around Bouts," *New York Times*, March 6, 1918.

11. "Trenton Bantamweight Who Meets Johnny Murray at T. A. C," *Trenton (NJ) Evening Times*, July 24, 1919; "Yarns from the Ringside," *Trenton Evening Times*, June 29, 1919.

12. "Johnson Anxious for Bell Which Will Start Bout with Champion Herman," *Trenton Evening Times*, April 21, 1919; "Pete 'Kid' Herman, 'Kid Williams Wins over Patsy Johnson,'" *Baltimore Sun*, May 25, 1920; "Heavies to Feature Newark Fight Card," *Washington (DC) Herald*, December 22, 1919; "Complete Chronology of Boxing during 1919," *Pittsburgh Press*, December 21, 1919.

13. Sussman, *Boxing and the Mob*, 44, 48.

14. "Triple Bouts to Be Feature at Fight Club," *Miami News*, March 14, 1925; "Mueller Will Tackle Toughest Boy in His Career in Meeting Patsy Johnson," *Buffalo (NY) Times*, September 25, 1924.

15. Private Patsy A. Petta, Surgeon's Certificate of Disability (SOD), service no. 6691901 (discharged May 27, 1927), Official Military Personnel Files, Infantry Panama, Army, National Personnel Records Center, St. Louis, Missouri. The center did not provide me with Petta's Personnel Files but only with one photocopy of his SOD, and this without citation. Petta had served in the military previously. Patsy Anthony Petta, 1917–1918, in "United States World War I Draft Registration Cards, 1917–1918," database with images, *FamilySearch*, accessed December 12, 2014, https://familysearch.org/ark:/61903/1:1:KXBX-ZSL, citing Syracuse City no. 1, New York, United States, NARA microfilm publication M1509 (n.d.), FHL microfilm 1,819,041.

16. "'P.J.,' Set Down for Good," *Trenton (NJ) Evening Times*, September 13, 1929.

17. "Stumpy Jacobs Wins Decision: Outsmarts Mike Marshall in Feature Bout on Oasis Card at Portsmouth," *Virginian-Pilot and Norfolk Landmark*, November 21, 1931. Banks served in the US Navy on the USS *Vestal*, a navy repair ship in service from 1913 to 1946. "Ship's Bell USS Vestal (AR-4)," Naval History and Heritage Command, accessed January 9, 2021, https://www.history.navy.mil/our-collections/artifacts/ship-and-shore/ShipsBells/vestal-bell-content-page-test.html.

18. "Jacobs Score at Oasis Club: Hopewell Star Wins Decision over Stetz after Giving Away Five Pounds," *Virginian-Pilot and Norfolk Landmark*, December 4, 1931.

19. Sam Roberts, "Norman T. Hatch, Who Filmed Grisly World War II Combat, Dies at 96," *New York Times*, April 28, 2017, https://www.nytimes.com/2017/04/28/us/norman-hatch-dead-filmed-war-in-the-pacific.html.

20. Cline, *Dashiell Hammett*, 16; Hardy, *The BFI Companion to Crime*, 156.

21. Friedman, *The Pinkerton Labor Spy*, 11; Cline, *Dashiell Hammett*; Hammett, *Selected Letters of Dashiell Hammett*, 3.

22. "Help Wanted—Male: Intelligent Person," *Baltimore Sun*, January 9, 1915.

23. Most likely Johnson was still working for the Pinkerton National Detective Agency, which was providing security in 1937 for the Ford Motor Company. According to the *Syracuse Journal*, Johnson was given the security job by former boxer and Holly-

wood actor Charles "Kid" McCoy (Norman Selby) following his release from prison. American Council of Learned Societies, *Dictionary of American Biography*, 396; "Bob Kenefick Says," *Syracuse (NY) Journal*, August 4, 1937; "Bass Arranges Five Bouts," *Syracuse Journal*, April 10, 1933; "Parents of Former Boxers 50 Years Wed," *Syracuse Sports Journal*, May 17, 1937; "Ring and Mat Gossip," *Syracuse Journal*, August 17, 1932.

24. The Burns Detective Agency (William J. Burns National Detective Agency) was established in New York City in 1909 by Baltimore native William J. Burns (1861–1932), a pioneering American private investigator and law enforcement official who would go on to conduct private investigations of several notable cases following his work in the King Johnson case in 1911, including the 1913 lynching of Jewish business owner Leo Frank, whom he would eventually clear of the murder of Mary Phagan. Beginning in 1921, he served as the first director of the Bureau of Investigation. Dray, *At the Hands of Persons Unknown*, 210; Hunt, *Front-Page Detective*, 117.

25. The investigation was covered heavily in the *Baltimore Sun*. "Recalls a Christmas Crime: Governor Gives Cost of Investigating King Johnson's Lynching," *Baltimore Sun*, January 14, 1914; "Used Many Disguises," *Baltimore Sun*, August 6, 1912; "Burns Men Closing In," *Baltimore Sun*, August 7, 1912; "Burns Men Expect to Tell Work in Lynching Case Saturday," *Baltimore Sun*, August 8, 1912; " 'Chief Erwin' Shadowed,' " *Baltimore Sun*, August 8, 1912; " 'Liar!,' Shouts Gleason," *Baltimore Sun*, August 11, 1912; "Two Go Free: Frank Schwab and Howard Herring Acquitted of Participation in Lynching," *Baltimore Sun*, August 11, 1912; "Attributed to Tom," *Baltimore Sun*, August 11, 1912; "Governor and Burns Confer in New York," *Baltimore Evening Sun*, August 13, 1912; "Gleason Brothers Free," *Baltimore Sun*, November 9, 1912; and "Detectives on Secret Work: Brooklyn Lynchings Said to be under Investigation Again," *Baltimore Sun*, November 13, 1912.

26. E. L. Patterson to Hon. William Preston Lane Jr., December 31, 1931, Attorney General (Transcripts), Correspondence, MSA: S T 2282-5.

27. E. L. Patterson to Hon. William Preston Lane Jr.

28. "Invoice for Services and Expenses in Case of Lynching Salisbury, Maryland," Pinkerton National Detective Agency (March 31, 1932), Correspondence, MSA: S T 2282-5.

29. "Thompson's Grill," in *Wicomico County Telephone Directory*, Fall 1930, 54; "Round Trip: Excursion," *Salisbury Times*, February 25, 1932; "Red Star Deluxe Motor Coaches," in Thurston, *Industrial Salisbury*, 1934, 42.

30. B.J. Reports, 1, Tuesday, January 5, 1932, MSA: S T2282-5; Ralph E. Wimbrow, 1930 U.S. Federal Census Record, Wicomico County, Maryland, population schedule, digital image, Ancestry.com, accessed July 9, 2017, https://www.ancestry.com/interactive/6224/4606979_00127/105687914?backurl=https://www.ancestry.com/family-tree/person/tree/113286080/person/280113960422/facts/citation/860293840886/edit/record; "Wimbrow's Garage," in *Wicomico County Telephone Directory*, Fall 1930, 23.

31. "Mayflower Grill," in *Wicomico County Telephone Directory*, Fall 1930, 53.

32. B.J. Reports, 1, Tuesday, January 5, 1932. Joe Fusco is not to be confused with the famous high-ranking associate of Al Capone of the same name, the man behind Capone's Prohibition-era beer-manufacturing operation. Born in Italy around March 14, 1887, Joe Fusco immigrated to Syracuse, New York, in 1905. He and his wife, Angeline Di Vito Fusco, welcomed their first son, Donald, in 1913 and daughter Dolores a year later.

33. As in much of the Prohibition-era South, bootlegging was rampant in Ocean City. Local historian George Hurley conducted oral history interviews with locals who

remembered the seamen active in bootlegging. According to George many of the hotels at the time were known to sell whiskey in tea cups at customers' request. According to these same sources, Capone is said to have provided the money to construct the George Washington Hotel, though no other evidence substantiates this claim. Hurley and Hurley, *Ocean City*; "Stories of Prohibition in Ocean City," Ocean City Life-Saving Station Museum, accessed July 6, 2017, http://www.ocmuseum.org/index.php/site/video _article/stories_of_prohibition_in_ocean_city; Year: 1930, Census Place: Syracuse, Onondaga, New York, Roll 1627, Page 11A, ED: 0061, Image 856.0, NARA, FHL microfilm 2,341,361; "New George Washington Hotel Opens," *Salisbury Times*, June 11, 1931.

34. Year: 1930, Census Place: Ocean City, Worcester, Maryland, Roll 880, Page 7B, ED 0008, US Census, 1930, NARA, FHL microfilm 2,340,615; "Funeral Rites Today for Capt. W. B. S. Powell: Special to the Morning News," *Ocean City Morning News*, October 10, 1933.

35. B.J. Reports, 1, Tuesday, January 5, 1932.

36. B.J. Reports, 2, Tuesday, January 5, 1932; "Arcade Bowling Alley," in *Wicomico County Telephone Directory*, Fall 1930, 55; "Arcade," *Salisbury Times*, February 25, 1932.

37. B.J. Reports, 1, Wednesday, January 6, 1932.

38. B.J. Reports, 1, January 6, 1932. Guthrie continued to fight until 1938. When Harry James "Kid" Guthrie was born on August 28, 1909, in Salisbury, his stepfather, Alfred Elliott, was sixty-three, and his mother, Daisey Guthrie, was twenty-one. Guthrie remained in Salisbury for the majority of his life. When he registered for the draft in 1940 at the age of thirty-two, he stood five feet, six inches and weighed around 140 pounds. He listed Irene Bennett Guthrie as his next of kin. Irene Bennett Guthrie, Year: 1930, Census Place: Salisbury, Wicomico County, Maryland; Roll 882; Page 3A; ED 0011; Image 203.0, US Census, 1930, NARA, FHL microfilm 2,340,617; Delaware, Marriage Records, 1806–1933, Delaware Vital Records, Microfilm, Delaware Public Archives, Dover, DE; Harry James Guthrie, Draft Registration Cards for Maryland, 10/16/1940–03/31/1947, RG 147, National Archives in St. Louis, MO; 1910 United States Federal Census, Census Place: Wilmington, Ward 8, New Castle, Delaware, Box 207, Roll T624_147, Page 18B, ED 0051, Records of the Bureau of the Census, RG 29, NARA; "Goldie-Novak Top Tonight's Fistic Card at the 'Audt,'" *Wilmington (DE) Morning News*, May 19, 1932; "Death and Funerals: Harry J. Guthrie," *Salisbury Times*, May 9, 1966; "Harry James Guthrie," Certificate of Death, Division of Statistical Research and Records, Maryland State Department of Health, Annapolis, MD; "Stumpy Jacobs Kyos Zinkman in Second," *Salisbury Times*, March 11, 1938; BoxRec, s.v. "Kid Guthrie," accessed July 7, 2017, http://boxrec .com/boxer/262526. See "Kid's Not Hungry, Don't Like to Fight, Veteran Says," *Salisbury Times*, August 9, 1951.

39. B.J. Reports, Wednesday, January 6, 1932, 1; Philadelphia Office (Pinkerton Detective Agency) Report, January 8, 1932, Attorney General (Transcripts); Year: 1930, Census Place: Berlin, Worcester County, Maryland, Roll 880, Page 1A, ED 0007, US Census, 1930, National Archives at St. Louis, MO, FHL microfilm 2340615; World War II Draft Cards (Fourth Registration) for the State of Maryland, RG 147, Series M1939.

40. Rodney Edvinsson, ed., Historical Currency Converter, Historicalstatistics.org, accessed January 1, 2017, http://www.historicalstatistics.org/.

41. B.J. Reports, Wednesday, January 6, 1932, 2; "Welter Featured Arena Fight Card," *Salisbury Times*, March 11, 1932; Year: 1930, Census Place: Parsons, Wicomico County, Maryland, Roll 882, Page 9B, ED 0012, US Census, 1930, NARA, FHL microfilm 2,340,617;

Lee Oland Harris, 1942, "United States World War II Draft Registration Cards, 1942," database with images, *FamilySearch*, accessed April 7, 2016, https://familysearch.org /ark:/61903/1:1:F387-GWR, citing NARA microfilm publication M1936, M1937, M1939, M1951, M1962, M1964, M1986, M2090, and M2097.

42. B.J. Reports, Wednesday, January 6, 1932, 2.

43. Born in 1908, Dennis was living in Parsons, Maryland, in 1920. In 1930, Russell lived in Salisbury and was listed as a prizefighter. Year: 1920, Census Place: Parsons, Wicomico County, Maryland, Roll T625_678, Page 10A, ED 122, US Census, 1920; B.J. Reports, January 7, 1932, 1.

44. B.J. Reports, Thursday, January 6, 1932, 1.

45. B.J. Reports, Thursday, January 7, 1932, 1.

46. "At Ritchie-for-Richie," *Salisbury Times*, January 7, 1932.

47. B.J. Reports, Thursday, January 7, 1932, 1–2; Year: 1930, Census Place: Salisbury, Wicomico County, Maryland, Roll 882, Page 11B, ED 0008, Image 74.0, US Census, 1930, NARA, FHL microfilm 2,340,617. Waller married Ruby Insley of Bivalve at Asbury Methodist Episcopal Church in Salisbury on October 6, 1934. "Local Happenings: Waller-Insley," *Salisbury Times*, October 8, 1934. Waller died in his home at age eighty-three on May 18, 1997, and is buried in the Bivalve United Methodist Church Cemetery in Bivalve, Wicomico County, Maryland. "Death Notices: Houston Elwood Waller," *Salisbury Times*, May 20, 1997.

48. Born in April 1883, Grier was a young boy when his father, F. A. Grier Sr., and his uncle R. D. Grier Jr. moved to Salisbury, establishing the Salisbury Machine Works after the fire of 1886. Their partnership in Salisbury dissolved in 1902, and one year later, at the age of twenty, Frederick Grier Jr. and his father went into business as F. A. Grier & Son to manufacture cranes that lifted boats from the water. Shortly thereafter, he began serving on the Salisbury Fire Department. He became chief engineer in 1916. In December 1923, after years of working alongside his father, Grier Jr. was elected to head the fire department, a position that he would hold for eight years until 1931, following the lynching of Matthew Williams. His public service extended to politics and he became a pillar of the Salisbury community, serving on the city council in the late 1920s and early '30s, when he served as president. In 1926, he was awarded for his service to the community as the first recipient of the annual Salisbury Award. James Terry White, "Robert David Grier," in *The National Cyclopaedia of American Biography*, 307; Jacob, *Salisbury in Vintage Postcards* (1988), 53; "F. A. Grier Jr. Dies at 87 in Nursing Home," *Salisbury Times*, April 9, 1971; "Grier Named Head Fire Department," *Salisbury Times*, December 8, 1923.

49. The next day, several New York state papers covered the lynching in detail, including the *Brooklyn Daily Eagle*, *Poughkeepsie Eagle-News*, *Rochester (NY) Democrat and Chronicle*, and *Ithaca Journal*. The *New York Times*, however, ran what it called a special to the *New York Times* under the headline "Mob Lynches Negro Seized in Hospital: Wounded Slayer Is Dragged to Salisbury (Md.) Courthouse and Hanged as 2,000 Look On," on December 5, 1931.

50. B.J. Reports, Thursday, January 7, 1932, 2.

51. B.J. Reports, Thursday, January 7, 1932, 2.

52. "Lankford's Sporting Goods," in *Wicomico County Telephone Directory*, Fall 1930, 53. The directory has Lankford's, as well as Campbell Sporting Goods, located at the corner of Market Street and Camden Avenue.

53. B.J. Reports, Friday, January 8, 1932, 1.

54. B.J. Reports, Saturday, January 9, 1932, 1.

55. "Preston Economy Store," *Salisbury Times*, December 7, 1931; "Preston Economy Store," in Thurston, *Salisbury*, 60.

56. B.J. Reports, Sunday, January 10, 1932, 1.

57. "Noted Fighter at Local Gymnasium," *Salisbury Times*, January 11, 1932.

58. "Noted Fighter at Local Gymnasium."

59. "Veterans Sponsor Boxing at Arena Wednesday Night," *Salisbury Times*, November 12, 1931; "Veterans Will Put on Fights Fortnightly," *Salisbury Times*, November 17, 1931; "Danny Russell Meets Geffner Here Tomorrow," *Salisbury Times*, December 24, 1931; "Smallwood, Turner Fight to a Draw," *Salisbury Times*, March 19, 1932.

60. B.J. Reports, Monday, January 11, 1932, 1.

61. According to the World War II Draft Registration Records from the 1940s, Buck Johnson may also have been known as Charles Buck Wheeler Johnson, born in Wicomico County around 1888. "Charles Buck Wheeler Johnson," World War II Draft Cards (Fourth Registration) for the State of Maryland, RG 147, Series M1939, National Archives at St. Louis, MO.

62. B.J. Reports, Monday, January 11, 1932, 1.

63. B.J. Reports, Tuesday, January 12, 1932, 1.

64. "Ulman's Theatre: Tonight, Tuesday, and Wednesday," *Salisbury Times*, January 12, 1932.

65. B.J. Reports, Wednesday, January 13, 1932, 1.

66. "Russell and Journee Top Card at Arena," *Salisbury Times*, January 14, 1932.

67. B.J. Reports, Thursday, January 14, 1932, 1.

68. Ellwood Charles Guthrie was born in Salisbury on May 15, 1891, to Charles H. Guthrie and Annie Elizabeth Farlow. Guthrie was one of seven children, including Ernest C. (1880–1917), Lillian H. (1883–1937), Clara E. (1885–1963), Daisy Pearl (mother of Harry "Kid" Guthrie) (1888–1958), James Walter (1892–1908), and Edna Susan (1896–1940). Guthrie remained in Salisbury for the majority of his life. He registered for the draft in 1917 at age twenty-seven, when he was living on Pine Street and working as a merchant. He married his wife, Cathie, in 1909, and their son, Charles Benjamin Guthrie, was born in 1927. Guthrie died on May 6, 1941, in Salisbury, Maryland. Charles Benjamin (d. 2010) married Nelda Elizabeth Davis on October 4, 1948, in Salisbury. In 1930, one year prior the lynching of Williams, Guthrie and his family were living in the Camden district of Salisbury, where, according the US Census, Guthrie was renting a home for $10 a month and was a grocery store merchant. Ellwood Guthrie, Salisbury, Wicomico County, Maryland, ED 11, sheet 3B, line 87, family 79, US Census, 1930, NARA microfilm publication T626, roll 882, FHL microfilm 2,340,617; Ellwood Charles Guthrie, 1917–1918, "United States World War I Draft Registration Cards, 1917–1918," database with images, *FamilySearch*, accessed August 24, 2019, https://familysearch.org/ark:/61903/1:1:KZ8F-27R; Ellwood Charles Guthrie, 1941, Burial, Salisbury, Wicomico County, Maryland, Parsons Cemetery, *Find a Grave*, http://www.findagrave.com, citing record ID 58453585.

69. B.J. Reports, Friday, January 15, 1932, 1.

70. "Russell and Journee Will Fight Friday," *Salisbury Times*, January 9, 1932; "Journee Takes 8 Around Bout from Journee," *Salisbury Times*, January 16, 1932;

71. B.J. Reports, Saturday, January 16, 1932, 1; Sunday, January 17, 1932, 1.

72. B.J. Reports, Monday, January 18, 1932, 1.

73. "Court Denies Lee New Trial," *Salisbury Times*, January 28, 1932; B.J. Reports, Wednesday, January 20, 1932, 1.

74. Martin and Ware to Captain Charles H. Burns, January 23, 1932, Attorney General (Transcripts), MSA: S T2282-5, MdHR: 87W9.

75. B.J. Reports, Wednesday, January 20, 1932, 1; "Sheriff History," Sussex County, Delaware, accessed March 15, 2018, https://sussexcountyde.gov/sheriff-history. A year later a Black employer who was a coworker of Williams recalled the mob cutting up his body, castrating him, and cutting off his toes, thereby creating "nigger Toes," which were used as ornaments. See "Historical Legend," Cambridge, Maryland, June 25, 1973, Box 7, Folder 5: Lynching Interviews, 1970–1973, PSP; "Lynched Man's Fingers, Toes, Used to Make 'Nigger Sandwich,'" *Baltimore Afro-American*, March 12, 1932.

76. "Sheriff's History," Wicomico County Sheriff's Office, accessed October 25, 2019, http://www.wicomicosheriff.com/pages/au-history.htm.

77. Thirty-two-year-old Dennis was a native of Salisbury, Maryland, born on May 28, 1900, at the turn of the twentieth century. He dropped out of high school in the eleventh grade and, by 1930, was living with his parents in Piankatank, Mathews County, Virginia, and working as a farmer. By 1940, Dennis had moved back to Maryland, where he was living on Busy Street in Berlin, Worcester County. He enlisted in the US Army on August 15, 1942, serving in World War II until he was honorably discharged on July 15, 1945. Dennis died on October 8, 1959, in Berlin. B.J. Reports, Thursday, January 21, 1932, 1; Dennis, Draft Registration Cards for Maryland, 10/16/1940–03/31/1947, RG 147, National Archives in St. Louis, MO.

78. Maslin graduated from Morgan College at Princess Anne Academy at age of seventeen or eighteen in 1915 with a degree in science and an Industrial Certificate in printing. *Year Book of Morgan College, 1914–1915* (Princess Anne Academy–Eastern Branch of the Maryland Agricultural College) (Baltimore: Morgan College Press, 1915), 7. Around this time, Maslin Pinkett began serving in the US armed services. He lived at 2101 W. First Street in Chester, Pennsylvania, where he worked at Chester Shipbuilding Company, owned and operated by retired US Navy captain Charles Jack. On his draft card, he lists Daniel J. Pinkett of Vienna, Maryland, as his nearest relative. Daniel Pinkett was an instructor of mathematics at Princess Anne Academy, where Maslin would soon join the faculty. Maslin Frysinger Pinkett, 1917–18, "United States World War I Draft Registration Cards, 1917–1918," database with images, *FamilySearch*, accessed February 23, 2021, https://familysearch.org/ark:/61903/1:1:K6V7-S5H.

In 1920, Maslin was living in Philadelphia, Pennsylvania, with his wife of two years, Martha, where they welcomed their first child, Geraldine V. Pinkett the year before. While in Philadelphia he worked a government job as a laborer, living as a boarder in Ward 32 of Philadelphia. In 1923, their second child, a boy, Maslin F. Pinkett Jr., was born, followed in 1925 by their second son, Grant "Robsol" Pinkett (1925–1991), the grandfather of award-winning actress, Jada Pinkett Smith. "United States Census, 1930," database with images, *FamilySearch*, accessed April 6, 2021, https://familysearch.org/ark:/61903/1:1:X34Y-H6F; Maslin F. Pinkett, Princess Anne, Somerset County, Maryland, citing ED 19, sheet 5A, line 19, family 3, NARA microfilm publication T626, roll 879, FHL microfilm 2,340,614.

By 1930 Pinkett and his family had made their way back home to Princess Anne, where he was now working as a teacher at the Princess Anne Academy. In the same year, they welcomed their third son, Marvin (Marlin) D. Pinkett. By 1940, all but two of his children had left their natal home, and he was still teaching at Princess Anne Academy. His son Maslin Jr., now eighteen, was working as a porter. Grant "Robsol" Pinkett was also living in the home, but was unemployed. Maslin Pinkett, 1920, in "United States Census, 1920," database with images, *FamilySearch*, accessed February 3, 2021, https://www.familysearch.org/ark:/61903/1:1:M6YP-4RP.

79. B.J. Reports, Friday, January 22, 1932, 1.

80. B.J. Reports, Saturday, January 23, 1932, 1.

81. B.J. Reports, Sunday, January 24, 1932, 1.

82. B.J. Reports, Monday, January 25, 1932, 1.

83. B.J. Reports, Tuesday, January 26, 1932, 1.

84. B.J. Reports, Wednesday, January 27, 1932, 1.

85. B.J. Reports, Thursday, January 28, 1932, 1.

86. B.J. Reports, Friday, January 29, 1932, 1.

87. B.J. Reports, Friday, January 29, 1932, 1.

88. B.J. Reports, Saturday, January 30, 1932, 1; "Maud Wilson," Year: 1930, Census Place: Parsons, Wicomico County, Maryland, Roll 882, Page 17A, ED 0012, Image 265.0, US Census, 1930, NARA, FHL microfilm 2,340,617; "Ralph 'Fats' Wilson," Year: 1940; Census Place: Princess Anne, Somerset County, Maryland, Roll T627_1560, Page 15A, ED, 20-2, database, *FamilySearch*, accessed March 15, 2016, https://familysearch.org /ark:/61903/1:1:Q29Y-XSHL; Ralph W. Wilson, 1949, Burial, Saint Andrew's Episcopal Cemetery, Princess Anne, Somerset County, Maryland, *Find a Grave*, February 10, 2019, http://www.findagrave.com.

89. Martin and Ware to Captain Charles H. Burns, report, January 30, 1932, MSA: S T2282-5, MdHR: 87W9. Lilian Serman (Sirman) was born in Camden, Wicomico County, Maryland, in 1909 to George and Florence Sirman. In 1930, one year before the lynching, Serman was living in Salisbury with her parents and was working as a bookkeeper. Later, by 1940, she moved to Baltimore and worked as a clerk. Lilian E. Serman, in household of George E. Serman, Salisbury, Wicomico County, Maryland, "United States Census, 1930," database with images, *FamilySearch*, accessed March 4, 2020, https:// familysearch.org/ark:/61903/1:1:X3H3-6G7, citing ED 16, sheet 3B, line 95, family 67, NARA microfilm publication T626, roll 882, FHL microfilm 2,340,617; Lillian Serman, in household of Leonara Baldwin, Ward 11, Baltimore City, Maryland, "United States Census, 1940," database with images, *FamilySearch*, accessed January 25, 2020, https:// familysearch.org/ark:/61903/1:1:K7X7-4V4, citing ED 4-259, sheet 3B, line 51, family 97, NARA digital publication T627, RG 29, roll 1518.

90. Martin and Ware to Captain Charles H. Burns, January 23, 1932.

91. A year later, a white high school teacher recalled having taken a bus from Pocomoke to Salisbury on the day of the lynching. His account also shows the lynching was planned and was to take place "before midnight." White Librarian, Cambridge High School (Age 63), Cambridge, Maryland, June 28, 1972, "The Salisbury Lynching," PSP.

92. John H. Williams, Trappe, Wicomico County, Maryland, "United States Census, 1920," database with images, *FamilySearch*, March 3, 2020, https://familysearch.org /ark:/61903/1:1:M677-XRN, citing ED 125, sheet 13B, line 98, family 157, NARA microfilm publication T625, roll 678, FHL microfilm 1,820,678; John H. Williams, ED 27, Wicomico County, Maryland, "United States Census, 1930," database with images, *FamilySearch*, accessed March 3, 2020, https://familysearch.org/ark:/61903/1:1:X3HQ-ZCT, cit-

ing ED 27, sheet 9A, line 30, family 208, NARA microfilm publication T626, roll 882, FHL microfilm 2,340,617; John H. Williams (obituary), *Salisbury Daily Times*, January 12, 1967.

93. John Martin Sr. was born on May 10, 1880, in Somerset County, Maryland. In 1903, he married Adel. John Henry Martin Jr., was born in 1907, one of five children. In 1920 Martin Sr. and his family were still living in Somerset County, in East Princess Anne, where he worked as laborer at a local sawmill. By 1930 John Jr. was no longer living at home, and his father was now working at a lumber factory. In 1942, John Henry Martin Sr. was living on Center Street in Fruitland, Maryland, and working for Conrad Oswald Long at Long Lumber Company on Tony Tank Road. Martin Jr. must have been illiterate as he signed an X by the signature line. His height was five, eight, and he weighed 135 pounds. "John H. Martin" (death notice), *Salisbury Daily Times*, May 23, 1959; John Martin, East Princess Anne, Somerset County, Maryland, "United States Census, 1920," database with images, *FamilySearch*, accessed March 5, 2020, https://familysearch.org/ark:/61903/1:1:M673-VJ6, citing ED 102, sheet 11A, line 8, family 224, NARA microfilm publication T625, roll 678, FHL microfilm 1,820,678; John Martin, ED 16, Wicomico, Maryland, United States, "United States Census, 1930"; John Henry Martin, 1942, "United States World War II Draft Registration Cards, 1942," database with images, *FamilySearch*, accessed March 9, 2018, https://familysearch.org/ark:/61903/1:1:F38P-8NR, citing NARA microfilm publication M1936, M1937, M1939, M1951, M1962, M1964, M1986, M2090, and M2097.

94. Conrad Oswald Long was born on August 15, 1891, in Fruitland, Maryland, to John and Cora Long. Conrad was the youngest male child of eight siblings. By 1930, one year before the lynching of Williams, Long, his first wife, Eva, and his two daughters, Pauline and Anne, were all living in Fruitland, where he was the owner and operator of Long Lumber Company. Most likely a wealthy man by then, Long served briefly in the military during World War II and raised over $20,000 in war bonds. Conrad Oswald Long, "United States, Veterans Administration Master Index, 1917–1940," database, *FamilySearch*, accessed October 23, 2019, https://familysearch.org/ark:/61903/1:1:WMT 5-BF6Z, citing Military Service, NARA microfilm publication 76193916, various roll numbers; Conrad O. Long in household of John I. Long, ED 7, Trappe, Wicomico County, Maryland, "United States Census, 1900," database with images, *FamilySearch*, accessed March 3, 2020, https://familysearch.org/ark:/61903/1:1:M32V-WYQ, citing ED 118, sheet 12B, family 187, NARA microfilm publication T623, FHL microfilm 1,240,629; "Loretta Long Spurs Sale of $62,400 in Bonds Here," *Salisbury Daily Times*, July 24, 1942; Martin and Ware to Captain Charles H. Burns, January 23, 1932.

95. Henry Yewell (Ewell) was born on March 19, 1889, in Westover, Maryland. Around 1915, he married Lillie. In 1930 he was working for the public utility department in Salisbury. In 1942, he lived at 308 Anne Street in Salisbury, Maryland, and was five foot, seven and a half and weighed 168 pounds. Ewell died of a heart attack in Salisbury in 1947; Henry P. Ewell, 1942, "United States World War II Draft Registration Cards, 1942," database with images, *FamilySearch*, accessed March 9, 2018, https://family search.org/ark:/61903/1:1:F3NQ-LX9, citing NARA microfilm publication M1936, M1937, M1939, M1951, M1962, M1964, M1986, M2090, and M2097, Henry P. Ewell (obituary), *Salisbury Daily Times*, July 18, 1947.

96. Attempts to find J. R. Waters in population schedules were unsuccessful. However, one Rev. J. R. Waters was identified in local newspapers and church reports as the

presiding elder of the Salisbury District in the Delaware Annual Conference of the United Methodist Church. *Minutes of the Session of the Delaware Annual Conference of the Methodist Episcopal Church* (Wilmington, DE: James & Webb Print and Stationery Company, 1904), 27; Penn and Bowen, *The United Negro*, 511; "Methodists Conference To Retire Ministers," *Salisbury Daily Times*, May 2, 1942;Martin and Ware to Captain Charles H. Burns, January 23, 1932.

97. By 1930, Corbin also worked as a painter and private contractor. He registered for the draft in 1942. B.J. Reports, Sunday, January 31, 1932, 1; Ralph A. Corbin, in "US Census, 1920," Census Place: Westover, Somerset County, Maryland, Roll T625_678, Page 13A; ED 100; Ralph A. Corbin, in "US Census, 1930," Census Place: Salisbury, Wicomico County, Maryland, Roll 882, Page 16B, ED 0011, Image 230.0, NARA, FHL microfilm 2,340,617.

98. Frederick Albert Grier Sr. and Frederick Albert Grier Jr., "US Census, 1930," Year: 1930, Census Place: Salisbury, Wicomico, County, Maryland, Page 4B, ED 0007.

99. Ifill, *On the Courthouse Lawn*, 77.

100. "Sheriff History," Sussex County, Delaware. Accessed March 15, 2018, https://sussexcountyde.gov/sheriff-history.

101. Chandler, *Brothers in Blood*, 168.

102. Ifill, *On the Courthouse Lawn*, 77.

Chapter 5

Epigraph: Mitchell quoted in "Senator Bruce Joins Defense Eastern Shore," *Salisbury Daily Times*, January 29, 1932.

1. Broadus Mitchell, interview with Mary Frederickson, August 14 and 15, 1977, interview B-0024, Southern Oral History Program Collection (no. 4007), University of North Carolina, Chapel Hill; Piper, "The Formation of the Social Policy of the Federal Council of Churches." The FCCCA practice of investigating lynching began around the time of the Williams incident. In his oral history, Mitchell suggests that the FCCCA maintained the practice throughout the United States whereby it would recruit a local citizen to develop a report detailing the events leading up to the extralegal mob action. Other sources, however, show that the FCCCA's interest in lynching dates back to at least 1916, when the issue was taken up at the Second Quadrennial Meeting by the newly established Committee on Special Interests of the Colored Denominations, which included such notable members as Booker T. Washington. It was during this meeting that the committee spoke out vocally against the evil of lynching, sparking a heated exchange in which a white member of the council suggested that the lynching of Black victims was justified by the need to protect white women.

2. "In Rebuttal to Prof. Broadus Mitchell" (editorial), *Salisbury Times*, February 6, 1932.

3. "Senator Bruce Joins Defense of Eastern Shore," *Salisbury Times*, January 29, 1932.

4. "To Pessimists, by Ritchie in Frankfort (Ky.) Address," *Cincinnati Enquirer* (Kentucky ed.), February 2, 1932.

5. B.J. Reports, Monday, February 1, 1932, 1. After not finding a Bill Davis in the census, I looked for William Davis. There were two William Davises listed in the 1930 census. One was born in 1904 and in 1930 was living at 415 Warks Street and working as

a farm laborer. The other Davis was born in 1898, and the census taker found him at 102 Monroe Street in Salisbury, working as a "Leatheror at a Whip Factory." William Davis, Census Place: Salisbury, Wicomico County, Maryland Roll 882, Page 12A, ED 0011, US Census, 1930, NARA, FHL microfilm 2340617; William Davis, Census Place: Salisbury, Wicomico, Maryland, Roll: 882, Page: 12A, ED 0011, US Census, 1930, NARA, FHL microfilm 2340617.

6. B.J. Reports, Monday, February 1, 1932, 1.

7. B.J. Reports, Monday, February 1, 1932, 1.

8. Bill Lankford Perry was born on September 14, 1896, in Maryland. He enlisted as a private in the US Army on August 27, 1918. By November 27, 1918, he was serving in Company One of the 72nd Infantry, 29th Division. On January 18, 1919, he was honorably discharged. By 1920 he was living with his parents on First Street in Salisbury and working at the local electric company. In 1930 he was living with his wife, Alice May, and his in-laws at 413 Barclay Street and was employed as a lineman at the local telephone company. By 1940 he and Alice had moved to Bishopville, Maryland, in Worcester County. Bill Lankford Perry, Census Place: Salisbury, Wicomico County, Maryland, Roll 629, Page 31A, ED 0123, US Census, 1930, FHL microfilm 1240629; Bill Lankford Perry, Census Place: Salisbury, Wicomico County, Maryland, Roll: T625_678, Page 12A, ED 136, US Census, 1920; Bill Lankford Perry, Census Place: Salisbury, Wicomico, Maryland, Roll 882, Page 21A, ED 0007, US Census, 1930, FHL microfilm 2340617; *Maryland in the World War, 1917–1919: Military and Naval Service Records*, 2 vols. (Baltimore: Twentieth Century Press, 1933); Perry draft registration card, World War II Draft Cards (Fourth Registration) for the State of Maryland, RG 147, NARA, series M1939.

9. Herman E. "Jack" Townsend was born on February 3, 1912. At age twenty-eight he was married and living with his parents at 510 Taylor Street in Salisbury, where he worked as a moving picture operator. According to census records, Townsend's salary was $1,300 a year. In 1942 he enlisted in the National Guard and was made a sergeant. Census Place: Salisbury, Wicomico County, Maryland, Roll T627_1563, Page 14A, ED 23-13, US Census, 1940, NARA; Electronic Army Serial Number Merged File, 1938–1946, ARC 1263923 World War II Army Enlistment Records, RG 64, National Archives at College Park, Maryland.

10. Herman E. Townsend, Census Place: Salisbury, Wicomico, Maryland, Roll T627_1563, Page 14A, ED 23-13, US Census, 1940, NARA; Electronic Army Serial Number Merged File, 1938–1946, ARC 1263923.

11. "Kellar Crawford" was actually born Crawford Keller on July 1, 1911, in Princess Anne, Somerset County, Maryland. He lived in Princess Anne until the late 1940s with his parents Frank and Beaulah Keller. In 1920 he lived in West Princess Anne, on Somerset Heights road. By 1930, one year before the lynching of Williams, Keller was eighteen, had quit school, and was working as a salesman in a hardware store. Keller took to boxing at an early age and, following the lynching, he would carry the Eastern Shore boxing legacy as a successful fighter, eventually becoming one of the most famous trainers and promoters in the region. It seems as if Keller saw Johnson and Harris and the older boxers as mentors. Crawford Keller, Census Place: West Princess Anne, Somerset County, Maryland, Roll T625_678, Page 19B, ED 84, US Census, 1920, NARA; Crawford Keller, Census Place: Princess Anne, Somerset County, Maryland, Roll 879, Page 8A, ED 0002, US Census, 1930, FHL microfilm 2340614; Crawford Keller, Find a Grave Index, 1600s–Current, Ancestry.com; "Through the Ropes," *Salisbury Times*,

March 21, 1936; "Rotary Arranges Boxing Bouts for Red Cross Benefits," *Salisbury Times*, January 28, 1937; Ed Nichols, "Shore Sports," *Salisbury Times*, April 8, 1947; "8 Bouts Scheduled at Memorial Field," *Salisbury Times*, June 25, 1948; "Former Boxer, Crawford Keller, Dies in Hospital," *Salisbury Times*, May 11, 1964.

12. B.J. Reports, Wednesday, February 3, 1932, 1.

13. Census Place: Salisbury, Wicomico, Maryland, Roll T627_1563, Page 14A, ED 23-13, US Census, 1940, NARA; Electronic Army Serial Number Merged File, 1938–1946, ARC 1263923, World War II Army Enlistment Records, RG 64, National Archives at College Park, Maryland.

14. B.J. Reports, Thursday, February 4, 1932, 1.

15. Born in Maryland, Beulah Smith was living as a boarder at 208 Ohio Avenue in Salisbury in 1930, where she worked as a waitress. Beulah Smith, Census Place: Salisbury, Wicomico County, Maryland, Roll 882, Page 8A, ED 0010, US Census, 1930, FHL microfilm 2340617.

16. B.J. Reports, Friday, February 5, 1932, 1.

17. B.J. Reports, Sunday, February 7, 1932, 1.

18. Fred Ruark was born on June 13, 1907, in Salisbury. By 1930 he was living with his wife and working as a farm laborer in Quantico, Maryland. By 1940, he had moved back to Salisbury and was employed as a government worker and was living on West Main Street with his wife, Catherine. During World War II he enlisted in one of the armed services. Census Place: Quantico, Wicomico County, Maryland, Roll 881, Page 3B, ED 0003, US Census, 1930, NARA, FHL microfilm 2340616; Census Place: Salisbury, Wicomico County, Maryland, Roll T627_1563, Page 1A, ED 23-10, US Census, 1940, NARA; Draft Registration Cards for Maryland, 10/16/1940–03/31/1947, RG 147, Box 445, National Archives at St. Louis, Mo.

19. B.J. Reports, Monday, February 8, 1932, 1.

20. B.J. Reports, Tuesday, February 9, 1932, 1.

21. John William Crockett was born in Dames Quarter, Maryland, May 24, 1895. During World War I, he enlisted in the US Army, Company G, 313th Infantry. He was honorably discharged on June 19, 1919. John William Crockett, World War II Draft Cards (Fourth Registration) for the State of Maryland, RG 147, Series M1939, National Archives at St. Louis, Mo.; Applications for Headstones for U.S. Military Veterans, 1925–1941, Microfilm publication M1916, ARC ID: 596118, RG 92, NARA.

22. B.J. Reports, Wednesday, February 10, 1932, 1.

23. B.J. Reports, Thursday, February 11, 1932, 1.

24. "100 to Be Called in Lynching Case," *Baltimore Sun*, March 14, 1932.

25. A native of Maryland, Kennerly was born around 1876. By 1930 he was living in Salisbury on Newton Street with his wife, Florence. He owned his home and ran a successful laundry business in Salisbury. Census Place: Salisbury, Wicomico County, Maryland, Roll 882, Page 6A, ED 0010, US Census, 1930, FHL microfilm 2340617. For a list of Salisbury mayors, see Wicomico County, Maryland," *Maryland Manual On-Line*, accessed January 5, 2018, http://msa.maryland.gov/msa/mdmanual/37mun/salisbury/html/smayors.html.

26. B.J. Reports, Friday, February 12, 1932, 1.

27. B.J. Reports, Friday, February 12, 1932, 1.

28. B.J. Reports, Saturday, February 13, 1932, 1.

29. B.J. Reports, Sunday, February 14, 1932, 1, and Monday, February 15, 1932, 1.

30. Sergeants Martin and Ware to Captain Charles H. Burns, February 12, 1932, Attorney General (Transcripts), MSA: S T 2282-5, MdHR: 87W9. Purnell was born on October 28, 1910, in Salisbury, Maryland, to Henry and Ola Purnell. He graduated from Salisbury Industrial High School (now Salisbury High School) in 1930. Three years following the Williams lynching, he married Mary Purnell. He would work at the Wicomico Hotel as a janitor and bellman until 1943. In November of that year, Purnell enlisted in the US Army in Baltimore and fought in World War II. He listed his occupation as bellman and claimed to have had five years of high school education. After the war, he worked for the C&P Telephone Company until his retirement. Except during his military service, Purnell lived in Salisbury all his life and was active in several local organizations, including the Wesley Temple United Methodist Church and the American Legion Spirit of Democracy Post 145. Howard Purnell in entry for Henry Purnell, "United States Census, 1920," database with images, *FamilySearch*, accessed February 1, 2021, https://www.familysearch.org/ark:/61903/1:1:M677-6N9; Howard Purnell in household of Henry Purnell, Salisbury, Wicomico County, Maryland, "United States Census, 1930," database with images, *FamilySearch*, accessed April 11, 2021, https://familysearch.org/ark:/61903/1:1:X3H3-LGX, citing ED 8, sheet 2A, line 27, family 23, NARA microfilm publication T626, roll 882, FHL microfilm 2,340,617; "Howard James Purnell" (obituary), *Salisbury Daily Times*, July 25, 2003.

31. Years later, one eyewitness to the lynching confirmed that the mob was made up not only of locals from Salisbury but also residents from Princess Anne. White Male Informant (Age 60), "During the Lynching," July 1970, Salisbury, Maryland, Box 7, Folder 5: Lynching Interviews, 1970–1973, PSP.

32. Sergeants Martin and Ware to Captain Charles H. Burns, February 12, 1932.

33. Linda Duyer, "Round the Pound," interview by Chris Ranck, *Delmarva Today*, July 11, 2014.

34. Duyer, "Round the Pound." Until Duyer's remembrance was published in 2014, it was long thought that Purnell took the memory of his classmate Williams's lynching to his grave.

35. Martin and Ware to Captain Charles H. Burns, February 12, 1932.

36. "News Bulletins," *Evening News*, February 5, 1932; "Philadelphia Is Being Combed for Slayer of Girl," *New Castle (PA) News*, February 9, 1932.

37. B.J. Reports, Tuesday, February 16, 1932, 1.

38. B.J. Reports, Tuesday, February 16, 1932, 1.

39. B.J. Reports, Wednesday, February 17, 1932, 1.

40. B.J. Reports, Thursday, February 18, 1932, 1.

41. "Johnson to Fight in Portsmouth, VA.," *The Salisbury Times*, February 17, 1932.

42. B.J. Reports, Friday, February 19, 1932, 1.

43. B.J. Reports, Friday, February 19, 1932, 2.

44. B.J. Reports, Friday, February 19, 1932, 1.

45. B.J. Reports, Saturday, February 20, 1932, 1; Sunday, February 21, 1932, 1.

46. "'Two Kinds of Women' at Arcade Theatre," *Salisbury Times*, February 22, 1932; B.J. Reports, Monday, February 22, 1932, 1.

47. B.J. Reports, Tuesday, February 23, 1932, 1.

48. B.J. Reports, Wednesday, February 24, 1932, 1.

49. B.J. Reports, Thursday, February 25, 1932, 1.

50. Bill Nichols lived in the "colored settlement" of Jersey. See "Veterans Sponsor

Boxing at Arena Wednesday Night," *Salisbury Times*, November 12, 1931; "Veterans Will Put on Fights Fortnightly," *Salisbury Times*, November 17, 1931; "From Reveille to Taps: The Veterans of Foreign Wars," *Salisbury Times*, November 30, 1931; William Nichols, Census Place: Salisbury, Wicomico County, Maryland; Roll T625_678, Page 2B, ED 134, US Census, 1920, NARA; William Nichols's draft registration, World War I Selective Service System Draft Registration Cards, 1917–1918, RG 147, NARA, M1509, 4,582 rolls, FHL microfilm.

51. B.J. Reports, Friday, February 26, 1932, 1.

52. B.J. Reports, Saturday, February 27, 1932, 1.

53. B.J. Reports, Sunday, February 28, 1932, 1; Monday, February 29, 1932, 1.

Chapter 6

1. "Editorial Notes," *Denton (MD) Journal*, March 5, 1932. Denton, in Caroline County, is less than seventy miles from Salisbury.

2. B.J. Reports, Tuesday, March 1, 1932, 1.

3. B.J. Reports, Wednesday, March 2, 1932, 1.

4. "Parsons Confectionery, Formerly Frank's, South Division Street," *Salisbury Times*, December 22, 1931; B.J. Reports, Thursday, March 3, 1932, 1.

5. "Dance Bradley Building: Percy Glascoe and His Plantation Orchestra," *Salisbury Times*, March 8, 1932.

6. Lawrence, *Duke Ellington and His World*, 69.

7. B.J. Reports, Friday, March 4, 1932, 1.

8. Attorney General Preston Lane to Levin C. Bailey, March 4, 1932, Attorney General (Transcripts), Correspondence, MSA S T 2282-5.

9. B.J. Reports, Saturday, March 5, 1932, 1.

10. Clifford Dreydon was born around 1903 in Maryland. In 1920, he was married and living in Salisbury. By 1930, Dryden had found a career as an oil agent. Apparently successful as a salesman, he owned a home in Salisbury, valued at $6,000, at 502 Saratoga Street, where he and his wife, Irma, lived. In 1940, the Drydens lived on Priscilla Street in Salisbury, and he was still working as an oil salesman, earning a little over $1,000 a year. See Clifford P. Dreydon, Salisbury, Wicomico County, Maryland, "United States Census, 1930," database with images, *FamilySearch*, accessed April 8, 2021, https://familysearch.org/ark:/61903/1:1:X3H3-GZC, citing ED 8, sheet 12A, line 19, family 86, NARA microfilm publication T626, roll 882, FHL microfilm 2,340,617; Clifford P. Dreydon, Salisbury, Wicomico County, Maryland, "United States Census, 1940," database with images, *FamilySearch*, accessed January 8, 2021, https://www.familysearch.org/ark:/61903/1:1:K7FT-V6X, citing ED 23-8, sheet 18A, line 13, family 376, NARA digital publication T627, roll 1563; B.J. Reports, Thursday, March 10, 1932, 1.

11. B.J. Reports, Saturday, March 12, 1932, 1.

12. B.J. Reports, Sunday, March 13, 1932, 1.

13. "75 Are Called in Lynching Case," *Baltimore Sun*, March 13, 1932.

14. For a list of those called to the grand jury, see "100 to Be Called in Lynching Case," *Baltimore Sun*, March 14, 1932.

15. "Many are Called in Shore Lynching," *Baltimore Sun*, March 15, 1932.

16. Paul Henderson, "On the Eastern 'SHO,'" *Baltimore Afro-American*, March 19, 1932.

17. Henderson, "On the Eastern 'SHO.' "

18. Henderson, "On the Eastern 'SHO.' "

19. "Text of Court's Charge to the Grand Jury," *Salisbury Times*, March 14, 1932.

20. "Salisbury Jury Opens Probe of Lynching Case," *Hagerstown (MD) Morning Herald*, March 15, 1932; "Witnesses Heard by Grand Jury in Lynching Probe," *Hagerstown (MD) Morning Herald*, March 16, 1932.

21. "Continue to Probe Shore Lynching Case," *Cumberland (MD) Evening Times*, March 16, 1932.

22. Sydney "Sid" N. Church was born in Connecticut in 1876. In 1930, he was living in Salisbury with his wife, Hannah, at 216 Williams Street. Church owned a furniture store. In 1930, he and his wife were also listed as living at 1900 Division Street. Census Place: Salisbury, Wicomico County, Maryland, Roll 882, Page 13B, ED 0008; Census Place: Salisbury, Wicomico County, Maryland, Roll 882, Page 21B, ED 0009, both in US Census, 1930, FHL microfilm 2,340,617.

23. Jewish Yiddish-speaking photographer Bird Sklar was born on April 1, 1895 in Tagancha, Ukraine, and arrived in the United States in 1914. By 1929, advertisements for his photography business began appearing in the *Salisbury Times*. The 1930 census recorded him as living at 204 Division Street in Salisbury. Eleven days following the lynching, Sklar began running a larger ad promoting photographs as ideal Christmas gifts. In March, just after the grand jury hearing, he ran another ad, this time pitching his photographs as the perfect Mother's Day gift. Sklar was most likely the Jewish photographer whom Sam Preston mentioned as having taken photographs of the lynching and been offered $1,000 dollars from New York reporters. In 1940, Sklar was still living in Salisbury. In 1942, at age forty-seven, Sklar registered for the draft. He and his wife, Mary, were living on Zion Road, and their photo studio was at 112 Main Street. Census Place: Salisbury, Wicomico County, Maryland, Roll 882, Page 24B, ED 0009, US Census, 1930, FHL microfilm 2340617; Census Place: Salisbury, Wicomico County, Maryland, Roll T627_1563, Page 15A, ED 23-14, US Census, 1940, FHL microfilm; ad for Sklar's photography service in *Con Survey City Directory: Salisbury, Maryland* (Columbus, OH: Mullin-Kille Company, 1948), 216; Sklar draft registration, World War II Draft Cards (Fourth Registration) for the State of Maryland, RG 147, Series Number M1939, National Archives at St. Louis, Mo.; B.J. Reports, March 15, 1932, 1.

24. B.J. Reports, March 15, 1932, 1.

25. B.J. Reports, March 15, 1932, 1.

26. B.J. Reports, March 15, 1932, 1.

27. B.J. Reports, March 15, 1932, 1.

28. "Makeup of Grand Jury Attacked by Labor League," *Cumberland (MD) Evening Times*, March 15, 1932; "Labor Defense League Protests Grand Jury," *Frederick (MD) News*, March 15, 1932; "Impeachment Asked," *Hagerstown (MD) Morning Herald*, March 16, 1932.

29. "Lynching Jury Is Expected to Report Today," *Baltimore Sun*, March 17, 1932.

30. B.J. Reports, Wednesday, March 16, 1932, 1.

31. "Grand Jury Reports It Found No One Remotely Connected with Lynching," *Salisbury Times*, March 18, 1932; "Lynching Jury Unable to Name Any Defendant," *Baltimore Sun*, March 19, 1932; "Eastern Sho' Lynch Probe Concluded," *Cumberland (MD) Evening Times*, March 18, 1932; "Two Detectives," *Baltimore Sun*, March 19, 1932.

32. "Grand Jury Starts Investigation in Salisbury Mob Burning," *Baltimore Afro-American*, March 19, 1932.

33. "I.L.D. Appeals to Ritchie for Lynching Probe," *Salisbury Times*, March 19, 1932; "Labor Defense Group Presents New Demands," *Baltimore Sun*, March 19, 1932.

34. B.J. Reports, February 1, 1932, 1.

35. T.J.F. Reports, March 5, 1932, Attorney General (Transcripts), MSA S T2282-5.

36. Investigation in Re Matthew Williams (Final Report), n.d., 6, MSA S T2282-5.

37. Investigation in Re Matthew Williams (Final Report), 6.

38. Investigation in Re Matthew Williams (Final Report), 6.

39. T.J.F. Reports, March 21, 1932.

40. *American Law Reports Annotated* (Eagan, MN: Lawyers Co-operative Publishing Company, 1938); *United States Code Service, Lawyers Edition: All Federal Laws of a General and Permanent Nature Arranged in Accordance with Section Numbering of the United States Code and the Supplements Thereto* (Eagan, MN: Lawyers Co-operative Publishing Company, 1936).

Chapter 7

1. Statement of Dr. Arthur D. Brown, 2.

2. Weiss, *Farewell to the Party of Lincoln*; Lisio, *Hoover, Blacks, and Lily-Whites*; Sherman, *The Republican Party and Black America from McKinley to Hoover*, 134–44.

3. John R. Lynch, quoted in Gosnell, *Negro Politicians*, 24–25.

4. "Get at the Roots," *Baltimore Afro-American*, October 21, 1933; "George Armwood (b. 1911, d. 1933)," MSA SC 3520-13750, Maryland State Archives (Biographical Series), accessed March 21, 2021, http://msa.maryland.gov/megafile/msa/speccol/sc3500/sc3520/013700/013750/html/13750bio.html.; "Mother's Heart Is Broken from Lynch Tragedy," *Baltimore Afro-American*, October 21, 1933.

5. *Eastern Shore of Delaware, Maryland, and Virginia Directory*, 1931–1932.

6. Sosna, "In Search of the Silent South," 55; Chappell, *Inside Agitators*.

Chapter 8

Epigraph: Scott, "Morning Remarks."

1. Natalie Sherman, Chris Kaltenbach, and Colin Campbell, "Freddie Gray Dies a Week after Being Injured during Arrest," *Baltimore Sun*, April 19, 2015, https://www.baltimoresun.com/news/crime/bs-md-freddie-gray-20150419-story.html.

2. Samuel C. Broughton, 217.

3. Levin, *The Fractured Republic*, 216; Rodgers, *Age of Fracture*, 6.

4. Maryland House Bill 307, regular session, 2019, *LegiScan*, https://legiscan.com/MD/text/HB307/2019.

5. Maryland House Bill 307.

6. Sotero, "A Conceptual Model of Historical Trauma." Public health practitioner Corey Henderson successfully utilized Michelle Sotero's model to chronicle the negative influence of historical trauma in Baltimore. His study revealed five themes that revealed resilience protective factors that Blacks used to counter the trauma of segregation and systemic racism. Henderson, "The Reverberating Influence of Historical Trauma on the Health of African Americans in Baltimore City."

7. Sotero, "A Conceptual Model of Historical Trauma," 99.

8. For discussion of these theories, see Roberts et al., "Race/Ethnic Differences in

Exposure to Traumatic Events"; Degruy, *Post Traumatic Slave Syndrome*; Gobodo-Madikizela, *History, Trauma, and Shame*; Fullilove, "Root Shock"; Roth, "How Traumatic Experiences Leave Their Signature on the Genome."

9. Sotero, "A Conceptual Model of Historical Trauma."

10. Maryland Case Files, Burnham Nobles Archive, Civil Rights and Restorative Justice Project, School of Law, Northeastern University.

11. "Terrorism of Mob Continues, Autoist Threatened, Curfew at Ridgely," *Baltimore Afro-American*, January 9, 1932.

12. Clarence Mitchell, "Lynching Shore Riots: Princess Anne Gang Attacks Towns-people," *Baltimore Afro-American*, September 15, 1934.

13. "AFRO Cameraman Shows Principals and Scenes in Near-Lynching at Stockton," *Baltimore Afro-American*, February 24, 1940.

14. "4 State Policemen Take Two Negroes from 1,000 After Jail Is Stormed, *Baltimore Sun*, February 14, 1940.

15. "Part O'Connor Played as Mob Stormed Jail," *Baltimore Sun*, February 14, 1940.

16. "4 State Policemen Take Two Negroes."

17. "Klan Roster and Other Secrets Salvaged from Waste Basket," *Atlanta Daily World*, January 31, 1950.

18. "Md. Refuses to Ratify 14th," *Baltimore Afro-American*, April 16, 1955; "The Week's Events in Legislative Halls," *Baltimore Afro-American*, April 18, 1959.

19. For more on the Cambridge riots, see Smith, *Here Lies Jim Crow*; and Levy, *Civil War on Race Street*.

20. Rhonda Y. Williams, "Black Women, Urban Politics, and Engendering Black Power," in Joseph, *The Black Power Movement*, 79–100. For more on Gloria Richardson, see Fitzgerald, *The Struggle Is Eternal*; Annette K. Brock, "Gloria Richardson and the Cambridge Movement," in Crawford, Rouse, and Woods, *Women in the Civil Rights Movement*, 121–44.

21. "Two Wounded in Cambridge Race Riots, Fires Flare," *Salisbury Times*, June 12, 1963; "5 Hurt, Stores Burned As Riots Flare in Maryland," *Chicago Daily Defender*, June 13, 1963; Ben A. Franklin, "S.N.C.C. Chief Shot in Cambridge, Md," *New York Times*, July 25, 1967.

22. Jersey Heights Neighborhood Association v. Tighlman et al., No. 98-1804 (4th Cir. April 5, 1999), https://caselaw.findlaw.com/us-4th-circuit/1022059.html.

23. G. Clinton Uhl, Bruce Howard, and John K. Shaw, *Report of the State Roads Commission of Maryland* (Baltimore: Maryland State Roads Commission, 1930), 66.

24. Cooper, *Salisbury in Times Gone By*, 179.

25. Ezra B. Whitman, P. Watson Webb, and W. Frank Thomas, *Report of the State Roads Commission of Maryland* (Baltimore: Maryland State Roads Commission, 1941), 25.

26. Russell H. McCain, Edgar T. Bennett, Bramwell Kelly, *Report of the State Roads Commission of Maryland* (Baltimore: Maryland State Roads Commission, 1954), 136–37; Robert M. Reindollar, Watson P. Webb, Russell H. McCain, *Report of the State Roads Commission of Maryland* (Baltimore: Maryland State Road Commission, 1947), 43; Robert M. Reindollar, Watson P. Webb, Russell H. McCain, and John J. McMullen, *Report of the State Roads Commission of Maryland* (Baltimore: Maryland State Roads Commission, 1956), 127; Cooper, *Salisbury in Times Gone By*, 263–64 (quotation).

27. "ACLU Complains about Proposed Salisbury Bypass," *Baltimore Sun*, April 22, 1994.

28. "Jersey Heights Residents File Appeal to Block Bypass," *Salisbury Daily Times*, May 29, 1998.

29. For more on the class-action law suit and Professor Ifill's involvement, see Krissah Thompson, "Sherrilyn Ifill Is to Be Head of NAACP Legal Defense and Educational Fund," *Washington Post*, January 22, 2013, https://www.washingtonpost.com/; Jersey Heights Neighborhd. Asso. v. Glendening, 174 F.3d 180 (4th Cir. 1999), https://casetext .com/case/jersey-heights-neighborhd-asso-v-glendening.

30. "Jersey Heights Residents File Appeal to Block Bypass."

31. "ACLU Complains about Proposed Salisbury Bypass."

32. "African American History and Cultural Resources at the Maryland Historical Trust," Maryland Historical Trust, Maryland Department of Planning, n.d., accessed April 11, 2021, maryland.gov, 3, 8, 9; Cooper, *Salisbury in Times Gone By*, 263.

33. Amber Green and James Yamakawa, interview with author, January 5, 2020.

34. Salisbury, Maryland, American Community Survey 5-Year Estimates, US Census Bureau, 2013–17; Maryland, American Community Survey 5-Year Estimates, US Census Bureau, 2013–17.

35. James Yamakawa, interview by author, October 9, 2019.

36. Don Pettijohn, "African Americans at Andersonville," Andersonville National Historic Site, National Park Service, updated April 14, 2015, https://www.nps.gov/ande /learn/historyculture/african_americans.htm; Davis, *Ghosts and Shadows of Andersonville*.

37. Jeremy Cox, "Confederate Marker Finds Support in Petition," *Delmarva Daily Times*, June 22, 2017, https://www.delmarvanow.com/story/news/2017/06/22/keep-salis burys-confederate-marker-theres-petition/420998001/; Singer, *The War Criminal's Son*, 6.

38. "Local History and Why We Need to Learn It" (a public statement from an unnamed Salisbury Citizen), in *The Sign*, directed by Torrez Wise and William Strang-Moya, produced by Mark Decker, William Strang-Moya, Torrez Wise, and Dan O'Hare (Delmarva, MD: Delmarva Film Collective, 2017).

39. "Local History and Why We Need to Learn It."

40. Kelly Powers, "Examining Gen. John Winder's History as Confederate Monuments Fall across the Country," *Delmarva Daily Times*, June 12, 2020, https://www.del marvanow.com/story/news/local/maryland/2020/06/12/confederate-monuments-gen eral-john-winder-history-maryland-wicomico/5341342002/; "A County on Maryland's Eastern Shore Quietly Takes Down a Confederate Memorial, after Years of Rejecting the Idea," *Baltimore Sun*, July 24, 2020, https://www.baltimoresun.com/maryland/east ern-shore/bs-md-salisbury-confederate-sign-20200724-hmlcbdh5gbgyza3viroy3aw mjq-story.html.

41. Taylor Lumpkin, "Salisbury University Students React to Racist Messages Written on Building Wall," 47 ABC, October 24, 2019, https://www.wmdt.com/2019/10/salis bury-university-students-react-to-racist-messages-written-on-building-wall/.

42. "Come Here from Here," interview with Mayor Jake Day, in *The Sign*.

43. Courtland Milloy, "A Young Man Died after Being Stopped by Police: Four Months Later, No One Knows Why," *Washington Post*, January 8, 2019; "Caroline County, Maryland: Municipalities—Greensboro," *Maryland Manual On-Line*, accessed January 6, 2021, https://msa.maryland.gov/msa/mdmanual/37mun/greensboro/html /g.html.

44. James Dawson, "Dover Pays Acquitted Officer $230k in Settlement," DPM: *Delaware Public Media*, February 24, 2016, https://www.delawarepublic.org/post/dover-pays-aquitted-officer-230k-settlement; Jeff Brown, "Dickerson Received $300,000 in Dover Legal Settlement," *Dover* (DE) *Post*, February 7, 2017, https://www.doverpost.com/news/20170207/dickerson-received-300000-in-dover-legal-settlement.

45. Glynis Kazanjian, "Questions Linger One Year after Anton Black's Death," *Maryland Matters*, September 13, 2019, https://www.marylandmatters.org/2019/09/13/questions-linger-one-year-after-anton-blacks-death/; Talia Richman, "In a Small Eastern Shore Town, Questions Remain after the Death of Anton Black," *Baltimore Sun*, January 24, 2019, https://www.baltimoresun.com/maryland/bs-md-anton-black-greensboro-20190124-story.html.

46. Kazanjian, "Questions Linger One Year after Anton Black's Death."

47. "Dr. Gail Christopher Addresses Helsinki Commission," National Collaborative for Health Equity, July 22, 2019, https://www.nationalcollaborative.org/dr-gail-christopher-addresses-helsinki-commission/.

[Bibliography]

Primary Sources

Manuscript Collections

Humphreys Family Papers. Edward H. Nabb Research Center for Delmarva History and Culture. Salisbury University, Salisbury, Maryland.

Maryland Case Files. Burnham Nobles Archive. Civil Rights and Restorative Justice Project. School of Law, Northeastern University, Boston.

Moore, Joseph, Collection. Edward H. Nabb Research Center for Delmarva History and Culture, Salisbury University, Salisbury, Maryland.

NAACP Papers. Part 7: The Anti-Lynching Campaign, 1912–1955. Library of Congress, Washington, DC.

NAACP Papers, Part 12: Selected Branch Files, 1913–1939. Library of Congress, Washington, DC.

Princeton University Graduate Alumni Index, 1839–1998. Department of Rare Books and Special Collections, Seeley G. Mudd Manuscript Library. Princeton University Libraries.

Ritchie, Albert, Papers. Special Collections, University of Maryland Libraries, Hornbake Library, College Park, Maryland.

Stewart, Polly, Papers. Edward H. Nabb Research Center for Delmarva History and Culture, Salisbury University, Salisbury, Maryland.

Thirty-Second Annual Catalog of the Officers and Students of the Leonard Medical School: The Medical Department of Shaw University, 1912, Raleigh, North Carolina.

Maryland State Government Records

Lane, William Preston. Records of the Attorney General. Maryland State Archives, Annapolis.

Ritchie, Albert C. Records of the Governor. Maryland State Archives, Annapolis.

New York State Census Population Schedules

New York. Onondaga County. New York State, 1905. Census, Population Schedule. New York State Archives, 2002. *Ancestry.com.* http://www.ancestry.com.

New York. Onondaga County. New York State, 1915. Census, Population Schedule. New York State Archives, 2002. *Ancestry.com.* http://www.ancestry.com.

New York. Onondaga County. New York State, 1920. Census, Population Schedule. New York State Archives, 2002. *Ancestry.com.* http://www.ancestry.com.

United States Government Publications

Emmett Till Unsolved Civil Rights Crimes Reauthorization Act of 2016. Pub. L. No. 114-325. 130 Stat. 1965 (2016). https://www.congress.gov/bill/114th-congress/senate-bill/2854/text.

France, Senator Joseph. Anti-Lynching Bill S. 2791, December. 6, 1921. 67th Cong., 4th sess. 62 Cong. Rec. S35 (1921).

United States Census Population Schedules

Delaware. New Castle County. US Census, Population Schedule, 1910. Washington, DC: National Archives and Records Administration, 2002. *Ancestry.com.* http://www.ancestry.com.

Delaware. Sussex County. US Census, Population Schedule, 1920. Washington, DC: National Archives and Records Administration, 2002. *Ancestry.com.* http://www.ancestry.com.

Iowa. Marion County. US Census, Population Schedule, 1850. *Ancestry.com.* http://www.ancestry.com.

Louisiana. Plaquemines County. US Census, Population Schedule, 1920. Washington, DC: National Archives and Records Administration, 2002. *Ancestry.com.* http://www.ancestry.com.

Maryland. Princess Anne County. US Census, Population Schedule, 1920. Washington, DC: National Archives and Records Administration, 2002. *Ancestry.com.* http://www.ancestry.com.

Maryland. Princess Anne County. US Census, Population Schedule, 1930. Washington, DC: National Archives and Records Administration, 2002. *Ancestry.com.* http://www.ancestry.com.

Maryland. Somerset County. US Census, Population Schedule, 1920. Washington, DC: National Archives and Records Administration, 2002. *Ancestry.com.* http://www.ancestry.com.

Maryland. Somerset County. US Census, Population Schedule, 1930. Washington, DC: National Archives and Records Administration, 2002. *Ancestry.com.* http://www.ancestry.com.

Maryland. Wicomico County. US Census, Population Schedule, 1900. Washington, DC: National Archives and Records Administration, 2002. *Ancestry.com.* http://www.ancestry.com.

Maryland. Wicomico County. US Census, Population Schedule, 1910. Washington, DC: National Archives and Records Administration, 2002. *Ancestry.com.* http://www.ancestry.com.

Maryland. Wicomico County. US Census, Population Schedule, 1920. Washington, DC: National Archives and Records Administration, 1992. *Ancestry.com.* http://www.ancestry.com.

Maryland. Wicomico County. US Census, Population Schedule, 1930. Washington, DC: National Archives and Records Administration, 1992. *Ancestry.com.* http://www.ancestry.com.

Maryland. Wicomico County. US Census, Population Schedule, 1940. Washington, DC: National Archives and Records Administration, 2002. *Ancestry.com.* http://www.ancestry.com.

Maryland. Worcester County. US Census, Population Schedule, 1930. Washington, DC: National Archives and Records Administration, 2002. *Ancestry.com.* http://www.ancestry.com.

Mississippi. Lowndes County. US Census, Population Schedule, 1920. Washington, DC: National Archives and Records Administration, 2002. *Ancestry.com.* http://www.ancestry.com.

Missouri. Nodaway County. US Census, Population Schedule, 1930. Washington, DC: National Archives and Records Administration, 2002. *Ancestry.com.* http://www.ancestry.com.

New York. Onondaga County. US Census, Population Schedule, 1930. Washington, DC: National Archives and Records Administration, 2002. *Ancestry.com.* http://www.ancestry.com.

Tennessee. Obion County. US Census, Population Schedule, 1920. Washington, DC: National Archives and Records Administration, 2002. *Ancestry.com.* http://www.ancestry.com.

Military Records

US World War II Draft Cards of Young Men, 1940–1947. *Ancestry.com.* http://www.ancestry.com.

World War I Draft Registration Cards, 1917–1918. *Ancestry.com.* http://www.ancestry.com.

World War II Army Enlistment Records. *Ancestry.com.* http://www.ancestry.com.

Reports, Inventories, and Studies of Private Organizations

Bureau of Labor Statistics, *Historical Statistics of the United States Colonial Times to the 1970, Part I.* Washington, DC: US Government Printing Office, 1975.

Equal Justice Initiative. *Lynching in America: Confronting the Legacy of Racial Terror.* Montgomery, AL, 2017.

Hill, T. Edward. *First Annual Report: Bureau of Negro Welfare and Statistics.* Charleston: State of West Virginia, Bureau of Negro Welfare and Statistics, 1922.

National Urban League. *The Forgotten Tenth: An Analysis of Unemployment among Negroes in the United States and Its Social Costs, 1932–1933.* New York, 1933.

Bibliography

Ritchie Citizenship League. *What Governor Ritchie Has Done for the Colored Race*. Baltimore: Ritchie Citizen Ship League, n.d. [1932?].

Touart, Paul B. *John Wesley Methodist Episcopal Church: Historic Site Inventory*. Crownsville, MD: Maryland Historic Trust.

Universities—National Bureau Committee for Economic Research. *The Measurement and Behavior of Unemployment*. NBER Special Conference Series 8, Princeton 1957.

Reference Works

American Council of Learned Societies. *Dictionary of American Biography*. New York: Scribner, 1946.

Con Survey City Directory: Salisbury, Maryland. Columbus, Ohio: Mullin-Kille Company, 1948.

Eastern Shore of Delaware, Maryland, and Virginia Directory, 1908–1909. R. L. Polk & Co. Publishers, 1908.

Eastern Shore of Delaware, Maryland, and Virginia Directory, 1931–1932. R. L. Polk & Co. Publishers, 1931.

The First Colored Professional, Clerical and Business Directory of Baltimore City, 1922–1923. 10th Annual Edition. R. W. Coleman, 1922.

Fitzgerald's Trenton and Mercer County Directory, 1920. Trenton, NJ, 1920.

Mather, Frank Lincoln. *Who's Who of the Colored Race: A General Biographical Dictionary of Men and Women of African Descent*. Chicago: N.p., 1915.

The National Cyclopaedia of American Biography. New York: James T. White and Company, 1922.

Onofrio, Jan. *Maryland Biographical Dictionary*. Somerset, 1999.

Papenfuse, Edward C., et al. *Archives of Maryland: Historical List*. Annapolis: Maryland State Archives, 1990.

Polk's Vicksburg (Mississippi) City Directory, 1929. Birmingham, AL: R. L. Polk and Co. of Alabama, 1929.

Thurston, W. C. *Salisbury: The Capital of the Eastern Shore—Homey, Hustling, Hospitable*. Salisbury, MD: Little Journeys, 1931.

Thurston, W. C., ed. *Industrial Salisbury, 1934: Business and Professional Directory*. Salisbury, MD: Little Journeys, 1934.

White, Frank F., Jr. *The Governors of Maryland, 1777–1970*. Annapolis, MD: Hall of Records Commission, 1970.

Wicomico Telephone Directory. Salisbury, MD: Chesapeake and Potomac Telephone Company of Baltimore City, 1930.

Wright, Richard R. *Centennial Encyclopedia of the African Methodist Episcopal Church*. Philadelphia: African Methodist Episcopal Church, 1916.

Published Primary Sources

Commercial Telegraphers' Journal. Milwaukee: Commercial Telegraphers' Union of America, 1918.

Department of Research and Department of Industrial Relations. *The Forgotten Tenth: An Analysis of Unemployment among Negroes in the United States and Its Social Costs, 1932–1933*. New York: National Urban League, 1933.

Earle, Alice Morse. *Curious Punishments of Bygone Days*. New York: Herbert S. Stone & Company, 1896.

Hammett, Dashiell. *Selected Letters of Dashiell Hammett, 1921–1960.* New York: Counterpoint, 2002.

Penn, Irvine Garland, and John Wesley Edward Bowen. *The United Negro: His Problems and His Progress; Containing the Addresses and Proceedings the Negro Young People's Christian and Educational Congress, Held August 6–11, 1902.* Atlanta: D. E. Luther Publishing Company, 1902.

P. G. H. Memories, 1904–54. Salisbury, MD: Peninsula General Hospital Medical Center, 1954.

Stenographic Transcript in the Case of Statements in Re Lynching of Matthew Williams. Baltimore: Lafayette P. Temple, Inc., 1931.

Waring, James H. N. *Work of the Colored Law and Order League: Baltimore, Md.* Cheyney, PA: Committee of Twelve, 1908.

Wells-Barnett, Ida B. "Lynch Law in America," *Arena* 23, no. 1 (1900).

Periodicals

Arena
Baltimore Afro-American
Baltimore Evening Sun
Baltimore Post
Baltimore Sun
Brooklyn Daily Eagle
Cincinnati Enquirer
Congressional Digest
The Crisis
Cumberland (MD) Evening Times
Delmarva Daily Times
Hagerstown (MD) Morning Herald
Indianapolis Star
Ithaca (NY) Journal
Literary Digest
Miami News
The Nation
Negro Associated Press
New Castle (PA) News
New York Times
Ocean City (MD) Morning News
Opportunity: A Journal of Negro Life

Pittsburgh Press
Poughkeepsie Eagle-News
Princess Anne Marylander and Herald
Rochester (NY) Democrat and Chronicle
Salisbury Advertiser
Salisbury Daily Times
Salisbury Times
Scribner's Magazine
Snow Hill (MD) News Journal
Syracuse (NY) Journal
Syracuse (NY) Sports Journal
Syracuse (NY) Sunday Herald
Time Magazine
Trenton (NJ) Evening Times
Twin-City Daily Sentinel
Virginian-Pilot and Norfolk Landmark
Washington (DC) Herald
Washington Post
Wilmington (DE) Morning News
Wilmington (DE) News Journal
York (MD) Gazette Daily

Secondary Sources

Dissertations and Theses

Harcourt, Felix. "Kleagles, Kash, and the Klan: Maryland and the Decline of the Klan, 1922–1928." Master's thesis, 2009.

Henderson, Corey Jermaine. "The Reverberating Influence of Historical Trauma on the Health of African Americans in Baltimore City." Doctoral dissertation, Morgan State University, 2017. https://doi.org/10.13016/M2HH6C83B.

Jackson, Cezar Tampoya. "A Comparative Study of Perceptions of the Media Relating to Lynchings on the Eastern Shore of Maryland, 1931–1933." Doctoral dissertation, 1996. Retrieved from ProQuest Dissertations & Theses.

Levin, James Benesch. "Albert C. Ritchie, a Political Biography." Doctoral dissertation, 1970. Retrieved from ProQuest Dissertations & Theses.

McCulley, Jessica LeKay. "Rape, Lynching, and Mythmaking in Missouri, 1804–1933." Master's thesis, University of Missouri–St. Louis, 2014.

Ross, John. "At the Bar of Judge Lynch: Lynching and Lynch Mobs in America." Doctoral dissertation, Texas Tech University, 1983. Retrieved from ProQuest Dissertations & Theses.

Smead, Edwin Howard. "The Lynching of Mack Charles Parker in Poplarville, Mississippi, April 25, 1959." Doctoral dissertation. ProQuest Dissertations & Theses.

Sosna, Morton Philip. "In Search of the Silent South: White Southern Racial Liberalism 1920–1950." Doctoral dissertation. ProQuest Dissertations & Theses.

Terry, David Taft (2002). "Tramping for Justice: The Dismantling of Jim Crow in Baltimore, 1942–1945." Doctoral dissertation. ProQuest Dissertations & Theses.

Books

Algren, Nelson. *Never Come Morning*. New York City: Harper & Brothers, 1942.

Allen, Barbara, and Schlereth J. Thomas, eds. *Sense of Place: American Regional Cultures*. Lexington: University Press of Kentucky, 1900.

Amidon, Stephen. *Something like the Gods: A Cultural History of the Athlete from Achilles to LeBron*. New York: Rodale, 2012.

Apel, Dora. *Imagery of Lynching: Black Men, White Women, and the Mob*. New Brunswick, NJ: Rutgers University Press, 2004.

Apel, Dora, and Shawn Michelle Smith. *Lynching Photographs*. Berkeley: University of California Press, 2007.

Armstead, Myra Beth Young. *Freedom's Gardener: James F. Brown, Horticulture, and the Hudson Valley in Antebellum America*. New York: New York University Press, 2012.

Armstrong, Julie Buckner. *Mary Turner and the Memory of Lynching*. Athens: University of Georgia Press, 2011.

Bailey, Amy Kate, and Stewart E. Tolnay. *Lynched: The Victims of Southern Mob Violence*. Chapel Hill: University of North Carolina Press, 2015.

Battat, Erin Royston. *Ain't Got No Home: America's Great Migrations and the Making of an Interracial Left*. Chapel Hill: University of North Carolina Press, 2014.

Beals, Carleton. *The Story of Huey P. Long*. Westport, CT: Greenwood Press, 1971.

Bernstein, Patricia. *The First Waco Horror: The Lynching of Jesse Washington and the Rise of the NAACP*. College Station: Texas A&M University Press, 2006.

Bevel, Tom, and Ross M. Gardner. *Bloodstain Pattern Analysis, with an Introduction to Crime Scene Reconstruction*. Boca Raton, FL: CRC Press, 2008.

Brawley, James S. *The Rowan Story*. Salisbury, MD: Rowan Print Co., 1953.

Brown, Dorothy Marie. *Setting a Course: American Women in the 1920s*. Boston: Twayne, 1987.

Brugger, Robert J. *Maryland: A Middle Temperament*. Baltimore: Johns Hopkins University Press, 1988.

Brundage, William Fitzhugh. *Lynching in the New South: Georgia and Virginia, 1880–1930*. Urbana: University of Illinois Press, 1993.

————, ed. *Under Sentence of Death: Lynching in the South*. Chapel Hill: The University of North Carolina Press, 1997.

Byford, Jovan. *Conspiracy Theories: A Critical Introduction*. New York: Palgrave Macmillan, 2011.

Calcott, Margaret Law. *The Negro in Maryland Politics, 1870–1912*. Baltimore: Johns Hopkins University Press, 1989.

Cameron, James. *A Time of Terror*. Baltimore: Black Classic Press, 1994.

Capeci, Dominic J., Jr. *The Lynching of Cleo Wright*. Lexington: University Press of Kentucky, 2015).

Carrigan, William D., and Christopher Waldrep, eds. *Swift to Wrath: Lynching in Global Historical Perspective*. Charlottesville: University of Virginia Press, 2013.

Cash, Wilbur Joseph. *The Mind of the South*. New York: Vintage Books, 1991.

Catledge, Turner. *My Life and the Times*. New York: Harper & Row, 1971.

Chandler, David L. *Brothers in Blood: The Rise of the Criminal Brotherhoods*. New York: Dutton, 1975.

Chappell, David L. *Inside Agitators: White Southerners in the Civil Rights Movement*. Baltimore: Johns Hopkins University Press, 1994.

Chisum, W. Jerry, and Brent E. Turvey. *Crime Reconstruction*. Cambridge, MA: Academic Press, 2011.

Clark, Charles B. *The Eastern Shore of Maryland and Virginia*. New York: Lewis Historical Pub. Co., 1950.

Clegg, Claude A. *Troubled Ground: A Tale of Murder, Lynching, and Reckoning in the New South*. Urbana: University of Illinois Press, 2010.

Cline, Sally. *Dashiell Hammett: Man of Mystery*. New York: Arcade, 2016.

Cooper, Richard W. *Salisbury in Times Gone By*. Baltimore: Gateway Press, 1991.

Corddry, George H. *Wicomico County History*. Salisbury, MD: Peninsula Press, 1981.

Crawford, Vicki L., Jacqueline Anne Rouse, and Barbara Woods, eds. *Women in the Civil Rights Movement: Trailblazers and Torchbearers, 1941–1965*. 1990. Reprinted, Bloomington: Indiana University Press, 1993.

Curtin, Philip D. *The Atlantic Slave Trade: A Census*. Madison: University of Wisconsin Press, 1969.

Davis, Robert Scott. *Ghosts and Shadows of Andersonville: Essays on the Secret Social Histories of America's Deadliest Prison*. Macon, GA: Mercer University Press, 2006.

DiLisio, James. *Maryland Geography: An Introduction*. Baltimore: Johns Hopkins University Press, 2014.

Domenico, Roy Palmer. *The Regions of Italy: A Reference Guide to History and Culture*. Westport, CT: Greenwood, 2002.

Dray, Philip. *At the Hands of Persons Unknown: The Lynching of Black America*. New York: Modern Library, 2003.

Duyer, Linda. *Mob Law on Delmarva*. Salisbury, MD: privately printed, 2014.

————. *'Round the Pond: Georgetown of Salisbury, Maryland; A History of the Georgetown and Cuba Neighborhood Communities Collectively Known as Georgetown*. Salisbury, MD: privately printed, 2007.

Earle, Swepson, and Percy G. Skirven. *Maryland's Colonial Eastern Shore: Historical Sketches of Counties and of Some Notable Structures*. Baltimore: Munder-Thomsen Press, 1916.

Eichengreen, Barry J. *Hall of Mirrors: The Great Depression, the Great Recession, and the Uses—and Misuses—of History*. New York: Oxford University Press, 2016.

Eltis, David, and David Richardson. *Atlas of the Transatlantic Slave Trade*. New Haven, CT: Yale University Press, 2015.

Epstein, Steven. *Speaking of Slavery: Color, Ethnicity, and Human Bondage in Italy*. Ithaca, NY: Cornell University Press, 2001.

Evans, Ivan. *Cultures of Violence: Racial Violence and the Origins of Segregation in South Africa and the American South*. Oxford: Oxford University Press, 2013.

Farrar, Hayward. *The Baltimore Afro-American, 1892–1950*. Westport, CT: Greenwood, 1998.

Feldman, Glenn. *Before Brown: Civil Rights and White Backlash in the Modern South*. Tuscaloosa: University of Alabama Press, 2004.

———. *The Irony of the Solid South: Democrats, Republicans, and Race, 1865–1944*. Tuscaloosa: University of Alabama Press, 2013.

———. *Politics, Society, and the Klan in Alabama, 1915–1949*. Tuscaloosa: University of Alabama Press, 1999.

Feldman, Glenn, ed. *Politics and Religion in the White South*. Lexington: University Press of Kentucky, 2013.

Fields, Barbara Jeanne. *Slavery and Freedom on the Middle Ground: Maryland during the Nineteenth Century*. New Haven, CT: Yale University Press, 1984.

Fischer, David. *Albion's Seed: Four British Folkways in America*. New York: Oxford University Press, 1989.

Fitzgerald, Joseph R. *The Struggle Is Eternal: Gloria Richardson and Black Liberation*. Lexington: University Press of Kentucky, 2018.

Foerster, Robert F. *The Italian Emigration of Our Times*. Cambridge, MA: Harvard University Press, 1919.

Franklin, John Hope, and John Whittington Franklin. *My Life and an Era: The Autobiography of Buck Colbert Franklin*. Baton Rouge: Louisiana State University Press, 1997.

Frazier, Harriet C. *Lynchings in Missouri, 1803–1981*. Jefferson, NC: McFarland, 2009.

Frederickson, Kari. *The Dixiecrat Revolt and the End of the Solid South, 1932-1968*. Chapel Hill: University of North Carolina Press, 2001.

Freedman, Estelle B. *Redefining Rape: Sexual Violence in the Era of Suffrage and Segregation*. Cambridge, MA: Harvard University Press, 2015.

Friedman, Morris. *The Pinkerton Labor Spy*. New York: Wilshire Book Company, 1907.

Frymer, Paul. *Uneasy Alliances: Race and Party Competition in America*. Princeton, NJ: Princeton University Press, 2010.

Gambino, Richard. *Blood of My Blood: The Dilemma of the Italian-Americans*. Lancaster, PA: Guernica Editions, 2000.

Gems, Gerald R. *Boxing: A Concise History of the Sweet Science*. Lanham, MD: Rowman & Littlefield, 2014.

———. *Sport and the Shaping of Italian-American Identity*. Syracuse, NY: Syracuse University Press, 2013.

Gems, Gerald R., Linda Borish, and Gertrud Pfister. *Sports in American History: From Colonization to Globalization*. 2nd ed. Champaign, IL: Human Kinetics, 2017.

Gilmore, Glenda Elizabeth. *Defying Dixie: The Radical Roots of Civil Rights, 1919–1950*. New York: W. W. Norton, 2009.

Glushakow, Abraham Dave. *A Pictorial History of Maryland Jewry*. Baltimore: Jewish Voice, 1955.

Gobodo-Madikizela, Pumla, ed. *History, Trauma, and Shame: Engaging the Past through Second Generation Dialogue*. Abingdon, UK: Routledge, 2020.

Godshalk, David Fort. *Veiled Visions: The 1906 Atlanta Race Riot and the Reshaping of American Race Relations*. Chapel Hill: University of North Carolina Press, 2006.

González-Tennant, Edward. *The Rosewood Massacre: An Archaeology and History of Intersectional Violence*. Gainesville: University Press of Florida, 2019.

Gosnell, Harold F. *Negro Politicians: The Rise of Negro Politics in Chicago*. Chicago: University of Chicago Press, 1935. Reprinted, New York: AMS Press, 1969.

Gualtieri, Sarah. *Between Arab and White: Race and Ethnicity in the Early Syrian American Diaspora*. Berkeley: University of California Press, 2009.

Gunning, Sandra. *Race, Rape, and Lynching: The Red Record of American Literature, 1890–1912*. New York: Oxford University Press, 1996.

Hale, Grace Elizabeth. *Making Whiteness: The Culture of Segregation in the South, 1890–1940*. New York: Pantheon, 1998.

Hall, Clayton Coleman, ed. *Baltimore: Its History and Its People*. New York: Lewis Historical Publishing Company, 1912.

Hardy, Phil. *The BFI Companion to Crime*. London: British Film Institute, 1997.

Harris, Trudier. *Exorcising Blackness: Historical and Literary Lynching and Burning Rituals*. Bloomington: Indiana University Press, 1984.

Hill, Karlos K. *Beyond the Rope: The Impact of Lynching on Black Culture and Memory*. New York: Cambridge University Press, 2016.

Hemstock, G. Kevin. *Injustice on the Eastern Shore: Race and the Hill Murder Trial*. Charleston: Arcadia, 2015.

Hossfeld, Leslie. *Narrative, Political Unconscious, and Racial Violence in Wilmington, North Carolina*. Abingdon, UK: Routledge, 2005.

Howes, Durward. *America's Young Men: The Official Who's Who among the Young Men of the Nation*. Los Angeles: Richard Bank Publishing Company, 1934.

Hunt, William R. *Front-Page Detective: William J. Burns and the Detective Profession, 1880–1930*. Bowling Green, OH: Popular Press, 1990.

Hurley, George M., and Suzanne B. Hurley. *Ocean City: A Pictorial History*. Virginia Beach, VA: Donning, 1979.

Ifill, Sherrilyn A. *On the Courthouse Lawn: Confronting the Legacy of Lynching in the Twenty-First Century*. Boston: Beacon Press, 2007.

Inikori, Joseph E., and Stanley L. Engerman. *The Atlantic Slave Trade: Effects on Economies, Societies, and Peoples in Africa, the Americas, and Europe*. Durham, NC: Duke University Press, 1992.

Irvin-Erickson, Douglas, Thomas La Pointe, and Alexander Hinton, eds. *Hidden Genocides: Power, Knowledge, Memory*. New Brunswick, NJ: Rutgers University Press, 2013.

Jacob, John E. *Salisbury in Vintage Postcards*. Chicago: Arcadia, 1988.

———. *Salisbury in Vintage Postcards*. Mt. Pleasant, SC: Arcadia, 1998.

Jaynes, David Gerald. *Branches without Roots: Genesis of the Black Working Class in the American South, 1862–1882*. New York: Oxford University Press, 1986.

Jones, Amelia, Andrew Stephenson Nfa, and Andrew Stephenson. *Performing the Body/ Performing the Text*. New York: Routledge, 2005.

Bibliography

Joseph, Peniel E., ed. *The Black Power Movement: Rethinking the Civil Rights–Black Power Era*. New York: Routledge, 2006.

Kneier, Charles Mayard. *Illustrative Materials in Municipal Government and Administration*. New York: Harper & Brothers, 1939.

Krech, Shepard, III. *Praise the Bridge That Carries You Over: The Life of Joseph L. Sutton*. Boston: G. K. Hall; Cambridge, MA: Schenkman Books, 1981.

Krehbiel, Randy. *Tulsa, 1921: Reporting a Massacre*. Norman: University of Oklahoma Press, 2019.

Lamon, Lester C. *Blacks in Tennessee, 1791–1970*. Knoxville: University of Tennessee Press, 1981.

Lawrence, A. H. *Duke Ellington and His World*. New York: Routledge, 2004.

Leary, Joy Degruy. *Post Traumatic Slave Syndrome: America's Legacy of Enduring Injury and Healing*. Revised ed. Portland: Joy Degruy, 2017.

Levin, Yuval. *The Fractured Republic: Renewing America's Social Contract in the Age of Individualism*. New York: Basic Books, 2016.

Levy, Peter B. *Civil War on Race Street: The Civil Rights Movement in Cambridge, Maryland*. Tallahassee: University Press of Florida, 2003.

Lightweis-Goff, Jennie. *Blood at the Root: Lynching as American Cultural Nucleus*. Albany: State University of New York Press, 2011.

Lisio, Donald J. *Hoover, Blacks, and Lily-Whites: A Study of Southern Strategies*. Chapel Hill: University of North Carolina Press, 1985.

Madison, James H. *A Lynching in the Heartland: Race and Memory in America*. London: Palgrave Macmillan, 2003.

Markovitz, Jonathan. *Legacies of Lynching: Racial Violence and Memory*. Minneapolis: University of Minnesota Press, 2004.

Mathews, Donald G. *At the Altar of Lynching: Burning Sam Hose in the American South*. Cambridge: Cambridge University Press, 2018.

McGovern, James R. *Anatomy of a Lynching: The Killing of Claude Neal*. Baton Rouge: Louisiana State University Press, 2014.

McGrath, John J. *The Brigade: A History; Its Organization and Employment in the US Army*. Fort Leavenworth, KS: Combat Studies Institute Press, 2004.

Moore, Joseph E. *Murder on Maryland's Eastern Shore: Race Politics and the Case of Orphan Jones*. Charleston, SC: History Press, 2006.

Morgan, Michael. *Ocean City: Going Down the Ocean*. Charleston, SC: History Press, 2011.

Morn, Frank. *"The Eye That Never Sleeps": A History of the Pinkerton National Detective Agency*. Bloomington: Indiana University Press, 1982.

Oakes, James. *The Ruling Race: A History of American Slaveholders*. New York: W. W. Norton, 1998.

O'Hara, S. Paul. *Inventing the Pinkertons; or, Spies, Sleuths, Mercenaries, and Thugs: Being a Story of the Nation's Most Famous (and Infamous) Detective Agency*. Baltimore: Johns Hopkins University Press, 2016.

Olson, James S., and Heather Olson Beal. *The Ethnic Dimension in American History*. New York: John Wiley, 2011.

Omo-Osagie, Solomon I. *Commercial Poultry Production on Maryland's Lower Eastern Shore: The Role of African Americans, 1930s to 1990s*. Lanham, MD: University Press of America, 2012.

Ore, Ersula J. *Lynching: Violence, Rhetoric, and American Identity*. Jackson: University Press of Mississippi, 2019.

Oswald, Diane L. *Fire Insurance Maps: Their History and Applications*. College Station, TX: Lacewing Press, 1997.

Pedersen, Vernon L. *The Communist Party in Maryland, 1919–57*. Champaign: University of Illinois Press, 2001.

Peninsula General Hospital Medical Center: Peninsula General Hospital Salisbury, Maryland; 75th Anniversary, 1897–1972. Salisbury, MD: Peninsula General Hospital, 1972.

Perman, Michael. *Struggle for Mastery: Disfranchisement in the South, 1888–1908*. Chapel Hill: University of North Carolina Press, 2003.

Pleck, Elizabeth Hafkin. *Domestic Tyranny: The Making of American Social Policy against Family Violence from Colonial Times to the Present*. Champaign: University of Illinois Press, 2004.

Radoff, Morris L., ed. *The Old Line State: A History of Maryland*. Hopkinsville, KY: Historical Record Association, 1956.

Raper, Arthur Franklin. *The Tragedy of Lynching*. Chapel Hill: University of North Carolina Press, 1933.

Rice, Anne P. *Witnessing Lynching: American Writers Respond*. New Brunswick, NJ: Rutgers University Press, 2003.

Roberts, Patricia L. *A Lynching in Little Dixie: The Life and Death of James T. Scott, ca. 1885–1923*. Jefferson, NC: McFarland, 2018.

Rodgers, Daniel T. *Age of Fracture*. Cambridge, MA: Belknap Press of Harvard University Press, 2011.

Roediger, David R. *Working toward Whiteness: How America's Immigrants Became White—The Strange Journey from Ellis Island to the Suburbs*. New York: Basic Books, 2006.

Rolph, Daniel N. *"To Shoot, Burn, and Hang": Folk-History from a Kentucky Mountain Family and Community*. Knoxville: University of Tennessee Press, 1994.

Sherman, Richard. *The Republican Party and Black America from McKinley to Hoover, 1896–1933*. Charlottesville: University of Virginia Press, 1973.

Singer, Jane. *The War Criminal's Son: The Civil War Saga of William A. Winder*. Lincoln: Potomac Books, 2019.

Sitkoff, Harvard. *A New Deal for Blacks: The Emergence of Civil Rights as a National Issue; The Depression Decade*. New York: Oxford University Press, 1978.

Skotnes, Andor. *A New Deal for All? Race and Class Struggles in Depression-Era Baltimore*. Durham, NC: Duke University Press, 2013.

Smead, Howard. *Blood Justice: The Lynching of Mack Charles Parker*. Oxford: Oxford University Press, 1986.

Smith, Asbury. *More than a Whisper*. Gaithersburg, MD: More Than a Whisper, 1985.

Smith, C. Fraser. *Here Lies Jim Crow: Civil Rights in Maryland*. Baltimore: Johns Hopkins University Press, 2008.

Smith, Jean Edward. *FDR*. New York: Random House, 2008.

Sommerville, Diane Miller. *Rape and Race in the Nineteenth-Century South*. Chapel Hill: University of North Carolina Press, 2004.

Stokes, Curtis, ed. *Race and Human Rights*. East Lansing: Michigan State University Press, 2009.

Sussman, Jeffrey. *Boxing and the Mob: The Notorious History of the Sweet Science*. Lanham, MD: Rowman & Littlefield, 2019.

Tindall, George Brown. *The Emergence of the New South, 1913–1945: A History of the South*. Baton Rouge: Louisiana State University Press, 1967.

Tolnay, Stewart E., and E. M. Beck. *A Festival of Violence: An Analysis of Southern Lynchings, 1882–1930*. Champaign: University of Illinois Press, 1995.

Touart, Paul B. *John Wesley Methodist Episcopal Church: Historic Site Inventory*. Crownsville: Maryland Historic Trust, 1999.

Townsend, Walter A., and Charles Boeschenstein. *Illinois Democracy: A History of the Party and Its Representative Members, Past and Present*. Springfield, IL: Democratic Historical Association, 1935.

Trotter, Joe William, and Joe William Trotter Jr. *Coal, Class, and Color: Blacks in Southern West Virginia, 1915–32*. Urbana: University of Illinois Press, 1990.

Truitt, Charles J. *Historic Salisbury, Maryland*. Garden City, NJ: Country Life Press, 1932.

Truitt, Charles J. *Historic Salisbury Updated, 1662–1982*. Salisbury, MD: Historical Books, 1982.

Tyson, Timothy B. *The Blood of Emmett Till*. New York: Simon and Schuster, 2017.

Valelly, Richard. *The Two Reconstructions: The Struggle for Black Enfranchisement*. Chicago: University of Chicago Press, 2004.

Waldrep, Christopher. *African Americans Confront Lynching: Strategies of Resistance from the Civil War to the Civil Rights Era*. Lanham, MD: Rowman & Littlefield, 2009.

Weiss, Nancy Joan. *Farewell to the Party of Lincoln: Black Politics in the Age of FDR*. Princeton, NJ: Princeton University Press, 1983.

Wennersten, John R. *Maryland's Eastern Shore: A Journey in Time and Place*. Centreville, MD: Tidewater, 1992.

Weston, Stanley, and Steven Farhood. *The Ring: Boxing in the 20th Century*. New York: BDD Illustrated Books, 1993.

White, Walter. *Rope and Faggot: A Biography of Judge Lynch*. Salem, MA: Arno Press, 1969.

Whyte, Kenneth. *Hoover: An Extraordinary Life in Extraordinary Times*. New York: Knopf, 2017.

Williams, T. Harry. "The Politics of the Longs." In *Romance and Realism in Southern Politics*. Athens: University of Georgia Press, 1961.

Williamson, Joel. *The Crucible of Race: Black-White Relations in the American South since Emancipation*. New York: Oxford University Press, 1984.

Willis, John T., and Herbert C. Smith. *Maryland Politics and Government: Democratic Dominance*. Lincoln: University of Nebraska Press, 2001.

Wilson, Vincent, Jr. *The Book of the States*. Brookville, MD: American History Research Associates, 1992.

Wood, Amy Louise. *Lynching and Spectacle: Witnessing Racial Violence in America, 1890–1940*. Chapel Hill: University of North Carolina Press, 2011.

Woods, Naruice F., ed. *Rooted in the Soul*. Dubuque, IA: Kendell Hunt, 2011.

Wright, George C. *Racial Violence in Kentucky: Lynchings, Mob Rule, and "Legal Lynchings."* Baton Rouge: Louisiana State University Press, 1996.

Zucchino, David. *Wilmington's Lie: The Murderous Coup of 1898 and the Rise of White Supremacy*. New York: Grove/Atlantic, 2021.

Bibliography

Journal Articles

Arnold-Lourie, Christine. "'A Madman's Deed, a Maniac's Hand': Gender and Justice in Three Maryland Lynchings." *Journal of Social History* 41 (2008).

Beck, E. M., and Stewart Tolnay. "The Killing Fields of the Deep South: The Market for Cotton and the Lynching of Blacks, 1882–1930." *American Sociological Review* 55, no. 4 (1990).

Berg, Manfred. "Black Civil Rights and Liberal Anti-Communism: The NAACP in the Early Cold War." *Journal of American History* 94, no. 1 (June 1, 2007).

Brown, Dorothy. "The Election of 1934: the 'New Deal' in Maryland." *Maryland Historical Magazine* 68, no. 4 (1973).

Castle, Taimi. "'Cops and the Klan': Police Disavowal of Risk and Minimization of Threat from the Far-Right." *Critical Criminology*, February 15, 2020. https://doi.org/10.1007/s10612-020-09493-6.

Chavis, Charles L., Jr. "Rabbi Edward L. Israel: The Making of a Progressive Interracialist, 1923–1941." *Southern Jewish History* 22 (October 2019).

Chepaitis, Joseph B. "Albert C. Ritchie in Power: 1920–1927." *Maryland Historical Magazine* 68 (1973).

Cohen, Michael. "'The Ku Klux Government': Vigilantism, Lynching, and the Repression of the I.W.W." *Journal for the Study of Radicalism* 1, no. 1 (2007).

Darby, M. R. "Three-and-a-Half Million U.S. Employees Have Been Mislaid: Or, An Explanation of Unemployment, 1934–1941." *Journal of Political Economy* 84, no. 1 (1976).

Darity, William. "The Numbers Game and the Profitability of the British Trade in Slaves." *Journal of Economic History* 45, no. 3 (1985).

Eltis, David, and David Richardson. "The 'Numbers Game' and Routes to Slavery." *Slavery and Abolition* 18, no. 1 (April 1, 1997).

Fullilove, M. T. "Root Shock: The Consequences of African American Dispossession." *Journal of Urban Health* 78, no. 1 (2001), 72–80.

Gault, Robert H. "Lynching, an Evil of County Government." *Journal of the American Institute of Criminal Law and Criminology* 11, no. 1 (1920): 127–31. http://www.jstor.org/stable/1133805.

Gibbs, Rabia. "The Heart of the Matter: The Developmental History of African American Archives." *American Archivist* 75, no. 1 (2012): 195–204.

Havel, Václav. "The Power of the Powerless." *International Journal of Politics* (October 1979).

Hovland, Carl I., and Robert R. Sears. "Minor Studies of Aggression: Correlations of Economic Indices with Lynchings." *Journal of Psychology* 9, no. 2 (1940).

Ishmael, Hannah J. M. "Reclaiming History: Arthur Schomburg." *Archives and Manuscripts* 46, no. 3 (September 2, 2018): 269–88. https://doi.org/10.1080/01576895.2018.1559741.

Johnson, J. R. "The Economics of Lynching." *Socialist Appeal* 4, no. 6 (February 10, 1940).

Konhaus, Tim. "'I Thought Things Would Be Different There': Lynching and the Black Community in Southern West Virginia, 1880–1933." *West Virginia History: A Journal of Regional Studies* 1, no. 2 (2008).

Levin, James. "Governor Albert C. Ritchie and the Democratic Convention of 1932." *Maryland Historical Magazine* 67, no. 4 (1972).

Levine, Mark V. "Standing Political Decisions and Critical Realignment: The Pattern of Maryland Politics, 1872–1948." *Journal of Politics* 38, no. 2 (1976).

Matthews, Donald G. "The Southern Rite of Human Sacrifice: Lynching in the American South." *Mississippi Quarterly* 61 (2008).

Nehls, Chris. "Sanborn Fire Insurance Maps at the University of Virginia." *Virginia Libraries* 46, no. 4 (2000).

Nowatzki, Robert. "Race, Rape, Lynching, and Manhood Suffrage: Constructions of White and Black Masculinity in Turn-of-the-Century White Supremacist Literature." *Journal of Men's Studies* 3, no. 2 (1994).

Pilkington, Charles Kirk. "The Trials of Brotherhood: The Founding of the Commission on Interracial Cooperation." *Georgia Historical Quarterly* 69, no. 1 (1985).

Piper, John F. "The Formation of the Social Policy of the Federal Council of Churches." *Journal of Church and State* 11, no. 1 (1969).

Roberts, A. L., S. E. Gilman, J. Breslau, N. Breslau, and K. C. Koenen. "Race/Ethnic Differences in Exposure to Traumatic Events, Development of Post-traumatic Stress Disorder, and Treatment-Seeking for Post-traumatic Stress Disorder in the United States." *Psychological Medicine* 41, no. 1 (January 2011): 71–83. https://doi.org/10.1017/S0033291710000401.

Roth, Tania L. "How Traumatic Experiences Leave Their Signature on the Genome: An Overview of Epigenetic Pathways in PTSD." *Frontiers in Psychiatry* 5 (2014). https://doi.org/10.3389/fpsyt.2014.00093.

Sotero, Michelle. "A Conceptual Model of Historical Trauma: Implications for Public Health Practice and Research." *Journal of Health Disparities Research and Practice* 1, no. 1 (Fall 2006). Available at SSRN, https://ssrn.com/abstract=1350062.

Stovel, Katherine. "Local Sequential Patterns: The Structure of Lynching in the Deep South, 1882–1930." *Social Forces* 79, no. 3 (2001): 843–80.

Tolnay, Stewart E., and E. M. Beck. "Black Flight: Lethal Violence and the Great Migration, 1900–1930." *Social Science History* 14, no. 3 (1990).

Webb, Clive. "The Lynching of Sicilian Immigrants in the American South, 1886–1910." *American Nineteenth Century History* 3 (2002).

"West Virginia, 1880–1933." *West Virginia History* 1, no. 2 (1972).

Williams, Yohuru R. "Permission to Hate: Delaware, Lynching, and the Culture of Violence in America." *Journal of Black Studies* 32, no. 1 (2001).

Oral History Resources

Du Bois, W. E. B. "The Reminiscences of W. E. B. Du Bois." New York: Columbia University Oral History Research Office, 1960.

Mitchell, Broadus. Interview by Mary Frederickson, August 14 and 15, 1977. No. 4007. Southern Oral History Program Collection, University of North Carolina, Chapel Hill.

Waller, Marie Johnson. Interview by Susan Holt, November 2009. Waller (Marie) Salisbury Lynching Oral History Collection. Edward H. Nabb Research Center for Delmarva History and Culture, Salisbury University, Salisbury, Maryland.

[Index]

Corbin, Ralph, 138, 145, 149, 154, 166, 171, 255n97
Cornish, Joseph, Sr., 30
Courthouse Lawn: Confronting the Legacy of Lynching in the Twenty-First Century (Ifill), 5–6
Creary, Nicholas M., 199
Creowell, Mr. and Mrs., 130, 137–38, 154; refused cooperation with system of silence, 137–38
Crockett, John William, 150–51, 170, 171, 257n21
Croswell, John, 182–83
Cuba. *See* Georgetown and Cuba

Dallam, Richard, 26
Dashields, Walter, 75
Dashiell, John, 23, 24
Daughtry, Luther, 201–2
Davis, Bill (of Fruitland, Maryland), 178
Davis, Bill (of Salisbury), 151, 157; biography, 255–56n5; as grand jury witness, 178–79, 183; in lynch mob inner circle, 130, 137, 145, 146, 147, 148, 149, 150, 153, 154, 160, 181, 183, 222
Davis, George, 32, 35–36, 106, 121, 158
Davis, Green K., 33–34
Davis, Jefferson, 208
Davis, Robert Scott, 208
Day, Jake, 210
Democratic Party, 23, 111, 189–90, 191–92
Dennis, Vincent Wheatley, 129, 252n77
Denton Journal, 164
Derritt, Andrew, 75–76
Dick, James McFaddin, *54*
Dickerson, J. N., 28
Dickerson, Lateef, 211
Diggs Amendment (1910–11), 84
Dillingham, Jack, 46
Douglass, Earl, 35
Douglass, Frederick, 2–3, 187
Downing, John, 71
Dreydon, Clifford, 170, 259n10
Du Bois, W. E. B., 241n144
Duer, Robert F., 36, 202
Duffy, Ralph C., 33, 155
Duyer, Linda, 22, 155, 197

Dyer, Leonidas C., 86, 87
Dyer anti-lynching bill, 86–89, 90

"Eastern Shore" term, 19
Easton, John Williams, 56–57
Eggleston, E. F., 27
Elliott Box and Crate Factory, 16, 43, 115, 121
Elliott, Daniel "D. J.," 3, 117, 121, 126, 158; biography, 48–49, 235n31; as difficult man, 153; photo, *49*; shooting of, 41, 43–45, 46–47; son as possible killer of, 46–47, 48, 237n67; will and testament of, 49–50; Williams work for, 16–17
Elliott, James Martindale, 158; biography, 236n41; and father's will, 49–50; as possible killer of father, 46–47, 48, 237n67; shooting of Williams by, 43
Ellis, Dallas M., 33
Emergency Committee for Employment, 39, 40
Emmett Till Civil Rights Crimes Reauthorization Act, 1
Equal Justice Initiative, 78, 242n167
Evers, Medgar, 203

Federal Bureau of Investigation (FBI), 9–10
Federal Council of Churches of Christ in America (FCCCA), 143, 255n1
Fenix Youth Project, Inc., 208
Fields, Barbara Jeanne, 5, 18
First Baptist Church (Salisbury), 30
Fisher, Helen E., 54, 57
Fitzhugh, William, 106
Floyd, George, 198, 210
Foote v. Maryland, 36
Ford, Richard, 32, 33, 106
Ford Motor Company, 110–11, 247–48n23
forensic reconstruction, 8, 229n27
France, Joseph Irwin, 87–88, *88,* 89, 90
Frank, Leo, 153
Franklin, Colbert "Buck," 43
Franklin, John Hope, 43
Furness, Sidney O., *73,* 178
Fusco, Joe, 113, 115–16, 154, 248n32

Gaddis, J. F., 26
Gadsby, Bob, 125, 170

Index

[281]

Index

House Bill 307 (HB307, Maryland), 199
Hurdle, S. H., 74
Huston, John, 21
Huston, Levin, 21
Huston, Solomon T., 25–26, 231n33

Ifill, Sherrilyn, xi, 140, 207; on intersection of memory and racial violence, 5–6; on system of silence, 6, 188
Igoe, Michael L., 93, 95
Insley, Wade W., 73, 100
International Labor Defense (ILD): and Euel Lee case, 28–29, 144, 178; and Williams lynching, 38, 177–78, 180
Irwin, George, 46
Israel, Edward L., 4

Jackson, Howard W., 95
Jackson, William P., 52
James, Charles, 92
James, George, 21
Janney, Stuart S., 84
Jean, Botham, 198
Jenkins, Charles, 57, 60
Jeon, Deborah A., 207
Jernigan, Rufus: disappearance of, 59, 179, 180; testimony by, 56, 57–58; as witness at hospital, 53, 54, 57–58, 60
Jersey Heights, 206
Jersey Heights Neighborhood Association (JHNA), 207
Jews, 153
Johnson, Benjamin, 164–65
Johnson, Buck "Petta," 146, 177; biography, 251n61; as grand jury witness, 171, 181; involvement of in Williams lynching, 123, 124, 144–45, 150, 222; killing of Black man by, 144
Johnson, Frederick Ernest, 143
Johnson, Jack, 2
Johnson, James L., 28
Johnson, James Weldon, 87
Johnson, King, 111
Johnson, Patsy, 8, 102, 195; in army, 108–9, 247n15; begins work as Pinkerton, 110–11, 247–48n23; boxing by, 108, 110; childhood and youth, 107–8; end of investigation by,

178, 182; establishing cover for, 112–15; gaining trust of locals, 124, 138, 147, 165, 181; and grand jury, 171, 174, 175, 183; photo, 109; week 1 of investigation by, 112–22; week 2 of investigation by, 122–27; week 3 of investigation by, 127–32; week 4 of investigation by, 132–37; week 5 of investigation by, 144–48; week 6 of investigation by, 148–56; week 7 of investigation by, 156–60; week 8 of investigation by, 160–63; weeks 9 and 10 of investigation by, 165–70
John Wesley Methodist Episcopal Church, 21, 25–26, 27, 207
Jolly, Levi, 17
Jones, Eugene Kinckle, 38
Jones, Tracey "Jeannie," 213–15

Keller, Crawford, 146, 223, 256n11
Kelly, Andy, 66
Kennerly, W. Arthur, 152, 155, 171, 175, 182, 257n25
Kent, Frank, 92–93
Kent County Nine, 92
King, Garfield: Black community response to lynching of, 25–27; lynching of, 23–25, 201
Knights of Columbus, 85, 108
Krech, Shepard, III, 47–48
Ku Klux Klan, 8, 85, 86, 111, 142, 203, 230n30; in Wicomico County, 33, 34
Kwedi, Julia, 210

labor conditions, 101–2
Lane, Preston, xi, 98, 99; and grand jury, 168–69, 173, 174, 182, 183; and Williams lynching investigation, 56, 93, 95, 101, 102, 168–69
Langston, Ulysses S. Grant and Julia, 30
Larmore, Talbot Louis "Toath," 132–33, 136, 145, 149, 152–54, 161, 163, 166, 167; biography, 128; breaks silence on Williams lynching, 128–29, 134, 140, 146, 156–57, 158, 181; and grand jury, 171, 174–77; involvement of in lynching, 129, 140, 223; on protection of lynchers, 147
Larmore, W. W., 129

Index

Index

Price, Marshall E., 232n38
Prohibition, 82, 144
Public Justice Center, 207
Purdue, Norman, 46
Purnell, Howard: biography, 258n30; as courageous Black witness, 7, 128, 154–55

Quillen, Raymond T., 35

Ralph, Randolph, 64
Reconstruction Finance Corporation (RFC), 37
Reid, Ira De Augustine, 40
Republican Party, 96; and Black vote, 83, 84–85, 191–92
Richardson, Gloria, 203
Rider, Thomas F. J., 23
Ridgely, MD, 201–2
Ritchie, Albert C., xi, 178; African Americans' challenging of, 93, 95–96; Baltimore's relationship with, 100–101; biography, 83–84; Black vote courted by, 84, 85, 90–91, 94–96, 102; and gubernatorial elections, 93, 192, 224, 225; investigation into Williams lynching launched by, 3, 9, 94, 97, 98, 102, 105–6, 132, 139, 165, 190–91; KKK denounced by, 85, 86; lynching condemned by, 79, 81–82, 94, 96, 97, 189–90, 193; photo, 91; Pinkerton detective agency hired by, 102, 105–6, 111–12, 120; presidential campaign of, 81, 83, 92–94, 120–21, 144; progressive racial stance taken by, 91–92, 102; Prohibition repeal supported by, 82, 144; refusal to support anti-lynching bills, 86–87, 89–90, 95; silence on grand jury decision, 180, 190–91; states' rights promotion by, 82, 90, 102, 144, 242n2
Ritchie, Kid, 167, 171, 174–75, 176
Robins, John, 193
Robinson, Thomas H., 98
Roosevelt, Franklin D., 81, 83; appeals to both Blacks and racist voters, 83, 190, 192; refusal to support anti-lynching bills, 90
Rope and Faggot (White), 44–45
Rosewood, Florida, Massacre (1923), 42, 188, 205
Ross, John, 8, 106, 117

Ruark, Fred, 149, 222, 223, 257n18
Russell, Danny, 125, 148, 160, 167, 171; as boxer, 116–17, 120, 123, 130, 158, 161, 163, 166, 167–68; involvement of in Williams lynching, 128, 129, 140, 223; tells of lynching, 117, 147, 156, 158

Salisbury, MD: Black businesses and churches in, 30–31, 207; Black professionals in, 42; Brown as Black community leader in, 30, 42–43, 77; class divisions in, 139–41; Confederate monuments in, 208–10; during Depression, 40; downtown, 61, 63, 210; and Garfield King lynching, 23–25; Georgetown and Cuba neighborhoods of, 17–18, 21–22, 204–8; history of, 20; legacy of racial violence in, 205, 208, 210; modern-day, 197; population of, 22, 23, 194, 221; powerbrokers in, 139, 147–48, 165–66; and Route 13 realignment, 205; and Route 50 completion, 205–6; segregation in, 204, 210; slavery in, 20–21; Stewart as Black community leader in, 29–30. See also lynching of Matthew Williams; Wicomico County
Salisbury Times, 39, 117, 127, 144, 203; on Elliott shooting, 48; on grand jury, 173–74; on Patsy Johnson, 122–23, 125, 158
Salisbury University, 210
Scottsboro Boys, 92, 178
segregation, 23, 43; in Salisbury and Wicomico County, 204, 206–7, 210
Selse, L. W., 102
Serman, Lilian, 137, 253n89
Shields, Roy, 201–2
Shipp, Thomas, 246n2
silence, system of: and Black witnesses, 188; Campbell breaking of, 140–41, 181; Creowells' breaking of, 137–38; and divisions in white community, 139–41, 180–81, 194–95; Harris breaking of, 121, 126, 127, 140–41, 158–60, 166; Ifill on, 6, 188; Larmore breaking of, 128–29, 134, 140, 146, 156–57, 158, 181; lynching as dependent on, 6–7, 106, 193–95; Perry breaking of, 146, 151, 181; surrounding Williams lynching, 7, 79, 118, 120, 132, 143, 150, 152, 166, 183–84;

Index